Redrawing the Western

World Comics and Graphic Nonfiction Series
Frederick Luis Aldama, Christopher González,
and Deborah Elizabeth Whaley, editors

Recent Books in the Series
Sam Langsdale, *Searching for Feminist Superheroes: Gender,
Sexuality, and Race in Marvel Comics*
James Scorer, *Latin American Comics in the Twenty-First Century:
Transgressing the Frame*
J. Andrew Deman, *The Claremont Run: Subverting Gender in
the X-Men*
Jeffrey Brown, *Super Bodies: Comic Book Illustration, Artistic Styles,
and Narrative Impact*
Peyton Brunet and Blair Davis, *Comic Book Women: Characters,
Creators, and Culture in the Golden Age*
Mark Cotta Vaz, *Empire of the Superheroes: America's Comic Book
Creators and the Making of a Billion-Dollar Industry*
Anna Peppard, ed., *Supersex: Sexuality, Fantasy, and the Superhero*
Allan W. Austin and Patrick L. Hamilton, *All New, All Different? A
History of Race and the American Superhero*
Jorge Santos Jr., *Graphic Memories of the Civil Rights Movement:
Reframing History in Comics*

Redrawing the Western

A History of American Comics and the Mythic West

WILLIAM GRADY

UNIVERSITY OF TEXAS PRESS ❧ *Austin*

Requests for permission to reproduce material from this work should
be sent to permissions@utpress.utexas.edu.

♾ The paper used in this book meets the minimum requirements of
ANSI/NISO Z39.48–1992 (R1997) (Permanence of Paper).

Library of Congress Cataloging-in-Publication Data

Names: Grady, William, PhD, author.
Title: Redrawing the Western : a history of American comics and
the mythic West / William Grady.
Other titles: World comics and graphic nonfiction series.
Description: First edition. | Austin : University of Texas Press, 2024. |
Series: World comics and graphic nonfiction series | Includes bibliographical
references and index.
Identifiers: LCCN 2023049619
ISBN 978-1-4773-2998-6 (hardback)
ISBN 978-1-4773-2999-3 (pdf)
ISBN 978-1-4773-3000-5 (epub)
Subjects: LCSH: Western comic books, strips, etc.—United States—History and
criticism. | Western comic books, strips, etc.—Social aspects—United States—
History. | Western comic books, strips, etc.—United States—Influence. |
Western stories—History and criticism.
Classification: LCC PN6725 .G725 2024 | DDC 813/.087409—dc23/eng/20231214
LC record available at https://lccn.loc.gov/2023049619

doi:10.7560/329986

This book is dedicated to the memory of Andrew Barlow
(1989–2000)

"When the sun appears on the horizon
Night starts to run away"

Contents

PART 2

A GOLDEN AGE OF WESTERN COMICS, 1940s–1970s

93

LIST OF ILLUSTRATIONS

Redrawing the Western

Rethinking the Western Genre through Comics

THE WESTERN IS ONE OF America's most discernable genres. It pulls together a mix of unmistakable archetypes, symbols, formulas, and themes. These remain largely unaltered in the countless versions from the genre's beginnings in folklore and fiction and throughout the various media it has since inhabited. The Western's grandiose landscapes and rugged terrains (desert plains, rich prairies, mountains, and forests) and its recognizable cast of characters (farmer, schoolmarm, outlaw, saloon girl, sheriff, Native American, and endless variations thereof) form part of the genre's allure. For some, the period is everything. Jim Kitses notes that the Western is typically set between 1865 and 1890, and the parameters within which a particular Western is set can determine many things, from narrative focus to attire and weaponry.[1] In this respect, there is a rich history at the genre's disposal: historic epochs—like the coming of the railroad, the Indian Wars, the mining rushes, and the rise of cattle drives—become narrative backdrops; and historic figures, such as law enforcers like Wyatt Earp or the fearless Lakota war chief Sitting Bull, become larger-than-life heroes. However, some Westerns remain ambiguous about their geographic position or their historical period, presenting instead a mythical tale of adventure from a time long ago. What brings these raw materials together is a set of instantly identifiable narratives—from frontier community dramas to battles in the desert—and embedded within them is a series of foundational myths about violence and progress. Nevertheless, a key notion that underlies the genre in all its forms is its relationship to American society and historical change.

Earl Pomeroy once wrote that "every generation seems to define the West anew."[2] The concept of the American West has its origins in European settlement on the eastern edge of the North American continent by the sixteenth century. For these Anglo-European colonists, the West symbolized a point of encounter between order and chaos, progress and the wild. Through the process by which the frontier was conquered, as settlers steadily shifted westward across the continent, the defining elements of American national character were forged, such as courage, dynamism, and rugged individualism. Equally, Richard Slotkin observes that this very process of conquest and imperial adventure served as "the basis of [American] mythology" and describes the development of the narrative of "regeneration through violence," which presents "tales of strife between Native Americans and interlopers, between dark races and light."[3] These stories served to buttress and encourage the most morally troubling aspects of American expansion, justifying white settlers' acts of acquisition through genocide as a form of retaliatory aggression against a "savage" Indigenous enemy.

The lore of the West is pervasive in American culture, but it flourished most profoundly in the years following the American Civil War (1861–1865). Reunification heralded an intensely nationalistic period that placed an emphasis on the rebirth of the nation. The mythic West helped shape the national imagination through its connections to imperial aspirations of Manifest Destiny and its symbols of American preeminence. The frontier was, for many, the "wellspring of the independent, indomitable American spirit."[4] Such images of the mythic West found powerful reinforcement in popular culture. Writers would embellish American perceptions of the frontier through exciting popular Western fiction; artists created grand paintings that captured the landscape and its inhabitants in vivid detail. Between 1883 and 1916, Buffalo Bill's Wild West show presented various elements of the mythic West to audiences through action-packed performances across the United States and Europe.[5] These spectacular displays of the West served to enthrall and entertain the public, presenting a synthesized (and sanitized) history of the frontier that remained the cornerstone of the Western genre into the twentieth century. Essentially, the mythic West of the nineteenth century was a frontier teeming with threatening Native Americans and aggressive outlaws who fed the desire for a hero to emerge and tame this violent land. However, for others the mythic West was a symbol of cultural anxiety over an era of greatness that might have passed.

This tension was captured most articulately in historian Frederick Jackson Turner's seminal thesis, "The Significance of the Frontier in

American History," which he delivered to the American Historical Association in 1893. Turner identified how the symbol of the West served to define "the forces dominating the American character," and argued that the progressive mission of advancing the frontier and the reaches of civilization had established the core terms of American exceptionalism.[6] Simultaneously, Turner's thesis observed the closing of the frontier—the line that had defined the unsettled terrains of the nation had disappeared from the census map by 1890. Turner's lament about the erosion of the nation's past was culturally resonant. Its impact was best measured in sources of popular culture after 1890, which rendered a mythical West frozen in time. Between 1890 and 1920, those who captured the West both in established forms (like literature and painting) and in developing media (such as cinema and comics) served to nostalgically assuage the loss of this bygone agrarian age through the articulation of familiar images of sparsely populated, majestic landscapes peopled with distinctive individuals.

However, these representations underwent continual change and revision. As John Belton observes, "The Western was both a barometer of contemporary history and a site for the production and perpetuation of myths that are crucial to the larger ideological demand of sustaining a nineteenth-century American identity that was repeatedly under attack in the twentieth century."[7] This helps to explain how and why the American West was routinely dramatized and reimagined for successive generations across the twentieth century. Indeed, by the 1930s the Western genre reflected major concerns in the American character. In particular, it attempted to remedy the dreary existence of Americans during the Depression by turning toward former glories of a romanticized frontier past. After 1945 the Western provided reassurance in a time of domestic anxiety and international insecurity triggered by the Cold War, but it equally provided a shrewd self-examination of foreign policy and traditional social values and customs.

By the 1960s American responses to social pressures—the floundering war in Vietnam, the birth of the New Left, an upsurge in riots demanding racial equality and government accountability, and the rise of a questioning counterculture—subjected the Western myth to increasing criticism. Its creators revised components of the genre to reflect many of the ills from the contemporaneous milieu. While the Western participated in a self-critical endeavor—what Stephen McVeigh describes as "the destruction of the genre's vital centre"— the Western genre overcame this sense of self-doubt in the national mythos, finding renewed popularity and productivity after the 1970s through remarkable works that either revised the genre anew or blended it with other genres.[8]

Henry Nash Smith once asserted that the Western is our fullest "objectified mass dream."[9] However, the most compelling aspect of this "mass dream" is how it has been continually reshaped and reinvented over time. Attempts to define the relationship between the American Western and American society and politics have dominated many discussions about the genre. Indeed, the Western has maintained a powerful symbolic resonance in American popular culture precisely for its ability to concurrently look backward and forward. That is to say, the Western tells of a frontier past rich in action and adventure while also finding ways of forging links within the contemporaneous context of its publication. Slotkin suggests that the images of the Western, drawn from American history, "have acquired through persistent usage the power of symbolizing that society's ideology and of dramatizing its moral consciousness."[10] The glut of scholarship on the Western tends to read the genre in these terms. In particular, a wide range of critics, historians, and scholars have mapped out histories of the genre in literature,[11] film,[12] television,[13] painting,[14] performance,[15] and music.[16] Nevertheless, gaps still remain in this vast corpus. For example, few have sought to consider the Western in comics.[17]

Comics are a word-and-image narrative medium that brings together different signs (from written language to icons and symbols) and a form-specific vocabulary (gutters, panels, speech balloons, bleeds, splashes, and so on). Comics readers interact with the comics page differently than they would with a page from a novel or a painting or a scene from a film. In fact, the comics reader must actively participate in the reading process, stitching together the various visual and verbal elements to make narrative meaning. However, it is this very visual and verbal interplay that perhaps accounts for previous readings of the Western in comics and how it is often linked to other forms of the genre. For instance, Henry Nash Smith and Christine Bold have placed mid-twentieth-century Western comic books into a lineage of popular Western fiction, interpreted as a form that succeeded both dime novels and pulp fiction.[18] In particular, Western comics bore many thematic hallmarks of earlier popular Western fiction, such as simplistic moral conflicts, stereotypical characters, formulaic narratives of violent confrontations between pioneers and Native Americans, and tales of law and order. Others have focused on the visuality of comics. For example,

FIGURE 0.1. Everett Raymond Kinstler, "Western Marshal," *Four Color* #534, February 1954. Dell.

Maurice Horn suggests that Western films and comics "share a common vocabulary of images and a congruent syntax of sequences."[19] Underground comics artist Jack Jackson postulates that Western comic books extend the B-movie Western's propensity for "fast action."[20] Bold marries these intertextual readings and their associations with fiction and film when she posits that "the genre that finally linked the written Western to the movie and television version was the comic."[21]

Judging from such readings, one could argue a case for Western comics as a version of the genre that brings together an array of literary and cinematic influences into its distinct presentation. A clear expression of this appears in the story "Western Marshal" from *Four Color* #534, February 1954 (Dell). The plot follows Marshal Dan Mitchell, who must uphold the law in the wild and raucous trail town River Bend as warring factions within the community look to tear apart any sense of order. The cover reveals its literary influences—it is described as an adaptation of the Ernest Haycox novel *Trail Town* (1941). Haycox was a prolific, popular Western-fiction author and is perhaps best known for the short story "Stage to Lordsburg" (1937), which later served as inspiration for John Ford's classic Western film *Stagecoach* (1939). However, rifling through the comic's pages we find that the text transcends its literary source material. Indeed, opposed to dense written description from the original novel, the visual nature of comics adds new dimensions to the narrative, heightening the drama and extending the action. Take the example page in fig. o.1, which details a fight sequence where the marshal beats up a series of miscreants before chasing them out of town at gunpoint. The dynamic artistry of cartoonist Everett Raymond Kinstler has the action spill across each panel—we see the marshal's elbow and the butt of his revolver break the rigid frame of the comics panel at different points, as if his violent swings are not contained by the rules of the form. Breaking through the walls of the panels provides a sense of motion as the marshal shifts from punching to tripping and, finally, to pistol-whipping his foes into submission. Arguably this is indicative of what Jackson describes as Western comics' use of B-Western films' propensity for "fast action," as the artist toys with various aspects of comics sequencing to evoke all the thrills and excitement of a typical Western film shoot-out. But the page is infused with other cinematic references as well. For example, Kinstler visually replicates Gary Cooper's character Will Kane from the popular Western film *High Noon* (1952), released not long before the comic book was published, in his interpretation of the plot's central hero. We can easily recognize Kane's iconic attire from the film and Cooper's familiar scowl. This cross-pollination more generally reflects the porous nature of comics and the medium's ability to organically absorb and reimagine the surrounding popular iconography and culture of the Old West onto the comics page. In this example we see how the creator has incorporated various literary and cinematic references into the comic to increase its appeal to the reader.

Nevertheless, the complex tangling of Western comics with other forms of the genre raises larger questions about the medium's status. Indeed, various scholars have positioned comics at the center of the Western's rich intermedial lineage, so why have so few sought to explore this version of the genre more deeply?

As a hand-drawn medium, comics are naturally predisposed to amplify the most exciting aspects of Western adventure for their readers, with the artists' lines transforming and reimagining the genre in interesting and unusual ways. In particular, these idiosyncrasies—their illustrated presentation of the Old West—create one core distinction of Western comics. Opposed to the photorealistic world that the cinematic Western occupies, the comic artist's pen was not necessarily bound to reality, as we shall see through the course of this book. This freedom opened the form to some eccentric and bizarre possibilities. Added to this, the continued biweekly, monthly, or bimonthly printing of comics offers much more dynamic interactions with shifts in national mood than other sources of popular culture. In *Redrawing the Western*, I seek to bring these unique elements to the fore. Utilizing the brief historical chronology of the Western genre detailed earlier, this book charts a cultural history of the Western in American comics from the late 1800s up until the 1970s. This chronology represents the core years in which the genre was forged and prospered in a range of popular media.

Part 1 contains three chapters that explore the origins of the mythic American West. Chapter 1 considers the representation of the Indian Wars in reportage from nineteenth-century newspapers and magazines, whose illustrations and cartoons were precursors to the comics medium. The chapter pays considerable attention to how this word-and-image form stood at the center of the Western's mythmaking process and became a vital mode to assimilate readers to accept the United States' imperialist and genocidal agenda on the frontier. (See one example in fig. 0.2.) Chapter 2 considers the impact the closing of the frontier had on representations of the West in newspaper

FIGURE 0.2. Livingston Hopkins, "The True Solution of the Indian Problem," *Daily Graphic*, July 8, 1876.

comic strips (from the turn of the century up until the 1920s). Whereas symbolic images of Native Americans and beatific scenery in film and painting from this era portrayed a sense of loss for a way of life, newspaper comic strips instead captured a sense of longing and nostalgia through scenes that confronted modern-day American tourists with the mythic West. Chapter 3 considers the rise and renewed purpose of the Western genre in newspaper comic strips during the 1930s and Depression-era America and explores the development of the action-driven formula that would be carried over into comics books from the 1940s and 1950s.

Part 2 looks at the "Golden Age" of Western comics. Chapter 4 charts the rise of the Western genre in postwar American comic books. Chapter 5 keeps focus on Western comic books from the postwar decades and attempts to pinpoint how Western stories about heroic cowboys who tame the most unruly portions of the frontier can be understood as expressions of Cold War culture. It argues that these righteous and imperialist stories of frontier conquest helped to promote new ideological rationales of exceptionalism, hegemony, and consensus. Specifically, they reinforced national aspirations like the American penetration of foreign economies and politics after 1945.

Chapter 6 provides a counterpoint to the previous chapter and argues that just as the conservative mythology of the Western could support and adhere to Cold War American culture, simultaneously some comics from the 1950s used this mythos as a direct means to confront and critique these very same mainstream ideals and values. Chapter 7 examines the darker and grittier tenor that imbued Westerns in comics (and popular culture more broadly) in the 1960s and 1970s. It explores the rupture of the national mythos in mainstream and underground comics, which acerbically retold the history of American conquest on the frontier.

Amid a wider global context of changing values and critical alliances associated with postcolonialism, postmodernism, and New Left politics in the later decades of the twentieth century, various cultural critics identified the death of the Western, arguing that the genre had ceased to function in its current guise. In these terms, the book's coda examines the Western's "afterlife" in comics, exploring the genre's resilience in contemporary popular culture, alongside positing some directions for future research.

In its study of stories about cowboys and Indians and law and order on the frontier, this book serves to highlight how the ostensibly simplistic dramas that were common in Western adventure comics could disguise highly political undercurrents. Because the medium was aimed at a distinctly adolescent readership for much of the twentieth century, the study makes the case that Western comics gave their young readers a variety of ways to think about the current social and political milieu. Furthermore, by examining the historical distance afforded by stories about taming the Wild West, the book argues that Western comics allowed young readers to explore contentious subjects and rethink old histories in ways that other genres and narratives in popular culture did not.

Besides tracing the history, forms, and politics of the American Western in comics across the late nineteenth century and into the twentieth century, the book offers a bold and original reassessment of the important role of comics in the development of the Western genre on an intermedial basis, ranking the medium alongside popular fiction and film in this process. As noted, the diverse and rich potentials that comics storytelling provides in the narration of the Western genre remains largely untapped in Western American literary and cultural studies, and in comics studies, too, for that matter. In *Redrawing the Western*, I argue that in its engagement with prevalent anxieties masked under the cover of frontier struggle, Western adventure comics serve as a striking visual record of twentieth-century America. In addition, I suggest that the study of comics can enhance and extend our current understanding of the mythic West's significance to American society.

Redrawing the Western is a cultural history of the Western in comics. Therefore, the methodology is informed by preestablished approaches to both the genre and the form. In relation to the Western genre, Richard Slotkin's trilogy *Regeneration through Violence* (1973), *The Fatal Environment* (1985), and *Gunfighter Nation* (1992) developed a pertinent approach for close readings of the Western genre and its relationship to American history. In his far-ranging exploration of the meaning of the frontier in a variety of chronological settings and his charting of its adaptation to differing cultural situations over time, the introduction to the middle volume most clearly explains how Westerns appeal to audiences in the United States: "Myth is acquired and preserved as part of our language. We observe its operation in the quality of historical (or pseudo-historical) resonance that attaches to terms like 'frontier,' 'cowboys and Indians,' or 'last stand.' They implicitly connect the events they emblematize to a system of values and beliefs, and they are usually used in a way that suggests an analogy between the historical past and the present situation."[22] Slotkin broadly describes how Westerns can respond to variations in national mood in a manner that allows them to captivate their audience. He further elaborates on this process: "Producers offer their fables and images, consumers buy or refuse to buy them; producers respond to consumer choices. . . . What emerges at the end is a body of genres and formulas whose appeal has been commercially validated; and this body of genres and formulas may be taken as the myth/ideology of the mass culture that consumes it, a kind of 'folklore of industrial society.'"[23]

This approach is redolent of a working definition of formulas advanced by John G. Cawelti. He summarizes that formulas are "ways in which specific cultural themes and stereotypes become embodied in more universal story archetypes."[24] They offer a helpful framework for viewing sources of entertainment: formulaic stories that resonate with audiences are likely to endure while those that do not eventually fade away. In this respect, the narrative formulas that are deployed in popular culture shift in relation to social and historical change. There-fore, formulas can be read as a product of the demands and desires of pro-ducers and consumers, as well as the historical conditions that surround them. This notion shapes a number of cultural histories on comic books, as well as research that aims to use comics to deepen understanding of the interaction between politics, social change, and popular culture.[25]

For instance, in the introduction to Bradford W. Wright's history of American comic books, he notes that comics publishers relied heavily on formulaic stories that sold well and were easily replicated. Those that succeeded did so by "speak[ing] adequately to the concerns and expectations of their audience." This rationale helps inform Wright's focus on the narrative content rather than the graphic qualities of com-ics in his cultural history, in which he explores comic books' "crude, exaggerated, and absurd" glimpses into the American experience from the late 1930s to the turn of the twenty-first century.[26]

The process of appealing to readers' values and modes of thinking through their consumption of popular texts—in which implicit values and ideologies are woven into the fabric of the story—is described as "mythic" by Roland Barthes.[27] This helps inform the approach taken here, and throughout the course of the book I will consider the types of Western-themed stories being told in comics and how they shift rela-tive to historical factors surrounding their production and circulation. I emphasize how Western comics do not just reinforce but also challenge what we know about historical perceptions. However, as form cannot be divorced from content, the approach in this study differs from previ-ous cultural histories in that aesthetic appreciations are not completely absent from my reading of comics. While surface readings from close analysis of a comics story can reveal the process of mythmaking at work, a much more complex discourse is afforded by comics' visual and verbal forms. Therefore, it is instructive to observe the interplay of different signs (from written language to icons and symbols) and meth-ods of storytelling (from symbolism, iconography, themes, narrative structure, character, and so on), as well as considering a given text's relationship to the political and cultural context of its time.[28]

In this respect, this study will engage with formal issues and theories of comics put forward by Scott McCloud and Thierry Groen-steen.[29] It will also utilize the rapidly expanding body of comics schol-arship that explores the formal aspects of the medium, much of which is published in peer-reviewed journals dedicated to comics studies, as well as in various other online fora.

To further reinforce any findings from this type of content and context analysis, which serves to reveal political and ideological messages that are encoded into a text, it is important to place those comics that are analyzed into a framework of broader popular culture and interrelated discourses. For instance, in his overview chapter on the Western film, Corey Creekmur asserts that despite references to "the western" in his writing solely referring to the film genre, "western movies must be appreciated within a cultural context that include examples of the genre across popular media, including theatre, music, fiction, radio, comics, and television, among other formats."[30] His reference to the importance of Western comics within the genre canon contradicts the general consensus in the scholarly corpus, which tends to avoid considering comics within any study of the Western. Nevertheless, Creekmur's suggestion informs the approach taken here. This study takes care to place Western comics into a broader framework of Westerns across popular media. Furthermore, this type of study, which considers the constant revisions and reformulations of the Western genre in parallel to historical change, must rely on scholarship regarding cultural and American history to help demonstrate the complex interweaving of symbols, myths, and historical experience in popular texts.

This book's historical account of American Western genre comics is ambitious in scale and scope, covering a vast history that begins in the nineteenth century and comes right up to the present day. This sheer breadth of material naturally means that some subjects of focus are missing. Acknowledging some of the limitations of the study is important. Indeed, Western comics are vast in number and diverse in character, making it impossible to undertake a comprehensive approach. Jon Tuska points out a similar contention in the study of Western films: "A survey of the Western is no longer possible for me. I have seen 8,000 Westerns. I would not recommend that anyone else do it. . . . I do not think it is possible to generalize about Westerns as so many have done."[31] In response to Tuska's warning, Douglas Pye suggests that "the best that can be achieved in genre criticism is to identify and analyse tendencies within the tradition and to consider the variations developed by particular films or groups of films."[32] This approach can be extrapolated to the Western in comics, and we can discern that it would be both unhelpful and difficult to document every single American Western comic ever published. Instead, I have endeavored to incorporate a wide selection of comics from each era. While this means there will naturally be omissions of certain comics and series along the way, this approach allows for the identification and analysis of tendencies within the tradition of American Western comics through history.

Another glaring omission is a deep focus on the production and circulation of Western comics globally. As Horn asserts, "The production of the Western comics from foreign lands is immense and far outstrips . . . the American contribution to the field."[33] I was saddened not to include popular titles such as *Lucky Luke* and *Lieutenant Blueberry* (Belgium/France), *Tex Willer* (Italy), and *Sgt. Kirk* (Argentina), just to name a few. However, Western comics from around the globe deserve much more critical attention than I would be able to provide in this cultural history of American Western comics. My brief focus on Western comics from a variety of national (mainly European) comics traditions in the coda reflects the vast scale of this rich area and serves as a guide for future directions in the study of a comics genre that has been woefully overlooked in both comics studies and Western studies.

Neil Campbell asserts that a central concern in studying the American Western and its far-ranging and multifaceted manifestations "is how to think differently" about the genre.[34] This is a driving impetus of more recent Western studies, although academic engagement by and large still squarely focuses on the Westerns of fiction and film. Writing much later, Andrew Patrick Nelson suggests that "the next step in widening investigation of the Western" is to turn our attention to those texts "that fall outside or on the margins of the established canon but *within* its temporal boundaries."[35] This outward-looking viewpoint to refresh scholarly explorations of the genre is met by a similar impetus in comics studies, which is rich in investigations of the superhero genre and autobiography comics. Recent work by Bart Beaty and Benjamin Woo (2016) and Marc Singer (2019), and international conferences such as the First Annual Conference of the Comics Studies Society ("MIND THE GAPS! The Futures of the Field," 2018), have sought to challenge common practices in comics studies and in particular the repeated engagement with only a select canon of standout comics titles and genres, rather than what Beaty and Woo describe as "the typical output of the American comic book industry."[36] In this regard, this book provides new perspectives and readings in the study of the Western genre and in the history of comics. This is not to minimize the valuable contribution to the wider scholarship that studying Western films or the standard comics canon can provide. Rather, I argue that by virtue of examining a version of the genre largely overlooked by the corpus—the Western in comics—in *Redrawing the Western* I can provide a novel interpretation of a familiar chronology (that is, the history of the Western in and around the twentieth century). It would therefore be difficult to argue that this book is in direct competition with other histories of the popular West or comics storytelling. Rather, it stands alongside them and encourages us to think differently about the vibrancy of frontier adventure and the mythic potency of the Western narrative.

PART 1

The Origins of the Mythic West in Comics, 1800s-1930s

CHAPTER 1

"Print the Legend"

Imagining the American West in
the Nineteenth-Century Illustrated Press

IN THE 1962 WESTERN FILM *The Man Who Shot Liberty Valance*, director John Ford presents two stories about the life of the character Senator Ransom Stoddard (played by James Stewart). One is the long-accepted narrative that before his prestigious political career, Stoddard brought law and order to the frontier border town Shinbone by slaying the outlaw Liberty Valance. The other story, shown in a flashback near the film's close, reveals that it was in fact Stoddard's friend Tom Doniphon (John Wayne) who shot and killed Valance. The latter story of course undermines the legend that surrounds the senator as "the man who shot Liberty Valance," and a reputation that kick-started his political career. Upon being presented with the true story and realizing that Stoddard's legacy is built on myth, a local newspaper reporter who is interviewing the senator tears up his notes before throwing them into the fire. "This is the West, sir," he explains. "When the legend becomes fact, print the legend!" The reporter's remark and outright refusal to print the truth reinforces the process of mythmaking at work within the nineteenth-century American West and demonstrates how legends were developed through the continued reiteration of deceptions. In addition, the impulse to "print the legend" reaffirms the role of print media and the press in the manufacture of the imagined West of the nineteenth century.

Long before the popular fiction of Zane Grey, John Wayne films, Lone Ranger serials, and the Marlboro Man, nineteenth-century newsprint and its associated illustrations, cartoons, and pictorial reportage served as a vital, albeit unlikely, source in the visual development of the mythic West. Indeed, ahead of technological advancements such as the mass printing and circulation of photographs and the dawn of cinema, illustrated representations of the contested frontier shaped how many Americans conceived the West. In predecessors of American comics, like cartoon-based magazines and the lurid cover images from popular Western dime novels of the era, illustration became a primary mode of narrative justification for the United States' inexorable westward movement in the 1800s. And, in the twilight years of the nation's Western frontier, word-and-image forms captured the events and actual dangers of these concluding scenes (however fictionalized). This chapter examines the depiction of frontier conflict in the nineteenth-century illustrated press and sheds light on how these graphic enunciations forged some of the most basic tenets of the Western genre in the twentieth century.

Early Forays into the Popular West of the Nineteenth Century

In the stories of settlement on a new continent, which appeared first in literature and then in the movies, the natural world posed the possibility of both dangers and profit. . . . The need for land began the move from spiritual to secular goals of nationbuilding in a new world, and this adjustment also changed the American relationship with the environment. Westward expansion grew as the population grew (early in the tentative settlement of the continent). Thomas Jefferson took delight in the increase of Virginia inhabitants, noting, "In Europe the object is to make the most of their land, labour being abundant: here it is to make the most of our labour, land being abundant." Thus began the independent, landowning tradition that underpinned American identity—a yeoman agriculturist (albeit, today, a gardener in a suburban backyard) ready to advance and conquer a limitless continent of natural resources.[1]

While Deborah Carmichael acknowledges that the frontier experience was a dominant influence in shaping the Westerns of fiction and film, she clarifies how this was rooted in the expansionist program of the nation's Founding Fathers. Moving the line of settlement across the continent of North America was a momentous process (spanning the seventeenth, eighteenth, and nineteenth centuries). It molded the distinctive character traits idealized by the nation: individualism, hard work, and self-reliance. The largely untouched (at least by European hands) region of North America west of the Appalachian Mountains lay at the heart of this mythmaking. It served as a symbol of unlimited opportunities and freedoms and as a beacon of promise that spurred successive waves of migration for those escaping from harsh economic or political conditions of life in Europe. But the imaginations of colonists across New England and the Eastern Seaboard were also captured. The Louisiana Purchase of 1803 heightened this hunger for land, as the United States opened a vast region west of the Mississippi River to exploration and exploitation. Mass migration westward soon followed, as a torrent of people flooded this newly opened region in search of land and opportunity. Moreover, its accessibility allowed a series of authors and artists to transform the American West in their own designs.

Early accounts, such as the published journals documenting Lewis and Clark's expedition through the region between 1804 and 1806, alongside the visualization of Native Americans in the paintings of George Caitlin (in the 1830s) and the later writings of Washington Irving, Francis Parkman, and Mark Twain, would capture the attention of the nation back east and greatly influence the popular imagination about what the West was like. However, it was not until the end of the Civil War and the construction of the transcontinental railroads in the 1860s that the intrigue surged. Rail travel provided a far easier means of journeying to and from the West and brought numerous tourists to the region, as well as attracting a wide range of writers looking for inspiration. Of particular interest for this study are the numerous dime novelists who headed West in search of material to be incorporated into exciting adventure tales when their journeys were written up back home in the eastern cities.

The new publication venture of issuing inexpensive paperbacks, known as dime novels, was popularized by Irwin and Erastus Beadle in the 1860s. Coinciding with the renewed fascination with the American West, it is perhaps unsurprising that three quarters of the dime novels printed concerned Western adventure fiction. Individual titles sold in the millions.[2] Content largely narrated the endemic strife in the border regions of the West. For instance, the Indian Wars, which arose as the United States extended its borders farther west and displaced the tribal populations from their homelands, were transformed into a series of narratives that focused on white settlers' struggles against "savage" Indigenous aggressors. This formula drew on the national narrative of Manifest Destiny, which justified the settling of the West. Another example was the strand of dime novels that focused on banditry and the lawmen's capacity to uphold law and order, narrativizing that period in history when outlaws were defying authority and getting away with it. (Dime novels sensationalized the daring bank and train robberies of Jesse James and the James-Younger gang, amongst others.) The dime novels, in this respect, took the complex events unfolding in the West in the nineteenth century and reduced them into fictitious yet exciting plot formulas of violent action and frontier adventure. Their appeal lay in the immediacy of their printing. That is to say that a mass readership could enjoy current developments regarding westward expansion through fictionalized accounts of outlaws and law enforcers and conflicts between "righteous white frontiersmen" and "treacherous Indians."[3]

The Western dime novels refined common themes regarding the confrontation between wilderness and civilization into a series of dramatic action and adventure stories. They created some of the earliest plot formulas that would be repeatedly articulated in popular Western fiction into the twentieth century.[4] However, of particular interest here are the covers of the dime novels. The richly illustrated cover images provided some of the earliest graphic articulations of iconography and dramatic scenes commonly associated with the Western, giving visual life to these fictitious stories. Dime-novel covers offered a range of exotic iconographies and exciting scenarios: frontiersmen in buckskins, valiant heroes defeating scores of Native Americans, cowboys on horseback, shootouts, and daring escapes from the law. While the reader assuredly found all the thrills and excitement that came with these visualizations of the frontier within the pages of the dime novels, the cover images served as a visual guide for the reader regarding the storyworld they were about to enter.

Moreover, these exhilarating scenes are paired with dramatic titles. Captions such as "The James Boys in Peril" (fig. 1.1) and "Buffalo Bill's Death-Deal" (fig. 1.2) provided textual cues for the reader to further assimilate the images of heroic action and violent conflict, while advertising the adventures of real-life figures from the West who could be found within. In this respect, the interplay of word and image played a crucial role in authoring some of the themes and motifs of the fictive West, laying claim to westward expansion as the site of heroism and adventure. More importantly, some of the authors and mythmakers of the dime novel carried the stories, themes, and images of the fictive West over into different media.

Through the 1870s and 1880s, the famous dime novel author Ned Buntline (the pen name of Edward Zane Carroll Judson) and his popular

Entered according to Act of Congress, in the year 1893, by FRANK TOUSEY, in the Office of the Librarian of Congress at Washington, D. C.

Entered at the Post Office, at New York, N. Y., as Second Class Matter.

No. 548. {COMPLETE.} FRANK TOUSEY, PUBLISHER, 34 & 36 NORTH MOORE STREET, New York. New York, May 27, 1893. Issued Every Saturday. {PRICE 10 CENTS.} **Vol. I.**

The Subscription Price of DETECTIVE LIBRARY by the year is $5.00; $2.50 per six months, post-paid. Address FRANK TOUSEY, PUBLISHER, 34 & 36 North Moore Street, New York. Box 2730.

THE JAMES BOYS IN PERIL:

OR,

Carl Greene the Detective's Oath.

By D. W. STEVENS.

Siroc was on the edge of the tall bluff, and for a single moment hesitated. "On, Siroc! Liberty or death!" roared Jesse James. Siroc gathered himself up for a mighty spring, rushed to the edge of the

FIGURE 1.1. "Siroc was on the edge of the tall bluff," from D. W. Stevens, "The James Boys in Peril," *New York Detective Library* #548, New York: Frank Tousey, 1893.

THE NEW YORK DIME LIBRARY

Copyrighted, 1897, by Beadle and Adams. Entered as Second Class Matter at the New York, N. Y., Post Office. January 19, 1898.

No. 1004. PUBLISHED EVERY WEDNESDAY. BEADLE AND ADAMS, Publishers, 92 WILLIAM STREET, NEW YORK. TEN CENTS A COPY. $5.00 A YEAR. Vol. LXXVIII.

⊰ BUFFALO BILL'S DEATH-DEAL; ⊱

OR,

The Wandering Jew of the West.

BY

Colonel Prentiss Ingraham.

BUFFALO BILL RODE INTO THEIR MIDST, HIS REVOLVERS RINGING OUT DEATH-KNELLS AT EVERY SHOT.

FIGURE 1.2. "Buffalo Bill rode into their midst," from Colonel Prentiss Ingraham, "Buffalo Bill's Death-Deal," *The New York Dime Library* #1004, New York: Beadle and Adams, 1898.

subject Buffalo Bill (a character based on the frontier scout William F. Cody) made great efforts to extrapolate the dime novel's content and integrate it into theatrical productions. Buntline and Cody acted in numerous Western-themed stage performances in the eastern cities of the United States. Later Cody would develop his traveling Wild West show, which was a much more grandiose live spectacle than his former theater performances, employing hundreds of performers (including cowboys, sharpshooters, and Native Americans) in retelling the settling of the West to audiences across the United States and Europe. Cody's show mixed fact and fiction, using images and themes from popular Western fiction in its various historic reenactments, from the attack on the Deadwood stagecoach to Custer's Last Stand.

More importantly, Joy S. Kasson observes that live spectacle became filmed spectacle when Thomas Edison recorded some vignettes from Buffalo Bill's Wild West show in 1894, inevitably fusing the Wild West with cinema. These sequences offered glimpses into performances from the Wild West show, including a Native American Buffalo Dance, a shooting display by Annie Oakley, and a cowboy's riding demonstration. However, Edison continued his Western shorts into the twentieth century: 1904 witnessed the release of *A Brush between Cowboys and Indians*, *Western Stage Coach Hold Up*, and *The Little Train Robbery* (director Edwin S. Porter's parody of his own *Great Train Robbery* of the previous year). Mary Lea Bandy and Kevin Stoehr suggest that these early silent Western film productions were greatly influenced by popular literature of the previous century but also "contained elements that would be repeated throughout Western movies for decades to come: bold adventure, broad humor, impressive horse riding, outdoor-location shooting, and violent conflicts."[5]

This loose timeline helps to frame the processes of remediation and influence at work. Placing emphasis on the themes, narratives, and images used in the dime novel to convey the Far West as a site of thrilling adventure, we can begin to see how, next to the formulaic stories of frontier conflict narrated within its pages, the illustrated cover of the dime novel is an antecedent medium that offered readers a preliminary means of visualizing the fictive West—before it made a transition into stage performance and later into cinema.

While the dime novel in this respect appeared as a natural precursor of these later incarnations of the popular West, it can be placed into a broader framework of other word-and-image media that emanated from the nineteenth-century illustrated press. Indeed, the rich tradition of pictorial reportage and satirical cartooning can further illustrate the potency of the drawn imaginings of the American West from the 1800s. Pictorial news reportage and satirical cartooning in magazines and newspapers have long been common modes to visually bring news stories to life, but they also helped convey popular opinion surrounding current events. The coverage was no different in the late nineteenth century, and the form covered a wide range of current affairs.[6] However, of most interest here are those cartoons and illustrations that captured the twilight years of the United States' westward movement.

Visualizing the Contested Frontier in Cartoons and Illustrated Reportage

For most of the second half of the nineteenth century, the technology that allowed photographs to be reproduced and published in the press was still in a developmental stage.[7] Therefore, in a time before photographs could be reproduced and circulated to mass audiences, hand-drawn illustrations (which were then mass-produced as lithographs) played a vital role in capturing events happening across the American frontier. In addition, it provided a visual premise to the written accounts from news stories. For instance, when George Ward Nichols wrote an exposé on James "Wild Bill" Hickok's exploits, in an article for *Harper's New Monthly Magazine* (February 1867), Hickok was catapulted into the realm of national celebrity. The article's content was largely exaggerated, but it was the illustrations that added drama to the recounting of certain parts of Hickok's life. For example, details of Hickok's quick-draw shoot-out (one of few recorded instances in the Old West) with Davis Tutt in 1865 are paired with a dramatic image of a triumphant Hickok and his foe (in the throes of death) moments after the shooting (fig. 1.3). Another example can be found in "The Modern Dick Turpin" from *Harper's Weekly* (January 16, 1892), an article that discusses the efforts of the Pinkerton detectives to crack down on train robberies across the country. By the 1890s train robberies were a well-established part of life in the American West. Indeed, Jesse James and his gang had robbed their first train in Iowa in 1873, and as their exploits became much bolder, they became a regular feature in exciting dime-novel tales about banditry. It may be what artist Edward Penfield attempted to evoke in his image that was paired with the 1892 *Harper's* article in which he depicts a scene of bandits conducting a train heist (fig. 1.4).

"ARE YOU SATISFIED?"

FIGURE 1.3. "Are You Satisfied?," from George Ward Nichols, "Wild Bill," *Harper's New Monthly Magazine*, February 1867.

At this point, it is important to add that much gentler illustrated reportage about life in the American West was also popular.[8] However, the examples above demonstrate how drawn representations helped embellish certain wild and barbarous aspects of frontier life. This fitted into a broader pattern of representation of the American West (found in other forms such as dime novels and Wild West performances) that did not capture the quotidian but depicted the region as a site of violent action. Nevertheless, illustrations in magazines and newspapers, in particular editorial cartoons, did something more.

Elizabeth El Refaie describes editorial cartoons as "an illustration, usually in a single panel," that serves "to represent an aspect of social, cultural, or political life in a way that condenses reality and transforms it in a striking, original, and/or humorous way."[9] R. L. Craig argues that editorial cartoons can "create powerful critical narratives by caricature, by juxtaposing related but disparate events and people, by creating imaginary conversations between social groups . . . or symbolic types, and by using multiple images to create narrative and mix factual

HARPER'S WEEKLY

JOURNAL OF CIVILIZATION

Vol. XXXVI.—No. 1830.
Copyright, 1891, by Harper & Brothers.
All Rights Reserved.
NEW YORK, SATURDAY, JANUARY 16, 1892.
TEN CENTS A COPY.
FOUR DOLLARS A YEAR.

THE MODERN DICK TURPIN.—DRAWN BY EDWARD PENFIELD.—[SEE PAGE 63.]

FIGURE 1.4. Edward Penfield, "The Modern Dick Turpin," *Harper's Weekly*, January 16, 1892.

with speculative images."[10] Cartoonists were key players in popular image creation of the nineteenth century, with word-and-image media proving to be at the forefront in expressing popular opinions and summarizing situations and circumstances to the masses. And regarding the contested frontier, editorial cartoons largely focused on the ongoing tensions evoked by Euro-American inroads in the American West and the responses to the nation's colonial ambitions offered by Indigenous populations.

The United States rapidly expanded its presence in the American West in the decades following the Civil War. Treaties were made and then ignored, leading to Native Americans being driven from their homelands and forced onto reservations. To accomplish this, the US Army fought a series of Indian Wars in the West from the late 1860s into the 1880s. However, part of this process involved the production and circulation of cultural and political myths that justified the bloody conquest of the frontier. Through the lenses of Native American studies and settler colonial studies, Jodi Byrd has unpacked this process, suggesting that American Indians and other Indigenous people were framed as "lamentable casualties of national progress who haunt[ed] the United States on the cusp of empire." Byrd describes an empire born out of settler colonialism, in which discourses of Indigenous displacements from nineteenth-century conquest shaped the "Indian" as peoples and nations who stood in the way of US military and economic ambitions. As Byrd summarizes, "U.S. cultural and political preoccupations with indigeneity and the reproduction of Indianness serve to facilitate, justify, and maintain Anglo-American hegemonic mastery over the significations of justice, democracy, law, and terror."[11]

We can see how this culture of dominance is played out through the Western genre in the twentieth century, and particularly in those texts that use the Indian Wars as a narrative source, casting Native Americans as "savage" aggressors opposed to US prosperity. However, this cultural work was at play in precursors like the nineteenth-century illustrated press. During the Indian Wars of the late 1800s, editorial cartoons and illustrated reportage not only captured unfolding events but also reaffirmed the domination of the United States over the contested frontier. The illustrated press promoted the political rhetoric surrounding Manifest Destiny by using racist caricatures that emphasized Native American ferocity and narrative framing that avoided the ambiguities of conquest. This can be found at play in a number of examples of magazine cartoons that show how cartoonists deployed

FIGURE 1.5. William de la Montagne Cary, "The Battle on the Little Big Horn River—The Death Struggle of General Custer," *Daily Graphic*, July 19, 1876.

images of Indian cruelty and "Indianness" as a means to vindicate the nation's pursuit of greatness through its taming of the Wild West.

For John M. Coward, the death of George Armstrong Custer and the defeat of the US Cavalry at the Battle of the Little Bighorn (June 25–26, 1876) was a crucial turning point in the representation of Native Americans in editorial cartoons. Prior to this event, magazines such as the *Daily Graphic* had merely presented Native Americans in humorous racist caricatures, depicting them as inferior but not as a mortal enemy to the United States. Coward argues that Custer's defeat "challenged" this representation, "making it painfully clear that Western Indians remained a threat to American progress and underscoring the continuing dangers of the frontier."[12] The *Daily Graphic* was one of the first publications to circulate an image of Custer's Last Stand on July 19, 1876 (fig. 1.5).[13] Though completely imagined by the artist William de la Montagne Cary, who was nowhere near the battlefield, the *Daily Graphic* attested that the artwork was created "from sketches and description by our special correspondent."[14] The drawing imagines a gallant Custer at the center of a hopeless battle against a mass of attacking Native Americans, valiantly continuing the fight as his comrades are slaughtered around him. While establishing a heroic scene featuring Custer at center stage, most remarkable is how the illustration's framing is reminiscent of a grand, romantic painting of a battle scene. Its wide display captures the chaos of the war scene. This composition of the courageous Custer surrounded by menacing attackers was continually redeployed in the later epic paintings depicting the historic battle, from John Mulvany's *Custer's Last Rally* (1881) and Cassilly Adams's *Custer's Last Fight* (1884) to Edgar Samuel Paxson's *Custer's Last Stand* (1899).[15] The lasting impact of Cary's illustration owes to the immediacy of its printing—circulated in a matter of weeks after the event—ensuring that the symbolic image of the fearless soldier front and center in a losing battle of attrition would shape and influence countless visual imaginings of this American defeat in popular culture for years to come.

Moreover, like the Hickok illustration from *Harper's* (fig. 1.3), this example again indicates how the illustrated press incorporated the most exciting representations of heroism and violent action into reportage of events occurring on the American frontier. This point will be returned to shortly, as we look again at the influence of the nineteenth-century illustrated press on the development of the Western genre in the twentieth century. However, Cary's drawing signals to a wider point about how illustrated news stories were culpable in the mythmaking process associated with the American West and indeed in shaping the perceived role of Native Americans within this national myth.

Gerald Vizenor describes Indian "savagery" and the construction of "Indianness" as "simulations of dominance"—in other words, misnomers that are presented as authentic representations of Native Americans that have been enforced and naturalized by centuries of empire culture. Vizenor suggests that "the savage as an impediment to developmental civilization" was a "bankable" simulation "that audiences would consume in Western literature and motion pictures, [and] protracted the extermination of tribal cultures."[16] We can see this in the Cary illustration—the hopeless cause of the righteous national hero fighting off scores of attackers, thus emphasizing an urgent need for retribution. Goenpul scholar Aileen Moreton-Robinson argues that "simulations of dominance" (to take Vizenor's wording) are a tool "deployed in response to a perceived threat of invasion and dispossession from Indigenous people"; in the process, "paranoid patriarchal white sovereignty" manages its anxiety over dispossession and threat through a "pathological relationship to Indigenous sovereignty."[17] Byrd

FIGURE 1.6. H. Poland, "The Right Way to Dispose of Sitting Bull and His Braves," *Daily Graphic*, August 11, 1876.

adds to this by drawing on the writing of Judith Butler and the concept of the "derealization of the Other" as a means of describing how Native American bodies were targeted for surveillance and destruction by US patriotic pathology: "In the United States, the Indian is the original enemy combatant who cannot be grieved."[18] When read from this perspective, an examination of editorial cartoons can reveal how "simulations of dominance" were manufactured not only in the promotion of US settler colonialism but also as a response to any threats posed to its success. Indeed, the shocking nature of Custer's defeat in June 1876 led to a series of cartoons that vindicated and encouraged violent retribution against Native Americans.

A stark example is the cartoon captioned "The True Solution of the Indian Problem," which was printed in the *Daily Graphic* on the July 8, 1876, just two weeks after the defeat of Custer at the Battle of the Little Bighorn. It depicts Uncle Sam with a scythe (its blade emblazoned with the word "Extermination") looming large over a band of fleeing Native Americans. (See fig. 0.2 in the introduction.)[19] Its blunt message encourages the reader to support the nation's vengeance in the face of an embarrassing defeat. An August 1876 cover of the *Daily Graphic*, printed a month after the "True Solution" image appeared, offered "The Right Way to Dispose of Sitting Bull and His Braves" (fig. 1.6). It is much more hyperbolic in its emphasis on vengeance. It also reflects the creative and imaginative freedoms inherent in illustration: the artist of the piece transforms a Native American into a grotesque caricature of a centaur. We see this sinister half-man, half-beast in his death throes, trampling over a scalped soldier (presumably Custer), who lies next to the fallen American flag. A patriotic soldier, standing upright in triumph after shooting this embodiment of Indian savagery, is an idealized personification of the nation. The cartoon underscores that violence needs to be met with greater violence. However, the artist's dehumanizing, animalistic caricature of Native Americans also shows how the illustrated press othered Indigenous people through depictions of the unreal. By representing Native Americans through ugly caricature, editorial cartoons like the one discussed above this served not only to promote bloody vengeance as a response to American defeat but also to naturalize and make palatable the process of expansion and conquest that would cause the deaths of millions of tribal people from massacres, diseases, and removal. In these terms, magazine illustrations and editorial cartoons were a vital tool for the nation's imperial desires.

PATIENCE UNTIL THE INDIAN *IS* CIVILIZED—SO TO SPEAK.

SECRETARY OF THE INTERIOR. "There are two methods of Indian management possible: either to herd and corral the Indians under the walls or guns of a military force, so to speak, so as to watch them and prevent outbreaks; or to start them at work upon their lands, to educate them, and to civilize them...... There are in the Army a great many gentlemen who have good ideas about the Indian Service, but it is one thing to have ideas, and another to carry them out, and I think that the patient labor and care of detail necessary to raise the Indian tribes to a state of civilization would not be found among the officers of the Army."

FIGURE 1.7. Thomas Nast, "Patience until the Indian Is Civilized—So to Speak," *Harper's Weekly*, December 28, 1878.

These are some of the most extreme cases of editorial cartoons that vilify Native Americans and promote complete extermination of Indigenous populations. For instance, "Patience until the Indian Is Civilized—So to Speak" (*Harper's Weekly*, December 28, 1878), is much more subtle in its approach (fig. 1.7). It depicts Secretary of the Interior Carl Schurz lecturing a homesteader to wait for the American Indians to integrate into white American society. Around the settler's feet lie the dead bodies of his murdered family, and his home burns in the background. Meanwhile the culprits, a group of Native Americans, ride off into the distance. This cartoon was produced at a time when Schurz was introducing reform at the Office of Indian Affairs. He hoped to "civilize" Native Americans through education and introduce them to agricultural work, which conflicted with the War Department's aim of "pacification" through violence.[20] The effect of the cartoon is achieved through the tensions between word and image. The image of seemingly unprovoked violence belies Schurz's advice: "Patience until the Indian Is civilized."[21] The scene of slaughter undermines the verbal passivity of Schurz's policy; we see that his method of gradual change is rendered futile in the face of naked aggression of Native Americans toward the settlers. By implicitly nullifying alternative solutions to "the Indian problem," the cartoon becomes a powerful advocate of military force.

Some cartoons, on the other hand, were less stark in their presentation. For example, "Woes of the Western Agriculturist," by Frederick Burr Opper (*Puck*, July 20, 1881), takes this source material in a more unusual comedic direction (fig. 1.8). The cartoon betrays the idealism of the United States' inexorable westward movement by presenting the Western frontier as a site of all-out treachery. We see a farmer shot in the back by "renegades" and "bushwhackers" who steal his claim. Meanwhile, his family are murdered, scalped, and kidnapped; his cabin is set alight by Native Americans from a nearby reservation; and enormous grasshoppers feed on his crop. Opper subverts the tropes of adventure and heroism that were engrained in various mythmakers' conceptualizations of US westward expansion. The artistic line caricatures figures from the West to humorous effect, but by foregrounding a sense of futile drudgery, Opper undermines much of the political rhetoric, reportage, painting, and popular fiction that framed the American West as a site calling out to be conquered and cultivated. Indeed, his caricatured West is clearly bereft of such aspirational and idealist value. However, his representation of Native Americans as a threat to US prosperity is worth further consideration.

WOES OF THE WESTERN AGRICULTURIST.

"THE FARMER'S LIFE IS NOT A HAPPY ONE!"

FIGURE 1.8. Frederick Burr Opper, "Woes of the Western Agriculturist," *Puck*, July 20, 1881.

The representation of Native Americans in nineteenth-century cartoons is far broader than the sample used for analysis here. Indeed, Native Americans were represented through a range of awful stereotypes, from drunkards and imbeciles to victims of Indian agents' greed. Cartoonists regularly placed blame on the illegal sale (by Anglo-Americans) of alcohol and arms to Indigenous people as a root cause of Native American aggression.[22] Nonetheless, the themes and visual tropes caught in the sample of cartoons here articulate codes and cues that whites used to represent Native Americans in the twilight years of their struggle against white expansion. Coward notes that when measured next to American progress in this manner, "cartoons 'naturalized' the image of Indian savagery, . . . reinforc[ing] the idea of the threatening, hyperviolent Indian as a menace to civilization."[23] These images can be more broadly incorporated into the myths of conquest bound up in America's westward expansion. Printed during the ongoing American expropriation of Indian lands in the West, cartoons helped establish the representation of Native Americans as both "savage" aggressors and figures resistant to American progress, at a time when the nation was close to claiming the last of the frontier.

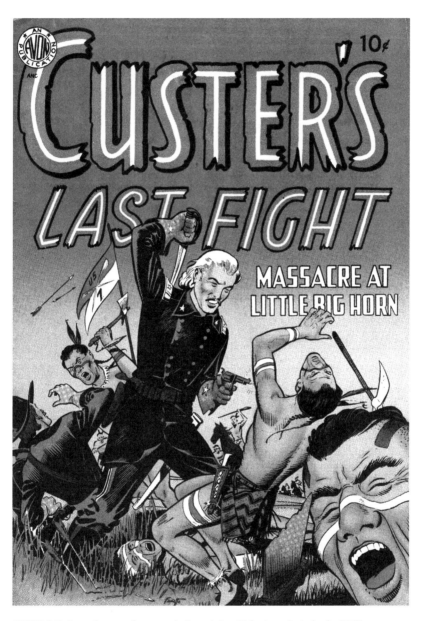

FIGURE 1.9. Gene Fawcette (cover art). *Custer's Last Fight*, Avon Periodicals, 1950.

However, more controversially, these simulations of dominance were carried over into the twentieth century, as this historical content was reproduced in popular new narrative forms such as cinema, comic strips, and comic books. Indeed, the twentieth-century Western genre often reimagined racial conflicts from the previous century for new audiences, depicting the frontier as a dangerous wilderness that was calling out to be tamed. This of course echoed the nationalistic themes found in earlier editorial cartoons of Native Americans as aggressors and saboteurs blocking the righteous white conquerors' quest for progress and nation building. One expressive example of this is the cover of Avon Periodicals, one-shot, *Custer's Last Fight*, printed in 1950 (fig. 1.9). We can see the lasting impact of editorial cartoons in how the artist visualized the contested frontier: Gene Fawcett frames a gallant Custer, surrounded by attackers, courageously fighting on against all odds, a trope that was originally imagined nearly seventy-five years earlier in Cary's 1876 illustration of the battle. Moreover, this example helps illustrate how the symbols and myths around Native American sabotage of American prosperity were continually rearticulated, finding resonance with new audiences in the twentieth century. Western adventure comic books will be a focus of later chapters, although their mention here points to some interesting associations between the nineteenth-century illustrated press, cartooning, and the development of the comics medium.

The Relationship between Cartoons and Comic Strips

In drawing together this sample of nineteenth-century illustrations and cartoons, we see that these early visualizations of dramatic frontier action and adventure—and racist imagery—established some enduring common myths about westward expansion. But we can also begin to draw out some broader links to the historical development of the newspaper comic strip. Patricia Mainardi asserts that the modern-day comics medium draws from developments in the illustrated press of the nineteenth century, including the humorous drawing styles and methods of storytelling found in editorial cartoons (as well as book illustrations).[24] Comics historian Robert C. Harvey places a stronger emphasis on formal properties in his attempt to locate the influence of nineteenth-century editorial cartoons on the development of the newspaper comic strip at the turn of the twentieth century.

Harvey suggests that the interplay between word and image is the uniting factor of cartoon and comics history, and not sequencing, which problematizes the work of Scott McCloud. Indeed, McCloud suggests that comics are "juxtaposed pictorial and other images in sequence."[25] However, much of the importance placed on sequencing between individual panels in a series is lost in single-panel cartoons. Instead, Harvey looks to the economy of expression at a cartoonist's disposal, or the process of "blending" verbal and visual content to make meaning.[26] This is best exemplified by fig. 1.7, the cartoon depicting Schurz lecturing a white settler who has lost his family and home to a raid. The image itself tells a story, but it is through the caption's interaction with the scene that the overarching comprehension is achieved. In this case, the image of whites slaughtered by Native Americans subverts the caption, which details Carl Schurz's seemingly soft approach to the American Indians, thus revealing a strong critique of the secretary of the interior's policy. As Harvey surmises, the "impact" of cartoons derives from "the combined 'meaning' of the visual-verbal blend."[27] This core function of the cartoon's form was continued in newspaper comic strips at the turn of the century (namely through the panel images and corresponding speech balloons and captions). However, Harvey posits that comic strip artists moved beyond the moment captured within a cartoon's single frame, extending its content by breaking the narrative into successive panels, giving the comics a duration.[28]

The contention here is that a cartoon only captures a moment within its single panel. While such an assertion may be justified by the various cartoons that Harvey uses to illustrate his point, in the above examples (particularly in the shooting scenes captured in figs. 1.3 and 1.6), we can see different time frames coexisting within the panel. For instance, fig. 1.6 shows us the grotesque caricature of a Native American in the instant of being shot and rearing backward in pain. However, we do not see the US soldier in the act of shooting the man, as one would expect; the soldier is already in repose, offering a measured evaluation of his act of violence. Likewise, in fig. 1.3, we see a similar instance of a man (this time Davis Tutt) in his death throes, while the shooter, Hickok, is not facing his adversary with the gun aimed in his direction but is instead turned to face the onlooking crowd. Granted, the gaps between these two time frames are fairly minimal. They have perhaps been represented in this manner by the artist for dramatic effect: the shooter stands triumphant; nearby his foe is caught in the grip of death. Fig. 1.7 is a more interesting example of the stylistic interdependence of past and present that coexist on the page. In the immediate foreground we see Schurz lecturing a white settler to have patience. This setup is abstracted from the background scene of slaughter and the fleeing attackers. The plumes of smoke carving out this disconnect between the foreground and background create a hazy vision, as if the attack were a past memory that haunts the injured settler at the fore. These examples problematize Harvey's reading of the cartoon. Rather than reflecting a moment in time, these textured artworks ask their readers to fill in the gaps that are created by the disjuncture of time in the images. Nonetheless, these instances do corroborate Harvey's connecting cartoons and the comic strip.

Indeed, comics form unites varying semantic systems (largely textual and symbolic) into panels where meaning is made through a collaborative process: between word and image, in the gutters between the sequential frames, and between reader and writer. The above cartoons require the reader to unpack the image to make meaning, and comprehension is achieved via the negotiation of the verbal-visual blending at work. This is useful in signaling how cartoons deployed some of the common processes later found in comics.[29]

This should not be a revelation to anyone familiar with the history of the newspaper comic strip.[30] However, it does give credence to Roger Sabin's categorization of the nineteenth-century cartoon-based magazines as a form of "proto-comics" that shaped the development of the American newspaper comic strip.[31] In extrapolating this term, perhaps "proto–Western comics" may best be used to describe these early word-and-image retellings of microcosms of American Western history. Indeed, these instances contained some of the raw materials that would later be found in Western comics. Triumphal battle scenes featuring righteous white heroes standing against all odds amid surrounding savagery were still being redeployed in the various Western comic books of the mid-twentieth century. (See, for example, fig. 1.9.) These visual tropes celebrated the American experience through retelling tales of frontier heroes who must stave off threats to progress and nation building. (For more on this theme, see chapter 5.)

Likewise, Opper's style of artwork, which provided a caricatured and satirical rendition of the frontier, would be commonplace in comics. The comedic essence of Opper's West can be found in examples such as some of the comic strips from *MAD* magazine, which regularly subverted and lampooned popular Western films from the midcentury (discussed in chapter 6); and in the irreverent anti-Western strip *Tumbleweeds* (1965–2007). The latter emerged as the aspirational and heroic idealism of the Western ceased to function in a country mired in the war in Vietnam (as discussed in chapter 7). In this respect, Western comics can support and adhere to the grand narratives of the American West, but they also have license to satirize, subvert, and challenge them. These nuances will be brought out throughout the course of this history of American Western comics but are drawn upon here as a means of locating their origins in the cartoon-based magazines of the nineteenth century.

This postulation begins to provide a framework for this history of Western comics, as we start to see themes that continue through the form. However, one key theme of American West cartooning from the nineteenth century has not yet been touched on—but it would infuse the Western comics of the turn of the century: the morose sense of loss and nostalgia for a bygone age.

In Robert Fischer's history of "anti-Indian cartooning" in the nineteenth century, he suggests that a real turning point in its production was the tragedy at Wounded Knee on December 29, 1890, when soldiers of the Seventh Cavalry, Custer's old command, surrounded a Lakota Sioux encampment on Pine Ridge Reservation in South Dakota.[32] A rifle was fired (by whom and under what circumstance remain unclear), and by the end of the encounter twenty-five soldiers and several hundred Sioux (many of whom were women and children) lay dead. The event shocked and sobered the nation and found echoes in the weekly humor magazines, which broke with their troubled, vilifying representations of Native Americans and applied a gloomier tone in their reportage. For example, on January 3, 1891, the cover of *Judge* featured the cartoon "Ever Our Indian Policy," featuring Secretary of the Interior John W. Noble viewing the corpses of fallen Sioux people who lay on their funeral racks as vultures circle above. Next to this critical commentary on the government's Indian policy, *Harper's Weekly* (February 14, 1891) presented a more pared-down and somber image, "The Last Scene of the Last Act of the Sioux War," which featured a Lakota woman mourning a slain warrior lying on a burial platform (fig. 1.10). The stillness of the image certainly countered much of the exciting action-packed reportage of the Indian Wars, providing a powerful solemnity not often registered in American West illustrations of the era. Parallel to this softening, Fischer notes a number of unfortunate cartoons printed after Wounded Knee that continued to denigrate Native

FIGURE 1.10. H. F. Farny, "The Last Scene of the Last Act of the Sioux War," *Harper's Weekly*, February 14, 1891.

Americans. However, he suggests that "Wounded Knee did effect real change in anti-Indian cartooning, not because of tender consciences but because it rang down the curtain on newsworthy western warfare and ushered in a long period in which Indians were almost wholly out of sight and out of mind for artists and their audiences alike."[33]

The popular West had thrived in American culture of the late nineteenth century, but its development faced new challenges by 1890. Not only did the massacre at Wounded Knee mark the concluding act of the Sioux Wars and what Fischer observed as the end of "newsworthy western warfare," but the superintendent of the US Census announced that widespread settlement across the American West had erased the frontier line. This signaled the close of the Western frontier and the end of an epoch that had provided a wealth of exciting source material for artists, writers, and performers.

Frederick Jackson Turner was perhaps the most immediate, or, failing that, most conspicuous respondent, declaring in 1893 that a major era in America's growth had faded into history. At the Columbian Exposition in Chicago, marking the four-hundredth anniversary of Columbus's "discovery" of the New World, Turner argued that the end of the Western frontier marked the end of the nation's formative experience, a process that had shaped its character and values.[34] In one sense, his nostalgic appraisal also marked the passage of the United States from an agrarian society to an industrialized multicultural and multiethnic state, but his assessment did not go unnoticed. Gerald D. Nash suggests that "almost immediately the reverberation of his essay reached beyond the halls of academe." Turner's elegiac frontier theme was first acknowledged in political spheres before it crossed into writing, art, and music and finally entered "national consciousness and myth."[35]

The politically motivated representations of the America West commonplace in the magazine cartoon of the late 1800s were problematized in light of this reconceptualization of the frontier as a bygone world. However, things were changing in the newspaper industry also. Indeed, the 1890s witnessed the emergence of the newspaper comic strip. This new form did not supplant the single-panel cartoon but rather grew out of it. While Fischer encourages us not to think of some of the final cartoons that reported on the Indian Wars (such as fig. 1.10) as a product of "tender consciences," such illustrations in retrospect certainly captured the sense of deep regret and perhaps a realization that the American frontier—a time of great opportunity and adventure in American history (at least according to the mythmakers of popular culture)—had entered its twilight years. And it was the sense of loss and regret for the disappearance of the frontier that played a heavy influence upon those turn-of-the-century comic strips that represented the American West.

CHAPTER 2

The Spectacle of the Southwest

Postfrontier Imaginings of the Far West in
Newspaper Comic Strips

THE HISTORICAL WEST BECAME THE mythic West with the closing of the frontier in 1890. As William Bloodworth suggests: "Suddenly lacking an actual frontier as a place to demonstrate the triumph of civilization, Americans turned to imaginary frontier experiences."[1] Through a range of examples—from symbolic images of Native Americans in paintings to tales of frontier heroism detailed in fiction and film—scholarship has identified how presentations of the American West between the 1890s and the 1920s were imbued with a distinct sense of loss and nostalgia for this bygone age. However, one generally overlooked medium that entered into this cultural exchange is the newspaper comic strip.

Newspaper comic strips emerged on the heels of a series of antecedent media that came out of the illustrated press in the latter half of the nineteenth century (such as books, illustrated periodicals, and humor anthologies that included cartoons). Pascal Lefèvre writes that "the first convincing successful use of graphic narratives in a newspaper occurred in the weekly format of American Sunday supplements" in the late 1800s.[2] Content from this new narrative medium often took its setting from the domestic sphere, and early comic strips tended to reflect contemporary everyday life. In this regard, newspaper strips offer a unique insight into modern America's reaction to the changing mythic landscape of the West. Rather than playing out historically set action and adventure narratives like the Westerns of fiction and film, comics from the early twentieth century instead captured modern American's experiences with this recent bygone world: either through a character's surreal interactions with the cinematic Western or through strange tourist encounters with the geographical West. Indeed, cartoonists like James Swinnerton, Frank King, and George

Herriman would all visit the geographical American West, and they subsequently transfigured their experiences in the popular comic strips *Little Jimmy* (1904–1958), *Gasoline Alley* (from 1918), and *Krazy Kat* (1913–1944) (respectively). In their own unique ways, each artist's American West blended mythic Western figures with real geographical locations, and the interplay of fantasy and reality offered evocative commentary on the West's transformation into a mythic landscape. This chapter challenges conventional perspectives on the Western from this era through an examination of newspaper comic strips and traces the alternative responses that comics provided in reaction to the United States' passage from an agrarian society to a newly emerging urban-industrial state. While not Westerns per se, the Western themes and iconographies in such comics exemplify how both the genre and the form acted as a barometer for the national mood—in this case, the gnawing sense of dissatisfaction with accelerated modernization.

The Postfrontier Western

The 1890s was a pivotal decade during which many elements that constituted the experience of the Western frontier as a historical reality seemingly ended; and it was a decade during which the conceptualization of the West was irrevocably altered. Frederick Jackson Turner's frontier thesis of 1893 was an early catalyst in this revision. Turner's nostalgic appraisal argued that the era of mass migration and settlement across the frontier was the nation's formative experience, shaping its character and values. Likewise, his thesis gestured to the end of the independent, agriculturist tradition and the rise of modern industrial societies. The rapid growth of cities challenged the bounds of American identity, values, and social structures. Nevertheless, Thomas Schatz claims that this transformation was an important moment for the popular West, too, suggesting that "the cumulative effects of the Western storytelling in the face of contemporary civilisation's steady encroachment served to subordinate the genre's historical function to a mythical one."[3] The previous chapter revealed how this process was ongoing throughout the nineteenth century, as popular culture developed a narrative framework that justified American expansion across the frontier while cultivating an imagined American West as a source of high adventure and entertainment. This was expressed not only in magazine cartoons but also in fiction, painting, and stage performances (such as Buffalo Bill Cody's Wild West show). However, the

1890s was a key turning point for the Western precisely because live spectacle gave way to cinematic spectacle as Thomas Edison captured vignettes from Cody's shows in the films *Sioux Ghost Dance* (1894), *Annie Oakley* (1894), and *Bucking Broncho* (1894).

Backed by Turner's acknowledgment of the passing of the frontier in his 1893 thesis and underscored by the massacre of Lakota Indians at Wounded Knee in December 1890, which wrote a tragic epilogue to nearly four decades of Indian Wars, Edison's shorts captured fragments from a vanishing epoch in American history. The films highlighted all the things that had remained fascinating and exciting about the American West in the nineteenth century: exotic Native American culture, shooting displays, and galloping horses. While Edison's short action vignettes caught the attention of curious audiences, later directors added to this material, signaling that the Western could be a viable and sustaining source of narrative entertainment. Edwin S. Porter's *The Great Train Robbery* (1903) was perhaps the clearest example of this, distinguished by its plot in which a gang holds up a train and is subsequently hunted down by a posse. Filmed both in Edison's New York studio and on location in a forested area of New Jersey, Porter's film was more of a contemporary crime thriller, but it contained dominant motifs that would continually be found in Western films: outlaws conducting daring robberies, fistfights and gunplay, and chases on horseback over vast expanses of unspoiled wilderness.

Filmmakers from the early decades of the twentieth century already could tap a rich vein of prevailing themes, icons, and situations associated with the imaginary American West. For example, Owen Wister's novel *The Virginian* (1902) had crystallized much of the idealization of America's frontier heritage in the central figure of the cowboy. The novel inspired a trend of films that featured a heroic cowboy who comes to the rescue of women and children (starting with *Bronco Billy's Redemption* [1910]). Likewise, Native Americans posed an interesting subject for early filmmakers, who portrayed them as enigmatic and deadly. Filmmakers translated the political struggle between the Indian nations and the United States into a set of thrilling conflicts on screen. As Scott Simmon observes, the gun violence and war narratives found in silent Westerns like *On the War Path* (1911), *The Indian Massacre* (1912), and *The Massacre* (1912) shaped the pattern that Hollywood continued to adopt for years to come.[4] The Wild West was readily adapted to the dramatic pace and visual power of cinema, and the films proved hugely popular: around fifty Western one-reelers were released in 1909, and between one hundred and two hundred such films were released each year through 1914.[5]

However, the preeminence of the Western at the turn of the century was not due to cinema alone. Christine Bold clarifies that much of the formulaic content from Western-themed dime novels of the nineteenth century was continued in the subsequent pulp fiction of the twentieth century: notable writers like Zane Grey and Frederick Faust (better known by his pen name Max Brand) emerged in the 1910s and refreshed the genre through a heightened attention to violence, sexual thrills, and lavish scenic descriptions.[6] In terms of its cultural work, the intensive narrativizing of American history in exciting Western fiction and film at the turn of the twentieth century arguably forged a dominant format for how the American West was imagined in popular culture.

As mentioned above, the sustained popularity of the Western in the early years of the twentieth century was a response to the closing of the frontier and the opening of a new, urban environment. The Western helped reinforce and promote the mythic assumptions about this period while sharing a complex relationship with anxieties surrounding the dramatic social changes of its own time. Wister's *The Virginian* is one clear example of this process. It tells of the mysterious stranger, known only as the Virginian, who arrives in Sunk Creek, Wyoming. Throughout the course of the story, the Virginian wins the heart of the local schoolteacher, lynches a cattle rustler, and finally defeats his recurring nemesis in a gunfight, synthesizing both wild and civilized traits like individual freedom and loyalty to others, while demonstrating that the use of violence is necessary to rid evil from society and champion civilization. Wister's formulation of the cowboy hero, in terms of presentation, manner, and skills, defined the Western in the twentieth century. However, *The Virginian* was also discursive in its engagement with turn-of-the-century political and social debates. Indeed, the text reflected fin de siècle anxieties over a decline in traditional American values brought about by industrialization and mass immigration, appealing to the reader through both its setting in the romanticized rural West and its heroic Anglo-American protagonist.

Early silent Western films explored similar anxieties surrounding modernization. They largely articulated this regional history through violent action and adventure stories, although rooted among these films were a handful that portrayed a strong elegiac quality, which was achieved primarily through the cinematic framing of Native Americans and their natural harmony with the wilderness. As Richard Schickle observes, D. W. Griffith's "romanticizing of the savage and the natural environment" in some of his early silent Westerns coincided "with the nation's first awareness that the frontier had finally closed, [and] that it had just lost something it had always taken for granted—untamed, untouched lands to the West."[7] For instance, *The Mended Lute* (1909) imagines Native American life in a time before their contact with white settlers and makes effective use of the natural landscape in an impressive chase sequence that features canoes gliding down a series of rivers. In the film *The Redman's View* (1909), we see a group of white settlers—introduced as "The Conquerors" in the title card—mercilessly harass a tribe of Native Americans, banishing them from their home-land. Griffith frames the long trek away from their land against rolling hillsides, with shots often capturing the tribe looking ominously into the distance off-camera on their solemn retreat.

Bandy and Stoehr suggest that such films portrayed tensions and moral ambivalence about the United States' historical maltreatment of Native Americans, particularly as hindsight in these immediate years following the close of the frontier had made audiences aware that the characters on screen were subject to conquest and eventual genocide.[8] Moreover, Simmon suggests that Griffith's early silent Western films established a "tableau idyll" that captured the harmony between Native Americans and nature but also carried "a further aura of loss and melancholy." Indeed, so poignant was Griffith's framing of a Native American character ruefully looking off into the distant valleys (in *The Redman's View*) that Simmon suggests it was "enough to imply an entire narrative of civilization's advance and the native's demise."[9]

In 1908 Frederic Remington evoked this allegory in a painting he titled *The Last of His Race*, which similarly depicts a Native American man on a hillside looking off into the distance. Likewise, A. T. Crichton's comic strip *Little Growling Bird in Windego Land*, which ran in the *North American* between 1906 and 1907, also placed Native Americans in harmony with nature (fig. 2.1). The comic features the adventures of Little Growling Bird, a young Ojibwe boy who is filled with a sense of awe for the forest he lives in, and throughout the series he is found interacting with its natural ecology and wildlife. Each Sunday strip followed the boy and his talking animal friends as they completed a certain task or investigated a certain area of the forest. For instance, the inaugural comic strip involves Little Growling Bird and the crow, Aun-dak, hunting down the Giant Spirits, the Windegoes, who

Little Growling Bird in Windego Land

FIGURE 2.1. A. T. Crichton, *Little Growling Bird in Windego Land*, Darke County, OH: Coachwhip Publications.

used to wander the lands. Nevertheless, the story soon progresses from its telling of Little Growling Bird's preoccupation with Ojibwe lore and his natural surroundings after he meets and befriends a young white girl, Fanny Yellow Hair, who has become lost in the forest. The weekly printing of the pair's adventures in the wilderness gave an egalitarian quality to the series, and the focus on interracial friendship gave a softer and more humanizing view of Native Americans than what was often found in the Westerns of fiction and film from the time.

In one respect, the idyllic presentation of the tranquil landscape and Little Growling Bird's intimate connection with the surrounding natural world echoed the images found in the paintings of Remington and the early silent Westerns of Griffith. However, the Western was not alone in its cultural response to modern industrial life at the turn of the century, and the acknowledgment of Crichton's strip above usefully alludes to the entry of the newspaper comic strips into this discourse. Indeed, this period of dramatic change played a fundamental part in the development of the newspaper comic strip.

Early Newspaper Strips and the Western

Comics were still in their infancy in the late 1800s.[10] As discussed in the previous chapter, cartoon-based magazines and their cartoonists did much to develop various tenets found later in newspaper comic strips. However, this was formalized when the mass of cartoons, satirical drawings, and illustrations found in the likes of *Harper's Weekly* (1857), *Puck* (1877), *Judge* (1881), and *Life* (1883) caught the attention of the newspaper magnate Joseph Pulitzer. Biographer George Juergens observes how "Pulitzer and his staff came to see in illustrations a great, unexploited medium of communication."[11] Pulitzer not only elevated illustration from an occasional novelty in his *New York World* to an important tool in reporting the news, but with the help of the cartoonist Richard F. Outcault, he would develop the artistic dimensions of the newspaper comic strip. Indeed, Outcault blended a succession of child characters that had appeared in his cartoons for *Truth* magazine in 1894 to form a recognizable character, the Yellow Kid, who took a leading role in the comic strip *Hogan's Alley*. Dubbed "the Yellow Kid" by readers because of the color of the character's nightshirt, the comic appeared in Pulitzer's *New York World* newspaper between 1895 and 1896.

Although the lifespan of the Yellow Kid was short-lived, other comic strips soon followed, such as Rudolph Dirk's *The Katzenjammer Kids*

(1897) and Frederick Burr Opper's *Happy Hooligan* (1900), which ensured the success of the comic strip form. These early newspaper strips formalized most of the basic elements that continued to be used and further developed by future creators: among them color printing (replacing the previous black-and-white cartoons from magazines), sequential-panel narratives, use of speech balloons, and recurring characters.[12]

Newspaper comic strips were offered as colored supplements in the Sunday newspapers. Their purpose was to provide easily accessible humor for a mass readership of big-city-dwelling workers, immigrants, and children. As David Hajdu summarizes, "The comics offered their audience a parodic look at itself, rendered in the vernacular of caricature and nonsense language. The mockery in comics was familial—intimate, knowing, affectionate, and merciless."[13] Indeed, *Hogan's Alley* was set in the slums of Manhattan's Lower East Side, depicting the rowdy antics of a gang of young street urchins; *Happy Hooligan* followed a tramp's humorous scrapes with the law; and *Katzenjammer Kids* saw a pair of immigrant German twins causing havoc among various walks of society. Jared Gardner suggests that rather than disdaining the perils of modern life (urban poverty, overcrowding, and crime), comic strips celebrated these same forces, finding humor and humanity in the midst of these inhuman conditions.[14] This notion is echoed by Ian Gordon, who identifies how comic strips at the turn of the century can be viewed as both "an outcome of the process of modernization" and "as a humor-based response to the problems of representation faced by a society in transition."[15]

Initially circulated in big-city newspapers, it was not long before comic strips became nationwide fare, with strips syndicated across a vast range of newspapers. To appeal to a mass readership, content eventually moved beyond the eccentric presentations of life in urban areas and began to focus on more universal themes: the everyday (however exaggerated), the workplace, homelife, and family. Some standout series included Bud Fisher's *Mutt and Jeff* (1907), George McManus's *Bringing Up Father* (1913), and Sidney Smith's *The Gumps* (1917).[16] In this respect, the comic strip provided a window into modern America, offering humorous observations about society and culture. This of course was in stark contrast to the Westerns from this era.

At the turn of the century the Western was lamenting the very conditions of modernization that the newspaper comic strip celebrated, looking backward to a historical and romanticized rural setting that could not be recaptured. Gerald D. Nash outlines a certain zeitgeist that permeated people's perceptions of the American West in the early decades of the twentieth century. As he observes:

> The generation that wrote [on the subject of the American West] during the years from 1890 to 1920 were overcome with a profound sense of loss, a feeling of nostalgia for the disappearance of a world which they had cherished, a world which had been at the very center of the American Dream, of the national mythology which Americans used to explain themselves not only to each other, but to the rest of the world.[17]

The profound sense of loss and nostalgia that Nash outlines certainly imbued the aforementioned range of elegiac presentations in some of Griffith's films, the literature of Wister, the paintings of Remington, and comics of Crichton. Notwithstanding Crichton's saga about the life of a young Native American boy in the wilderness, newspaper comic strips in this same period provided a distinct counterpoint to this discourse, reveling in the very social conditions of modern life that Westerns bemoaned and presenting the everyday through hyperbolic and humorous accentuations. In this regard, those strips set in the American West, or that featured icons and themes relating to it, tended to present a very different perspective on the region than other sources of popular culture at the time.

Indeed, among the newspaper comic strip's reflections on modern American life and culture, the formidable translation of American Western history into exciting genre fiction and film at the turn of the twentieth century was not lost on this burgeoning narrative medium. Rather than rendering the American West as a historical site of action and adventure like the Westerns of fiction and film, comic strips instead captured modern America's strange interactions with the mythic West. And within some of these modern-day encounters with the mythic West, we can locate the same spirit of loss and nostalgia that Nash observes in Westerns from other sources of popular culture.

Out Our Way (1922–1977) by J. R. Williams is one such example. Williams had lived a varied life before becoming a comics artist; at different times he worked as a cowhand on a ranch in New Mexico and joined the US Cavalry in Oklahoma.[18] These experiences informed his depiction of American rural life from the perspective of various recurring characters, like the cowboy, Curly, and the ranch hand, Wes, producing a humorous yet affectionate depiction of cowboy life.

Out Our Way   *By Williams*

FIGURE 2.2. J. R. Williams, *Out Our Way*, Newspaper Enterprise Association, March 25, 1922.

Throughout the course of Williams's comics series, his work is punctuated by reappropriations of the heavily mythologized cowboy hero from popular culture, in which the artist foregrounds true-to-life facts and details about ranch life in the jocular situations amid which he sets his cowboy cast. The effect of this work presents a critical tension with the transformation of cowboy life into a narrative genre.

One arresting example of this at work can be found in an early cartoon that Williams produced for his *Out Our Way* series. It depicts an old man, Doc Teeters, who confuses a cowboy inviting people for a drink at the bar on the cinema screen in front of him with a real-life invitation (fig. 2.2). The scene is at once humorous in presenting the out-of-touch man's interaction with the cinematic medium, but it also reflects a surreal encounter with a way of life not too far removed from America's past. As with Williams (born in 1888), who had experienced this transition himself, we can presume that the "old absent minded" Doc Teeters in the 1922 cartoon personifies the gap between the actual nineteenth-century West and its contemporary simulation on cinema screens.

The historical conception of the American West by the early 1920s was largely the product of its representation in popular culture, whereby the historical landscape was not merely depicted but had begun to be written and constructed. Thus, Williams's sharp use of humor makes a more erudite comment about the point at which this historical "reality" and its media depictions have become fused and inseparable in Western films. Drawing on Baudrillard's notion of hyperreality, in which he argues that the "real" (in this case the historical West) is lost, can inform our reading of Williams's cartoon, which reveals an elegiac response to the fictional construction of the West.[19] Western films relied on an audience's hindsight in the years following the close of the frontier to convey tensions and moral ambivalence with westward expansion—or to evoke a "profound sense of loss, [and] a feeling of nostalgia," to use Nash's wording. By contrast, Williams creates a similar response in a much more wry and humorous manner, depicting Doc Teeter's seeming lack of hindsight as he confuses the "real" Western frontier for the one simulated on the cinema screen.

Another, more dominant, formula in turn-of-the-century comic strips that engaged with the Western was a narrative in which denizens from big eastern American cities confronted figures from the mythic frontier as they journeyed way out West. For example, Rudolph Dirk's *Katzenjammer Kids* had a continuing storyline through 1909 and 1910 that pitted the mischievous child characters against the dangers of the Wild West.[20] This could also be found in Winsor McCay's *Little Nemo in Slumberland* (1905–1911), which told of young Nemo's weekly adventures in a dreamworld as he shuts his eyes and goes to sleep; each strip concludes with his return to reality by waking up or falling out of bed. The strips were filled with magic and whimsy, as Nemo's dreams were peopled with an array of animals, giants, clowns, tribal figures, royalty, and strange creatures. They took place in a range of settings from vast cityscapes, exotic parades, bizarre circuses, and

FIGURE 2.3. Extract from Winsor McCay's *Little Nemo in Slumberland*, February 21, 1909.

other festivities rendered in Byzantine, rococo, and art nouveau styles. McCay's strip broke away from the urban comedies of the Yellow Kid and others before it. The dream imagery intersected with larger preoccupations with fantasy that dominated the popular culture of early twentieth-century urban America.[21] It is unsurprising, then, that the Western filtered into this dreamworld not as a fixed historical epoch but as an imaginative storyworld where icons and figures from the genre bled into the fantasies of the child protagonist.

In one strip from 1909 Nemo dreams about a journey around the world that he embarks upon with his friends, running through locales such as Egypt and the pyramids and passing Eskimos in their igloos at the North Pole. When Nemo eventually travels to the United States, he comes across cowboys on horseback and Native Americans beside wigwams (fig. 2.3). Like the patchwork of pyramids, igloos, and Eskimos that the artist uses as iconic representations of specific nations and cultures, he uses figures from the American West like cowboys and Native Americans to summarize and present an imagined America to his readers in the space of a couple of comics panels.[22] A similar artifice is employed in a later strip, in which Nemo and his friends become lost when traveling back to Earth from their adventures in outer space on a zeppelin. Unsure of their surroundings, it is only when the zeppelin almost lands directly on top of a band of Native Americans amid some tall redwood trees do the characters realize where they have landed: "This is America!"[23] The characters' instant recognition of these unmistakable figures and scenery from the West illustrates how uniquely American these visual markers are—a reliable source of iconography for McCay to draw upon when imagining and representing the nation to his readers.

In addition, McCay's use of such imagery provides a strong sense of just how influential the intensive narrativizing of American history into exciting Western fiction and film had become at the turn of the twentieth century. Indeed, the closing of the frontier in 1890 marked the end on an epoch in American history (not too distant from the publication of this early comic strip), yet the repeated reference to Western themes and iconographies in *Little Nemo in Slumberland* indicates how the frontier had become a natural setting for excitement and adventure. Just as Nemo's dreamworld adventures are situated in exotic locales like castles in the sky, surreal cityscapes, and distant planets, the mythic West appears amid this mixture, revealing how the American frontier had entered the realm of thrilling genre fiction and had become a symbol to readers of an enthralling narrative space filled with action and suspense. However, the arresting vignettes discussed above foreground larger cultural factors at work in comic strips about the American West.

In "Seeing and Being Seen: Tourism in the American West," Patricia Nelson Limerick locates the origins of the popular West in the nineteenth-century writing of Western explorers who extracted their experiences and published them as reports for easterners eager to know more. As she describes,

> Many of our ideas about the West originated in the minds of people who were just passing through. . . . For these travelers, their relationship to their audience made it necessary to cast the West as that exotic place "out there." To dramatize their own daring and mark their own achievement, these explorers had to dramatize the West's strangeness, novelty, unpredictability, and general wildness. The explorers of the first half of the nineteenth century thus built the foundation for later tourism. Offering an image of the West defined by its separateness from the familiar [and] a portrait of a place that was, if dangerous and threatening, also very interesting.[24]

By Limerick's account, nineteenth-century explorers not only laid the groundwork for how the frontier would be constructed and represented as the fabled West but also influenced the development of tourism in the American West that followed the growth of the railroads. We can see this played out through *Little Nemo*, which depicts some of the inflated assumptions about travel to the American West through one little boy's dreams. We are presented with how Nemo sees the region in his imagination: his wonderment with its strange and grandiose landscapes and of course his expectations that the West

FIGURE 2.4. Winsor McCay, *Little Nemo in Slumberland*, September 5, 1910.

is peopled with Native Americans and cowboys on horseback. Fig. 2.4 shows Nemo and his friends engaging two tourists in a conversation as their zeppelin lands on one of the geysers in Yellowstone National Park. This accounts not merely for the dominant influence of the popular West in encouraging a certain way of imagining the American West—not the actual region but rather a patchwork of icons and figures developed in popular culture—but also reaffirms that this is the very lived tourist experience that readers could expect to find if they, too, headed West.

If *Little Nemo* presented travel through the American West by emphasizing the region's "strangeness, novelty, unpredictability, and general wildness" (to use Limerick's wording), this was matched by a wider series of comics strips from this period that featured journeys through the modern-day West. These provided an assortment of alternative perspectives about the region, whether arising from a desire to find and experience adventure way out West or from awe inspired by the landscape and its people—or as a means of reclaiming the West and challenging how it had been constructed in popular culture. This is particularly indicative in the comics of James Swinnerton, Frank King, and George Herriman, who each visited the geographical American West on vacations and later reimagined their experiences with the region in their popular comic series (*Little Jimmy*, *Gasoline Alley*, and *Krazy Kat*, respectively). Arguably these comic strips involved similar cultural work as fiction and film from the early decades of the twentieth century. However, instead of nostalgically looking backward to the historical West, these comic strips achieved a sense of loss and melancholy through present-day tourist narratives in which characters go in search of a Wild West experience in a location that has since been tamed and reshaped in the aftermath of the frontier's close.

Nevertheless, these comics just as effectively represent, and even satirize, the main features of tourism in the American Southwest—a region that had been transformed into a desirable travel destination at the turn of the century, with its people and landscapes offered up as a form of spectacle for wealthy middle-class visitors.

Nostalgia, Loss, and the Tourist's West

Limerick describes how the rise of tourism at turn of the century was a watershed moment that represented the end of the frontier: "When places and people who were once frightening and threatening turned quaint and fun, when Indians did war dances for tourists at train stations . . . , when deserts, which had terrified overland travelers, turned pretty and appealing in their colors and clear lines, then . . . one could think, the violent history of conquest ended, and a new, tame history of buying souvenirs and taking photographs began."[25] The appeal of the mythic West cannot be understated here. Western fiction and film popularized the West as a romantic landscape: a mesmerizing wilderness peopled by cowboys, Native Americans, and pioneers and defined by thrilling narratives of action and adventure. This very imagery would prefigure visitors' tangible experiences with the West as the region was transformed into a tourist destination.

Turner's thesis, both a nationalist manifesto celebrating the frontier and a eulogy to its passing, was an early influence on this transformation in American culture. Marguerite S. Shaffer observes how the intersection of a yearning for a romanticized rural past and the emerging modern urban-industrial society "recast Turner's mythical frontier into a real place," helping to "reshape particular places across the West as frontier dreamscapes—landscapes of leisure dependent on an array of 'western' texts and images available for consumption."[26] Train companies took an early lead in manufacturing popular Western imagery to lure passengers to travel cross-continent (see, for example, fig. 2.5). Shaffer notes that as early as 1871 the Northern Pacific was hiring artists to create images of scenic wonders (such as Yellowstone) for promotional brochures and guidebooks, rendering "a West of pristine wilderness populated by rugged individuals and picturesque Indians."[27] By World War I (1914–1918), iconographic Western landscapes—Yellowstone, Yosemite, and the Grand Canyon being the most prominent—were transformed into brand-name tourist attractions "that offered the mythic frontier West up for display and pleasure."[28] However, broader scholarship on the tourist's West has examined this context through a range of examples—from early twentieth-century travel writing, promotional tourist material, the creation of national parks and mountain resorts, ranches, preserved Native American ruins, historic frontier towns, to casinos and theme parks—analyzing how these sites have objectified landmarks and figures from the popular West and constructed a space that mapped Western mythology onto the environment and landscape.[29]

The tourist's West, as Earl Pomeroy neatly describes, is a place

FIGURE 2.5. A sample travel brochure that conflated striking landscapes of the American West and modern-day tourists with popular figures from the Western: Northern Pacific Railroad, *The Land of Geysers: Yellowstone National Park*, St. Paul, Minnesota, 1916.

where the "West plays West."[30] Shaffer details this as a process whereby "myth and region are synthesized to create a hyperreality that fuses cowboys and Indians, abundance and opportunity, wilderness and perpetual sunshine with consumer desire."[31] It is the hyperreal space of the tourist's West and those complex exchanges between fantasy and reality, myth and region, that best aids our understanding as we look to the presentation of the American West in early newspaper comic strips. We can refer back to *Little Nemo in Slumberland*'s feature of Western iconography in a little boy's dreams as a reflection of this sense of yearning and desire to experience excitement and adventure in the Wild West. However, the tourist's West was captured in a wider set of fictional comic-strip stories set in the American Southwest, which were inspired by certain cartoonists' journeys through the desert regions in and around Arizona from the early decades of the twentieth century. Some travelers, like Frank King and George Herriman, experienced their encounters with the region as purely touristic fare. But others, like James Swinnerton, who moved to California in 1906, had much more personal interactions with the West.

Little Jimmy

James Swinnerton had been a prolific cartoonist for William Randolph Hearst since the 1890s, but he is perhaps best known for his enduring strip *Little Jimmy* (1904–1958), which appeared in the *New York Journal*. The comic strip began life, like many other newspaper comic strips from the turn of the century, reveling in the conditions of city living. However, unlike strips such as Opper's *Happy Hooligan*, which specialized in hyperbolic and slapstick appropriations of urban violence and crime, Jared Gardner suggests that *Little Jimmy* celebrated "the new urban *distractions* that shaped the daily lives of many newspapers' readers."[32] Each comic strip saw Jimmy given a certain errand by his parents, only for the young boy to get distracted by other denizens of the bustling city, concluding with Jimmy being spanked for not completing the set task. While this formula was a sustaining feature of the strip, Swinnerton's change of situation and location had a dramatic impact on the series. The artist was diagnosed with tuberculosis in 1906, and doctors gave him only a few weeks to live. He left New York City for Colton, California, a place of refuge for tuberculosis patients, where Swinnerton made a full recovery. He was so enamored with the region that he would not return to the city and spent the rest of his life residing in California and Arizona.[33]

Michael Tisserand writes that "in the years following his desert recovery, Jimmy Swinnerton had become an apostle of the Southwest, painting its hidden landforms and telling all who'd listen about its wonders." He adds that Swinnerton also changed his personal style: "He wore tall boots and kept his hair short, with one observer noting that he looked more like a gold panner than an 'off-kilter artist.' "[34] The move west dramatically changed the artist in more ways than one, and his comics work was no exception. The Southwest would become the definitive setting of *Little Jimmy* by the 1920s, but before then the desert landscapes of Arizona offered a vibrant destination for Jimmy and his family's vacations away from the city. In 1913, for instance, Swinnerton confronted Jimmy and his family with a range of locales and inhabitants from the region, visiting the Grand Canyon in one Sunday strip (fig. 2.6) and meeting Navajo Indians in another. There is a simplicity to Swinnerton's artwork, and through some basic lines and hatchings the artist evokes a strong sense of depth and vastness in his renderings of expansive desert locales. The "urban *distractions*" that Gardner suggests had shaped the series, whereby Jimmy is led astray

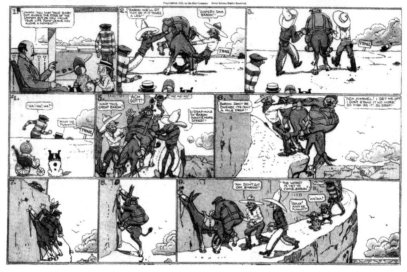

FIGURE 2.6. James Swinnerton, "Jimmy—He Sees the Grand Canyon," *Los Angeles Examiner*, April 27, 1913.

by the people that he meets and his surroundings in the city, was a formula that complemented the new setting in the American Southwest. Indeed, Swinnerton's depictions of mesmerizing desert vistas and his exotic presentation of the Navajo Indians in their ceremonial masks certainly instilled a sense of wonderment within Jimmy, who gets lost in various misadventures in the region. In a radio interview from 1963, Swinnerton recognized that the beauty of the deserts and the Native Americans from the region could be a source of fascination for his readership, many of whom would never get to experience the area for themselves. Therefore, his artwork, which captured the panoramic views of the rugged landscape, was paramount. In addition, the cartoonist stated that he wanted to move away from the "blood and thunder" presentations common in the Western genre and provide a wholesome source of entertainment for children and adults alike.[35]

FIGURE 2.7. James Swinnerton, "Jimmy—He Smokes the Pipe of Peace," *Seattle Times*, May 18, 1913.

FIGURE 2.8. James Swinnerton, "Jimmy—He's Among the Navajos!," March 23, 1913.

This reclamation of the region from the mythmakers of the Western genre is significant. Various authors and filmmakers were appropriating historical instances from the American West to develop a narrative genre rendered in "blood and thunder" (to use Swinnerton's wording). Here, however, the creator presents the region in a demythologized and more everyday manner while satirizing skewed perceptions of the American West and the Native American. One of the running jokes from the strip concerns Jimmy's friend who repeatedly anticipates the Navajo characters to be on the verge of war, only for his expectations to be trampled. For example, in the strip "Jimmy—He

Smokes the Pipe of Peace" (fig. 2.7), when Jimmy and his friends happen upon a group of Navajo men sitting in a circle smoking a pipe, one of the boys remarks: "Deyre smokin d'pipe o'peace dat means war!" On closer inspection, this observation is undermined as we see the men grumbling about the humdrum nature of everyday life: one complains, "Rents too high," another, "Me payum too much for gas for my auto."[36] In another strip, "Jimmy—He's Among the Navajos!," Swinnerton shows a group of Navajos participating in a strange kinetic activity, or what one of Jimmy's friends claims is a "war dance." Again, this observation is undermined in a following panel, which reveals that the men are in fact training for the school football squad (fig. 2.8).[37]

This configuration—conflicting genre expectations that are subverted across the comics page, blending the fantasy elements of the Western with the humdrum everyday of Western reality—coalesces to form Swinnerton's challenge to the fabled West, and he invites the reader to question the West's transformation into a site of mythic importance.

This slightly wry interpretation of region and myth was evident in how Swinnerton depicted the local tourism industry, too, and *Little Jimmy* can be read as a document chronicling the inelegance of Southwestern tourism. As a resident who lived and worked in the region, the cartoonist regularly used his strip to lampoon the travelers who visited the Southwest. Jimmy and his family were certainly part of this running joke, and at the close of the "Among the Navajos!" strip, we can see Jimmy's embarrassed father making his excuses to a group of disgruntled Navajo men who have been attacked by the family dog: "I'm doing the best I can for you!" he proclaims in his efforts to make things right (fig. 2.8).[38] However, it was not only Jimmy and his family who caused chaos while on vacation in the region. For example, in a strip from April 27, 1913, Swinnerton documents another buffoonish tourist's awkward experience (fig. 2.6). Indeed, after admiring the captivating scenery in the opening panel, Jimmy and his friends decide to follow a wealthy European visitor, the plump Baron, on his donkey ride into the Grand Canyon, with the comedy in the strip deriving from the rotund character's increasing discomfort as the perilous ride unfolds.

If Pomeroy described the tourist's West as a place where the "West plays West," *Little Jimmy* gives a much less pristine vision. While Swinnerton seems obliged to show all the wonderment that can be found when visiting the Southwest, amid the hijinks and humor of Little Jimmy's misadventures, the artist displays a distinct irreverence, as if duty bound to unmask some of the untruths about the tourist's West experience, providing splashes of reality in his representations (the Navajo characters' grumbles about the cost of living being a most evocative example). This ambivalent point of view was echoed in other strips from the time, too, such as *Gasoline Alley*.

Gasoline Alley

The Western in fiction and film gave a counterpoint to the overcrowding of city life, presenting a nostalgic look at a rural way of life fast fading after the frontier's close in 1890. However, physical travel to these natural and remote regions provided a much more tangible experience. Primarily, the automobile opened up America to mass tourism, further satisfying the urge to visit the mythologized landscape of the West.[39] Frank King (1883–1969), a cartoonist who resided in the Chicago area, regularly indulged in this source of adventure, taking a number of car journeys to the Southwest region and a range of national parks. He would subsequently translate his travel experiences into his comic strip, *Gasoline Alley*.[40] The series started out in 1918 as a single panel cartoon, "Sunday Morning in Gasoline Alley," which featured a group of men—Walt Wallet, Bill, Avery, and Doc—who spent their spare time working on, and talking about, cars. So popular was this setup that the following year *Gasoline Alley* debuted as daily comic strip. When baby Skeezix was abandoned on Walt's doorstep in 1921, this added a familial element to the series, and for the last century *Gasoline Alley* has stood as a humorous chronicle of family life in small-town America, following the everyday lives of the Wallet family.

Jeet Heer has suggested that car journeys and vacations were a vital part of the series in its formative years: "King, seeking to capture the texture of middle America, used long car trips as a way of showing how his characters behaved when removed from the familiar world of their neighborhood."[41] Of particular interest is the journey that King took in 1923, when he visited the pioneering couple John and Louisa Wetherill, who operated a trading post and lodge in Kayenta, Arizona. Erected in 1910, the Wetherills' lodge was embedded in the desert landscape, close to the vast natural sculpture garden of sandstone, siltstone, and shale known as Monument Valley. The couple offered pack horse excursions to Rainbow Bridge and the rocky ruins of an Ancestral Pueblan civilization for a variety of city-dwelling visitors. Their most notable clients included Theodore Roosevelt, author Zane Grey, and various cartoonists, including James Swinnerton and George Herriman (whose work will be discussed shortly).[42] King's personal visit in 1923 placed him in contact with the Grand Canyon, Monument Valley, and the Rainbow Bridge in Utah, and the artist would later use the grandiose desert landscape as the stage for Walt and Skeezix's retreat to the Southwest in 1924. Arriving at the Wetherills' lodge in one strip, from June 1924, Walt and Skeezix are then guided deep into the surrounding desert by a cowboy. King transformed personal photographs from his own vacation into panels in his comic, ranging from actual people (like the Wetherills), to the most remarkable natural rock features that he came across. The *Gasoline Alley* dailies typically adhered to a rigid, foursquare panel setup. But when Walt and Skeezix headed to the Southwest, King frequently broke this pattern, sometimes using only two or three wider panels to provide a more panoramic view of the expansive locale.

King's own fascination with the region is clearly enacted through Walt and Skeezix, who are often found gazing at the natural wonders and staring at the colorful locals. Nevertheless, a strange tension persists in this visit, and one that echoes a tension that Shaffer locates in the tourist's West: in a space where frontier mythology has spawned its own reality, "the mythic West vies with the real West."[43] Foremost, King's illustrated translations of his personal photographs ground his drawn storyworld with a loose sense of realism. However, it is his inclusion of the cowboy character, who guides Walt and Skeezix through the desert, that challenges these seemingly fixed boundaries of the region and reveals larger cultural forces at work. Indeed, as Walt questions their guide about the impressive landmarks that they encounter, the cowboy's explanations draw on the myths and lore of the region and border on the ludicrous. In figs. 2.9 and 2.10 we see a couple of these encounters. The cowboy proclaims that the Rainbow Bridge, a natural stone formation in Utah, is the "cup handle of the world," used to hang the globe out to dry, whereas he suggests that Paul Bunyan (a giant lumberjack of American folklore) was most likely responsible for the rock formations in Monument Valley.[44] On the one hand, these recounted legends can be read as King's way of undermining the mythic West, with the cowboy rendered in caricature in his lengthy ruminations on the lore of the region, framed as out of touch next to the suburban visitors. Indeed, Walt later recalls his interaction with this figure from the mythic West: "He's a good ol' scout! I'll bet he thinks I believe all the stories he told me. He tells them so well I almost do, at

FIGURE 2.9. Frank King, *Gasoline Alley*, June 21, 1924.

FIGURE 2.10. Frank King, *Gasoline Alley*, June 30, 1924.

that."[45] On the other hand, King's arrangement of regional lore, figures from the popular West, and real geographical points reflects a hyper-real encounter with the West; the coexistence of fantasy and reality in the comics panels accentuates how the mythical West has helped shape and give meaning to the tourist's West.

This tension between fact and fiction was certainly present in the *Little Jimmy* strips discussed earlier, and especially in those instances in which Jimmy's friend expects to witness Wild West conflict, only for these desires to be trampled when they actually encounter the peaceable and friendly locals. However, this theme was dealt with in an entirely different manner by another cartoonist, George Herriman (1880–1944), who, like Swinnerton and King, was a visitor to John and Louisa Wetherill's lodge. However, Herriman's reinterpretation of personal tourist experiences with the American Southwest in his comics was almost unrecognizable. Patrick McDonnell, Georgia Riley De Havenon, and Karen O'Connell suggest that Herriman's lengthy stays with the Wetherills was a means to escape his routine in the city (for twenty years Herriman was a repeat visitor), but so influential was the trading post's desert setting that it formed the backdrop to the artist's comic strip *Krazy Kat* (1913–1944).[46] Where Walt and Skeezix's journey through the American Southwest emphatically reflected the artist's own lived experience with the tourist's West, Herriman's West emphasized all that he found fascinating with the region (particularly the sublime desert landscape and Navajo lore), but he buried this beneath a comic strip focused on a cat and a mouse who inhabit a distinctly surreal version of the American Southwest.

Krazy Kat

Krazy Kat centers on a simple-minded cat named Krazy and Ignatz the mouse. Ignatz is often found scheming about ways to throw bricks at Krazy's head, a violent act that the cat confuses as a sign of love. A third character, Officer Pupp, is affectionate toward Krazy and acts as the cat's protector, often placing Ignatz in jail for his antics. This bizarre love triangle formed the basic formula reenacted throughout the comic's history, with Herriman accentuating and reworking this setup in more surreal and eccentric ways. Herriman's comic is rich in its reference to the arts, literature, and intellectualism masked under surreal cartoon art, slapstick humor, and clever toying with language (mixing slang, accents, and phrasings). Tisserand admits that "Herriman's philosophical musing, literary allusions, . . . and enigmatic lead character made for a challenging read," but these very elements perhaps account for *Krazy Kat*'s popularity within art and literary circles: avid readers of the strip included T. S. Eliot, E. E. Cummings, and Gilbert Seldes.[47] The series reached its height in popularity by 1920, making an appearance in a series of commercial products such as animated cartoons and toys, and estimates suggest that the series was read by an impressive ten million readers in newspapers across the country.[48] But of interest to this chapter is *Krazy Kat*'s setting, a strange and dreamlike version of Coconino County, Arizona.

Herriman was captivated by the American Southwest desert, and it was a key component in the artist's strip. As he described: "That's the country I love and that's the way I see it. . . . I like it nearly as well as the characters themselves."[49] However, Herriman reimagined and subverted this setting in ways almost beyond recognition. Herriman's West is a semifictional space in Arizona, complete with dreamy night sequences and desert backdrops that change from panel to panel. Desert mesas and buttes became abstract blocks and squares, and the desert backdrop repeatedly changed across panels to mirror the shifting

FIGURE 2.11. George Herriman, *Krazy Kat*, King Features Syndicate, September 4, 1927.

light patterns Herriman witnessed in the Southwest landscape. These strange observations about the setting are commonplace throughout the series. Nevertheless, a much more profound message underlies Herriman's West. Take, for example, this panel from a *Krazy Kat* strip printed in 1927 (fig. 2.11): it shows Ignatz in jail, set against a Western landscape—an open desert vista, complete with buttes and cacti. But what stands out here is what Herriman drew around the margins of his image: a patterned frame inspired by Navajo design.

Shaffer suggests that "the longing for the physical and imaginary geography of the multifaceted mythical western frontier embodied by cowboys and Indians, wilderness and sunshine, abundance and leisure" are manifest in the tourist's West; a place where "myth and region are synthesized into a hyperreality."[50] This is certainly evoked by the tourist experiences found in Swinnerton's and King's comics and even in the dreamworld of *Little Nemo*, which shared in this interplay of fantasy and reality (mixing tourist encounters with a way of life that had been dramatically altered, if not erased entirely). The Native Americans' tacit presence in Herriman's West—circumscribed to the borders of his strip—arguably gives a more troubling view of the tourist's West. Fig. 2.11 is just one example of many where the artist makes use of Navajo designs and motifs, which can act as a decorative border to a comic panel, appear on a piece of pottery, or ornament the trim on a house.[51] In one respect, Herriman's West is a sanitized version of the region, where cacti are taken from their natural setting in the desert and are growing in pots and Native American culture now offers nothing more than decorative designs for ceramics and architecture. This is not the mythic West of cowboys and Indians but rather a postfrontier landscape in which only residual elements remain. The use of Navajo designs and motifs can be read as Herriman's way of hinting at the region's transformation into a tourist destination where Native American arts and crafts are offered up as a commodity. Alternatively, Herriman's use of Navajo motifs can be read through the lens of modernist art cultures.

US modernism as both an aesthetic and a mode of cultural critique gained considerable traction among a set of artists and writers in the 1910s and 1920s in response to what they saw as the staleness of modern American life—its rampant materialism and commercialization and the rise of a mass culture with no depth. The solution to this lack of depth and authenticity could be found among "primitive" societies (especially Native Americans), which modernists thought represented a simpler way of living, divorced from the issues of modern American life. In addition, they sought inspiration from Native American arts and crafts, which promised to reinvigorate culture. A series of artists and writers expanded on this fascination and began to incorporate Native American graphic and verbal expressions into their work.[52] However, as Leah Dilworth points out, in their use and promotion of Native American art, American modernist artists and writers overlooked the condition of Indigenous populations as subjugated and oppressed peoples, and modernist representations displayed an overall lack of concern for the meaning of Native American expression.[53] The aesthetic practice of using "modernist primitivism" (to take Dilworth's description), or rather appropriating Native American art, was purely about demonstrating the authority and authenticity of the artist's experience; it was "an attempt to recoup . . . the direct, unmediated experience with primitive societies" as Marianna Torgovnick describes.[54] Indeed, modernists held the belief that their art was the result of the individual's experience of reality. In this regard, we can postulate that Herriman's use of Navajo motifs in *Krazy Kat* intersected with the cultural work of modernist writers and artists working out of the American Southwest.[55] If, as Dilworth describes, modernists used Native American art as a means of showing an aesthetic affinity with Native American arts and culture, it could be argued that Herriman too was capturing his authentic lived experience with the American Southwest and its Indigenous populations through his repeated references to Navajo patterns and designs.

However, while modernists' use of tribal art avoided engagement with the impact of settler colonialism on Indigenous populations in the American Southwest, as it held no romantic or exotic appeal to those writers and artists, the tacit presence of Native American life on the margins of Herriman's West arguably gives a more engaged point of view. Tisserand observes that throughout the series, Herriman dealt with interrogations of identity and social status, and some strips explicitly engaged with race—"or as explicitly as possible in an all-animal comic."[56] Herriman's treatment of Native Americans was certainly bound up within this social interrogation. Indeed, the absence of Native Americans from *Krazy Kat* can be read as a critique of US policy toward its Indigenous population, whereby only subtle traces of tribal cultures remained in the tragic aftermath of frontier imperialism.

Such a reading intersects with the range of responses to modernization and the accelerating transformation of the United States from a rural to an urban-based nation that have been emphasized throughout the chapter. Comics, as Gordon notes, were "an outcome of the process of modernization"; the Western, as Bloodworth suggests, emerged in this milieu: "Suddenly lacking an actual frontier as a place to demonstrate the triumph of civilization, Americans turned to imaginary frontier experiences"; while Shaffer describes how nostalgia for the frontier's passing would recast the "mythical frontier into a real place," helping to "reshape particular places across the West as frontier dreamscapes—landscapes of leisure dependent on an array of 'western' texts and images available for consumption."[57] In pulling these perspectives together—from the popular West to the tourist's West—I argue that a similar, overarching project unites these example texts that depicted the American West in the early twentieth century. The silent films of D. W. Griffith, the paintings of Remington, the literature of Wister, and the comics by Swinnerton, King, and Herriman (which play out, however covertly, their visits to the geographical Southwest) can all be understood as expressions of what anthropologist Renato Rosaldo has termed "imperialist nostalgia": an innocent yearning for what one has helped intentionally to efface or destroy.[58]

In conclusion, I return to Nash's observation about the Western genre texts that emerged between the 1890s and the 1920s, which reflected a dominant idiom "of loss, [and] a feeling of nostalgia for the disappearance of a world." We can see how this context is enacted and sometimes challenged through a range of sources. Scholars tend to explore this context through the Western in fiction and film, which evoked fin de siècle anxieties about the closing of the frontier by looking back to a romanticized historical setting. However, comics allow us to look at this context in a very different way. Through the lens of the tourist's West, strips like *Little Jimmy*, *Gasoline Alley*, and *Krazy Kat* can be read as extensions of their artists' actual experiences with the American West. These comics synthesize myth and region to create a hyperreal version of the geographical locale, fusing icons and figures from the mythic West with the real-life terrains the cartoonists encountered. While these comics are not Westerns per se, they are important artifacts that reflect the changing Western landscape, accentuating how the mythical West helped to shape and give meaning to the geographical West, reflecting a strange tension between popular myth and reality.

The construction of the Southwest landscape in comics, contrasting natural rock forms with deliberately contrived and artificial figures from the popular West, was a stark deviation from its more common associations in the later frontier epics of cinema. Indeed, if we look at King's use of Monument Valley in his *Gasoline Alley* strip from June 30, 1924 (see fig. 2.10), we are reminded of director John Ford's later framing of this locale in his popular Western films: the characters on horseback form small specks in the frame next to the cluster of vast sandstone buttes. Nevertheless, both versions represent different perspectives. For King, Monument Valley was a site inwhich to question the American West's transformation into myth. Using the presence of the otherworldly, yet very real, rock formations from the region alongside a caricatured cowboy figure from the Western, the artist revealed a complex interplay between fantasy and reality implicit in the formulations of the tourist's West. Ford, on the other hand, used Monument Valley as the setting of his Western epics; the powerful backdrop added a tremendous cinematic quality to his films and provided the symbolic staging ground for his vision of the triumph of social order over untamed territory.

This point is indicative of how constructions and conceptualizations of the American West are not fixed and have continually altered with the changing forces of culture and society. Where Westerns in the early decades of the twentieth century were imbued with a sense of loss and nostalgia for a bygone age, by the 1930s the Western negotiated the conflicts and contradictions of American life in the Depression, offering audiences escapist entertainment. The following chapter examines this context through adventure comic strips.

CHAPTER 3

Saddling Up in the Slump

Retooling the Western during the Depression

THE OPENING PANEL TO Garrett Price's (1896–1979) comic strip *White Boy* (1933–1935) sees a group of young Native American characters sitting on a cliff edge, observing warriors from their tribe embarking on a raid in the valley below (fig. 3.1). As the reader soon finds out, the band of warriors on horseback are hunting a group of white settlers who have wandered onto the plains near the tribe's encampment. The opening panel is clear about the comic strip's narrative point of view: the conflict with white settlers is somewhere far off in the distance, all the while observed by Native American teenagers in the foreground. Indeed, *White Boy* is a Western told from the Native American's perspective and is set in the world of the Rainbow Indians, a fictional tribe that lived in the nineteenth-century American West.

While conflicts from the Indian Wars remain ever-present on the periphery of the series, the central storyline is about the assimilation of an outsider, a white boy, into Native American society. After his pioneer family is wiped out by a group of Sioux Indians, "Whiteboy" (the moniker bestowed on him) is taken in by the Rainbow Indians. The comic follows the many adventures of Whiteboy and his friends Chickadee, Woodchuck, and Starlight, featuring dramatic episodes that highlight the characters' survival and mastery of their natural surroundings as they stave off threats from rival tribes.

I open with Price's *White Boy* because it acts as a thematic bridge from earlier presentations of the Western genre in newspaper comic strips to the stronger focus on action and adventure that was realized more fully in a wide range of Western strips from the 1930s. Indeed, Price was not averse to devoting full pages of his weekly strip to Native American lore and employed expressive artwork to capture the Rainbow Indians in harmony with vast untamed wilderness. While the

FIGURE 3.1. Garrett Price, *White Boy*, October 1, 1933.

strip evoked similar themes expressed in earlier strips like *Little Growling Bird in Windego Land* (1906–1907) and *Little Jimmy* (1904–1958), the
attention paid to Western action on the contested frontier (hinted at in
the opening panel from the series) reflects a taste for adventure-fueled
narratives that comic strip readers came to expect during the 1930s.
White Boy's narrative focus changed multiple times in its short tenure
(by the end of the strip the story was set in the present day and Native American folklore had given way to outlaws, masked heroes, and
dinosaurs), which perhaps indicates the pressures from a readership
who desired something more intensely action-packed.[1] Nevertheless,
while *White Boy*'s success was short-lived, other Western comic strips
emerged in the 1930s that devoted pages to white-Indian conflict, cowboy heroics, and exciting Western gunplay and developed a sustaining popular formula that lasted for years to come in the newspapers'
"funny pages."

The decade of the 1930s presented tests for the United States and
its people. The earlier years were characterized by the hardships that
arose from the Great Depression; toward the end of the decade the
developing war in Europe and the external threats that this posed to
national interests loomed large. Wearied by harsh realities, the nation
sought escapism in popular culture, and the Western genre delivered
in this capacity. The melancholy that had previously imbued the Western had ceded ground to a mode of storytelling much more orientated
toward bold action and frontier adventure. Through the genre's central positioning in a range of popular forms (comics, fiction, films, and
music), the Western offered its audience as much potential cultural
self-reflection as escapist entertainment.

The combined daily circulation figures for American newspapers reached highs of over forty million by the 1930s.[2] This widespread reach placed a specific cultural value on the array of cowboy comic strips that emerged in this decade. In their continued efforts to uplift a downtrodden frontier community from the dangers posed by an array of dastardly villains, the daily printing of righteous cowboy justice in comic strips provided narrative solutions to the problems of everyday life and cultural reassurance for Depression-era America.

The Adventurous Decade: Retooling the Western in Newspaper Strips

Comedy had always been at the heart of the newspaper comic strip's formative years.[3] As Pascal Lefèvre notes, "Newspaper strips didn't generally have the space to develop various parallel plot lines in the short daily episodes"; therefore, the medium was well suited to the raucous gag strips that were widely accessible to a national readership.[4] However, this changed in the 1930s, a period characterized by Ron Goulart as the "Adventurous Decade" precisely because of how successfully adventure-fueled genres flourished in the comic strip medium.[5] Chapter 2 gave a largely closed account of how newspaper comic strips from the early decades of the twentieth century captured modern America's reaction to the end of the frontier, often through humorous present-day tourist encounters with the Southwest region. However, there were instances during this period when Western adventure appeared in the comics pages, too. Two early examples are found in the work of Vic Forsythe (1885–1962) and his strips *Bad Bill the Western Wildcat* (1911) and *Tenderfoot Tim* (1912–1914), both of which featured in the *New York World*. As a native of California, Forsythe had a good knowledge of the region, but in his strips his version of the Wild West was often imbued with a sense of humor. This is particularly evident in *Tenderfoot Tim*, which sees a derisible easterner head West to live life as a cowboy. Each strip saw the local ranch hands playing practical jokes on this outsider, which often involved lively riding, roping, and gunplay sequences.

Another, more expressive, example can be found later in J. Carroll Mansfield's series *Highlights of History*, which ran in American newspapers from 1926 to 1939. The series can best be described as an educational comic recounting various stories from history (and usually those most dramatic episodes from the past), but in 1927 Mansfield covered a wide range of events from American Western history, from Civil War battles to life on the prairie. Likewise, as part of the series

Mansfield began an ongoing daily strip, *Buffalo Bill, Scout of Scouts*, in October 1927, which recounted the formative years of a young Billy Cody before his life as a star of the traveling Wild West show. The daily strips charted Cody's development as a skilled hunter and scout but were punctuated by a variety of skirmishes he experienced with Plains Indian tribes, giving the comics a sense of excitement amidst the dense biographical account. Nevertheless, these instances of more standard Western adventure were few and far between in early twentieth-century American comic strips. And it was not until the 1930s that frontier action and adventure became the dominant formula when narrating the fabled West. As one comics historian describes: "The stock market crash of Oct 1929, and the long depression that followed, helped guarantee [a] new serious note in comics. . . . Readers wanted more than laughs, they also wanted images of strong men taking control of their world."[6]

The 1930s were presaged by the Great Depression, and for the first three years of this new decade the economy spiraled further downwards: hourly wages dropped by 60 percent, 86,000 businesses failed, more than five thousand banks closed, industrial output halved, and unemployment reached fifteen million people. As President Herbert Hoover reflected on his final day in office in March 1933, "We are at the end of our string. There is nothing more we can do." However, the new president, Franklin D. Roosevelt, offered renewed hope. Within the first one hundred days in office Roosevelt delivered on the promise of "direct, vigorous action" from his inauguration speech. Congress passed fifteen major bills, affecting unemployment relief, industry, agriculture, labor, transport, banking, and currency. This "New Deal" for the nation helped farmers, financed homebuyers, created jobs, guaranteed bank deposits, and provided tangible results for relieving the nation's debilitated economy.[7] While Roosevelt helped bring the United States out of one of its worst crises, David Reynolds observes how the Depression caused lasting psychological damage to the nation, causing "a loss of faith in the American Dream."[8]

One remedy for this ideological crisis was through a mass retreat into popular culture. Americans wearied by economic devastation found solace in escapism, and cultural industries obliged through a stream of outputs: from comedies, musicals, crime dramas, and animated cartoons unfolding on cinema screens across the nation to swing and American folk music, which reached a wide audience over the radio.[9] The 1930s also saw a growth in popular fiction, which introduced a new kind of sensationalist storytelling in cheaply produced pulp novels, including genres such as the Western, crime capers, and science fiction.

In *The Myth of the American Superhero*, John Shelton Lawrence and Robert Jewett document the emergence of a type of character—an American hero who transcended mere heroism to become superheroic: this character could relieve the deep social problems afflicting the weak and dispossessed. In pulp fiction this was evident through a range of crime fighting heroes such as the Shadow (in 1929), and his widely popular imitators Doc Savage and the Phantom (both from 1933).

However, newspaper syndicates quickly took note of this rise in bold heroic figures and began to print comic strip versions of popular pulp fiction heroes, such as United Feature Syndicate's *Tarzan* and National Newspaper Syndicate's *Buck Rogers* (both from 1929). In addition, press syndicates licensed the production of a series of new and iconic heroes, such as Chester Gould's master crime detective, *Dick Tracy* (from 1931), and Jerry Siegel and Joe Shuster's *Superman* (from 1938).[10] The preexisting range of domestic comedy strips (including the likes of *Gasoline Alley*) continued to offer reassurance through humorous family features of domestic stability insulated from the destitution that was a reality for many Americans in early 1930s. Nevertheless, it was the advent of the adventure strip that really began to shift the medium away from the traditional "funny paper" material.

The adventure strip offered distractions from everyday life, transporting its readers to exotic locations, from the darkest jungles to the far reaches of outer space, in a range of science fiction, fantasy, espionage, and detective comics. The thrilling plotlines of adventure strips often saw good do battle with evil, and the superhuman title hero always triumphed against seemingly insurmountable odds, quelling threats to the established order. Alongside aforementioned series like *Tarzan* and *Dick Tracy*, some of the standout comic strips of the decade included Alex Raymond's science fiction strip *Flash Gordon* (from 1934), Milton Caniff's far-flung adventure series *Terry and the Pirates* (from 1934), and Hal Foster's medieval fantasy *Prince Valiant* (from 1937). These comics moved beyond the cartooned lines and comedic content that had previously characterized the comic strip medium, portraying exciting action-filled narratives through realistic artwork, three-dimensional characters, and vivid settings. Alongside taking inspiration from the characters, themes, and formulas of popular genre fiction, some scholars have observed how the heavily stylized artwork from adventure strips took influence from cinematic composition, which added to the pace and presentation of the story.[11] For example, Pierre Couperie observes how comics artists adopted "stylistic innovations from the cinema," toying with perspectives (using an array of "down shots," "up shots," "long shots," and "close ups"), contrasting variable panel sizes to meet with the dynamic action sequences, and using chiaroscuro lighting to create dramatic effects.[12]

The appeal of the adventure comic strip lay not only in its fluid and dynamic artistry but also in its ability to transport the reader to exotic storyworlds filled with excitement and thrills. Amid this adventurous output, newspaper syndicates also licensed a host of Western comic strips. The Western provided tremendous appeal to Americans in its offer of comforting and familiar images of the mythic West. This new breed of Westerns did away with the more pared-down and gentle adventures set in the West found in earlier comic strips, which sought to reflect a sense of wonderment with the region. The adventure strips instead emphasized bold cowboy heroics, fistfights, shoot-outs, and chases on horseback; they backgrounded vast expanses of unspoiled wilderness. Some of the standout Western strips from the period included Harry F. O'Neill's *Broncho Bill* (1928–1950), Ed Leffingwell's *Little Joe* (1933–1972), Vic Forsythe's *Way Out West* (1934–1936), Fred Harman's *Bronc Peeler* (1933–1938) and *Red Ryder* (1938–1964), and King Features Syndicate's *The Lone Ranger* (1938–1971).

On the flip side of this, a number of parodic Western comic strips also emerged in this period, including Ferd Johnson's *Texas Slim* (1925–1928; 1940–1958), a gag strip about two ranch hands, Texas Slim and his rambunctious friend Dirty Dalton, who wreak havoc on a cattle ranch in Texas; and Elmer Woggon and Allen Saunder's *Big Chief Wahoo* (from 1936). The latter series struck a pleasing chord with readers, as it followed the humorous exploits of Big Chief Wahoo and his life on the Indian reservation, Teepee Town, before eventually seeing the character branch out on a tour around the country seeking easy money as a medicine salesman. Although Wahoo was presented as a harmless buffoon and the humor in each strip derived from the comedic scrapes the character got into on his travels, artist Elmer Woggon continued the racist strand of cartooning in his representation of native peoples, exaggerating racial signifiers of difference (such as the character's nose and the use of broken English).

Nevertheless, for the most part, the Western in comics had been retooled as a vehicle of highly formulaic adventure fiction by the 1930s, and strips often featured an interchangeable lone hero on the Western range who fights against cattle rustlers, outlaws, crooked businessmen, and various other miscreants who were driven by simple imperatives of greed and evil.

In a similar manner to the absorption of visual vocabularies and storytelling techniques from other media, which was evident in a variety of adventure comics from the 1930s, Western strips also took inspiration from surrounding popular culture. A most blunt example of this in practice can be found in the Register and Tribune Syndicate's series of comic strip adaptations of Zane Grey's popular Western adventure novels, which were illustrated by Jack Abbott (including *Riders of the Purple Sage* [1932], *Nevada* [1932], and *Desert Gold* [1933], among others). Zane Grey was a household name by the 1930s, having authored many immensely popular adventure novels and pulp fiction stories that presented a romanticized image of the rugged Old West. The daily serialization of the prolific writer's work in newspaper comic strips certainly reflected how newspaper syndicates attempted to capitalize on the boom in adventure fiction in the 1930s (in a similar manner to United Feature Syndicate's *Tarzan* and National Newspaper Syndicate's *Buck Rogers* before it). Unfortunately, little can be said for Jack Abbott's flat artwork, which failed to carry the pace and drama of Grey's Western adventure stories and relied on bloated captions below each image to tell the story (fig. 3.2).

But the potential was there for images to help deepen the imaginative storyworlds that had been conjured in popular fiction, adding a new dimension to the written Western. Indeed, if we consider that a key tenet of the adventure comic strip was how its artists reappropriated "stylistic innovations from the cinema" (to take Couperie's wording), it can be argued that visual storytelling was vital in the new look for Western comics and was an important facet in the comic strips offered to readers eager for escapist frontier adventure. And there were other comics that united dynamic, cinema-inspired artistry with the themes and formulas of Western fiction in a much more nuanced and exciting manner. Take for example Fred Harman's *Red Ryder*.

Fred Harman (1902–1982) had at different times worked as a cowhand, an animator for Walt Disney, a painter of the West, and an intelligence agent for the US government, tasked with using his artistic talents to document what he witnessed on a mission through a series of Eastern Bloc countries during the Cold War.[13] However, the cowboy-artist-turned-spy is perhaps best known for his frontier adventure comics. After the limited success of his first strip about a tough

FIGURE 3.2. Zane Grey and Jack Abbott, *Riders of the Purple Sage*, Register and Tribune Syndicate, 1932.

cowboy, *Bronc Peeler*, Harman teamed up with the business-savvy producer Stephen Slesinger to create *Red Ryder*. Syndicated by Newspaper Enterprise Association, *Red Ryder* ran from November 1938 until 1965. Harman's drawing was inspired by his ranch in the Colorado wilderness, and the strip followed the adventures of a red-haired cowboy who herded cattle and regularly helped local law enforcement. Ryder is joined on his adventures by the resourceful and brave Little Beaver, an Apache orphan adopted by Ryder, and his loyal black steed, Thunder. The artist produced a dazzling vision of the Wild West, and his arresting strips often ended on an exciting cliff-hanger.

Take for example the opening storyline of the series, in which the red-haired hero looks to put a stop to the Devil's Hole Gang—a group of outlaws who have pulled off a series of stagecoach heists in the area. Fig. 3.3 is taken from this inaugural storyline. The sequence sees the Devil's Hole Gang plotting to murder the zealous upholder of the law by rolling a keg of gunpowder toward the cabin that Ryder and his friends occupy. Unlike the separation of word and image in the clunky retellings of Zane Grey novels, Harman transcends any previous literary representations of Western action and adventure, maximizing the potential of comics form—particularly image sequence and negotiations of word and image. In this instance, the strip opens with Little Beaver warning his friends about the rolling keg of gunpowder, setting off a series of events, from Red Ryder and his friends jumping into the safety of a mine shaft below the cabin to the villainous outlaws' elation over the presumed demise of Ryder and his friends with the cabin's explosion. The visual flicking between the impending danger from the rolling keg outside of the cabin and the action within, as Ryder hurries his friends to safety, offers a heightened dramatic

FIGURE 3.3. Fred Harman, *Red Ryder*, Newspaper Enterprise Association, December 18, 1938.

foregrounding beyond typical Western literature. And, of course, the closing panel of the strip shows Red Ryder hinting at a cunning plan to get payback against his rivals, encouraging readers to return for the next installment of the saga the following week.

Harman's pairing of dynamic artistry with the lavish thrills and excitement of popular fiction is indicative of the unique brand of Western action and adventure that comics can provide. In its over-twenty-five-year tenure, *Red Ryder* became a hugely successful comic strip, published in 750 newspapers, collated and reprinted in comic books, translated into ten different languages and circulated globally, and reaching an American readership of fourteen million.[14] Alongside this, *Red Ryder* spawned radio spin-offs, thirty-eight movies, television appearances, books, and forty commercial products—most notably the Red Ryder BB Gun that Harman designed, which is still in production today.[15] In this respect, the series represented a successful mix of fluid and well-paced artistry and exciting Western adventure, attaining a wide appeal both at home and abroad.

Furthermore, *Red Ryder* provides a useful starting point in considering the distinctive version of Western adventure that could be delivered in comics in the 1930s. Beyond their offer of enthralling action-driven storylines set in the historically distant Old West, Western comics reminded their readers of the nation's unique promise. Indeed, the Depression had shaken some of the oldest and strongest of American cultural myths, particularly the assurance of the American Dream that hard work and perseverance would bring success. To counter this, Robert Sklar suggests, "In politics, industry and the media there were men and women, as often of liberal as of conservative persuasion, who saw the necessity, almost as a patriotic duty, to revitalize and refashion a cultural mythology."[16] The Western genre was an active participant in this mythmaking, alluding to American triumph against all the odds.

The Western in the Thirties

Peter Stanfield suggests that the effects of the Great Depression were paramount to the Western's vitality in the 1930s. With an unprecedented movement of rural workers to urban centers and continued migration as American defense industries geared up to meet the demands of the war in Europe, Stanfield notes: "The sense of dislocation faced by rural workers was by all accounts immense, but was alleviated, if only momentarily, by a nostalgic and sentimental reckoning with the recent past."[17] Stanfield is primarily concerned with country music in his essay, looking at how its associations with the South were minimized as it garnered more universal appeal through the foregrounding of Western motifs. (For instance, stars like Gene Autry were transformed into singing cowboys.) He suggests that the great popularity of country music in the 1930s (in no small part owed to increasing radio ownership among rural Americans) was due to the genre's infusion with the Western: "In their search to regain a sense of purpose, many Americans may have found comfort in identifying with a reassuring symbol of independence and mastery, a collection of traits that the nation had once possessed."[18] However, Stanfield's rationale can be extrapolated. Indeed, the 1930s also witnessed the absorption of Western Americana from the diverse worlds of Native Americans, pioneers, and cowboys into American classical music, most notably Aaron Copland's ballet *Billy the Kid* (1938) and Roy Harris's Symphony No. 3 (1939).[19] Likewise, despite the commercial failure of Raoul Walsh's *The Big Trail* (1930), which left Hollywood more cautious about investing in big-budget Western pictures throughout the decade, the rise of B-Westerns ensured the continued presence of the genre in the American film market.

A proliferation of low-budget, quickly produced B-Westerns from the 1930s dealt in populist stories of economic survival and clashes between decent, hardworking Americans and greedy corporate land-grabbers set on taking away individuals' property and livelihood. The cowboy heroes that come to society's aid in these films, driven to help those in need for the sake of the common good, echo the general sentiments behind Roosevelt's "New Deal" programs, which attempted to rescue the American people from economic catastrophe.[20] In this respect, B-Western content resonated within the context of 1930s America. However, its fictive patterns and formulas were inherited from the Westerns of pulp fiction. Christine Bold observes how pulp fiction magazines that specialized in Western stories had steadily expanded in print across the 1920s and 1930s.[21] Richard Slotkin notes that the pulp Westerns' heroes identified with "the People," and "the plots frequently have a distinctly 'populist' bias against malefactors of great wealth."[22] However, he argues that B-Western films took these basic formulas from pulp fiction and imbued them with a "metaphorical connection to contemporary concerns." Regarding the array of villainous characters corrupted by greed from the B-films (crooked bankers or politicians, wealthy ranchers and outlaws preying on outlying communities or farms), Slotkin suggests that these were coded as

"villains from the modern world" (including gangsters, corrupt politicians, greedy corporations, and, after 1936, Nazi agents).[23]

The effect of expanding the mythic Western space in this manner,
whereby heroes from this historical epoch allegorically do battle with
the evils of the present day, gave the Western a profound sense of rele-
vancy to Americans in the 1930s. But Western adventure comic strips
added to this context too, providing a similarly cavalier use of the Western's raw materials, pulling an array of stock characters, settings, and
situations together to produce often absurd, always simplistic, but exciting action and adventure stories. However, the primary innovation of
the Western strips was their unique positioning in newspapers. Readers
would absorb the horrific news stories from the week regarding economic devastation (and later the concerning activity occurring across
Europe in the buildup to World War II), but with the turn of a page they
were transported to the mythical realm of cowboy heroes and frontier
adventure in a variety of Western strips. The Western's situation in a
historical setting somewhere in the untamed frontier provided a favored
articulation of escapism during the Depression. At the same time, the
strips were able to provide cultural reflections of this difficult existence,
offering optimistic resolutions to a fractured nation. Primarily, the Western offered a sense of consolation to audiences struggling with the harsh
realities of life in Depression-era America through its numerous retellings of trail blazing and community building, reminding readers how
the great nation had arisen from a constant struggle against unforgiving
wilderness and adversity. A variety of Western strips encapsulated this
spirit amid serial storylines of relentless escapades and perils.

Myth and Formula in Depression-Era Western Strips

Roosevelt's New Deal represented a potent cultural ideal, which blamed
Wall Street and big business for causing the Depression, even as it supported underrepresented working-class groups (small farmers, urban
workers, and ethnic minorities) through a range of policies that targeted
public welfare and security.[24] In tackling corporate greed and uplifting
a downtrodden America, the New Deal represented an inclusive concept of American identity. But it is noteworthy that this spirit flowed
through popular culture from the era. The variety of heroes who stood
up for the vulnerable and oppressed across comic strips, radio dramas,
and the pages of pulp fiction underscored the New Deal ethos. Most
often this was achieved through the heroes targeting the corrupt forces

of greed that threatened society, echoing Roosevelt's rhetoric against "economic royalists" who exploited hardworking Americans.[25] We can situate this within the inaugural 1938 storyline from *Red Ryder*, with the title hero selflessly championing an outlying frontier community threatened by the vicious Devil's Hole Gang.

Nevertheless, Red Ryder was just one representative of a range of square-jawed, fervent guardians of justice and champions of the weak and dispossessed that emanated from the rugged Western adventure strips of the 1930s. Each displays a selfless dedication to upholding law and order in the Old West. They champion virtuous frontier communities, whose freedoms and livelihoods are being infringed upon by villainous landgrabbers, outlaws, or corrupt officials. The heroic westerner's commanding mastery of any given problem in the Old West gave direction and shape to Americans in search of solutions in overcoming the obstacles of injustice and adversity in the face of economic troubles.

Harry F. O'Neill's Western strip for the United Feature Syndicate was printed under a couple of different titles before it landed on *Broncho Bill* (1928–1950); storylines from the strip's formative years strongly evoked the Depression-era milieu. The series is set in a fractured post–Civil War America and invites readers to identify with the themes of survival amid great hardship at a time when the United States was recovering from the devastation of the financial crash of 1929. The discontent of the 1930s is implicitly alluded to in the comic; however, it is presented in much more hyperbolic terms. Law enforcement is unable to cope with the influx of outlaws, claim-jumpers, cattle rustlers, and bank robbers that look to capitalize on the disarray of the war-ravaged American West. The strip endorses the need for outside intervention and tacitly stresses the common interest for public welfare, as Broncho Bill and his youthful vigilante troupe, known as "The Rangers," are called upon to defeat these threats to societal prosperity. O'Neill seamlessly connects each adventure, as we can see in one 1938 story arc (initiated with the September 30 daily strip, "Hell Doesn't Approve") when outlaws pull off a heist on a train that Bill and his friends are traveling on. After Bill and his gang capture these bandits and return the gold to the small local business that it belongs to, there is no time to spare as the Rangers are immediately confronted with another crime: a robbery of money and important papers from the local Wells Fargo office (a story arc initiated with the strip of November 3, 1938, "Back Home Again"). They are plunged into another action-packed caper to resolve.

The strip in figure 3.4 is part of a broader story arc—which features

FIGURE 3.4. Harry F. O'Neill, "Broncho Bill—The Smash Up," United Features, October 5, 1938.

a train crash, horseback pursuits, and gunfights in a range of locales from rivers and forests to frontier towns—and hints at the wide narrative possibilities afforded to Western comics. In a comparison with other popular media from the mid-twentieth century, William W. Savage observes how the comic artist's line could "carry heroes beyond the limits of possibility imposed by radio (sound without pictures . . .) and film (. . . constrained by technology)."[26] In the context of *Broncho Bill*, O'Neill was not limited by the technical or creative restraints of other media and could naturally conjure exciting, action-filled scenes and scenarios fluidly with a stroke of his pen. Moreover, the seamless connections between each adventure undertaken by Bill and his cohort—and crime-fighting in the West more generally—reflects the possibilities afforded by serialized media, offering a mass audience daily doses of escapism and cultural reassurance. However, this was heightened further by media franchises such as the Lone Ranger, a masked rider who was simultaneously defeating villainy and corruption across the panels of newspaper comic strips and thundering on his mount at incredible speeds across the sound-effects stage of radio in the 1930s.

The Lone Ranger character first appeared on a radio show in Detroit in January 1933. However, it was not long before the show was being broadcast across the nation. By the end of the 1930s the hero's adventures had been syndicated in comic strips and published in books written by the character's creator Fran Striker, with films and comic books about his daring deeds soon to follow. The legend goes that the Lone Ranger was a former member of the Texas Rangers and the sole survivor of a troop of Rangers who are ambushed and murdered by the treacherous Cavendish gang. Nursed to recovery by a passing Native American, Tonto, he dons a mask and takes up the moniker, "the Lone Ranger," vowing to bring the Cavendish gang to justice. Once he has sought his revenge, the Lone Ranger turns his attention to the wider plains of the Wild West, continuing his campaign to selflessly defeat crime wherever it may rear its ugly head throughout the land. In aid of his mission, the Lone Ranger is accompanied by his loyal companion, Tonto, and his noble white steed, Silver. Likewise, his occupation of a secret silver mine means that the masked vigilante's escapades as an unofficial agent of law enforcement are never without funding and that his guns are never without ammunition—indeed, the Lone Ranger crafts his bullets from the plentiful veins of silver ore in his mine.

Lawrence and Jewett outline a range of crucial elements that define the Lone Ranger mythos: racial reconciliation through the hero's friendship with Tonto; Silver's rapid mobility, which provides a characteristic form of freedom coveted by Americans; the Lone Ranger's restrained use of violence, which means disarming his opponents rather than killing them, invariably leading to the crooks being captured and handed to the proper authorities for punishment.[27]

Although it emerged in the 1930s, *The Lone Ranger* comic strip was printed from 1938 until 1971, meaning that over the years his adventures would be responsive to a variety of different moments in history. For example, Lawrence and Jewett read the Lone Ranger's ability to disarm his foes through his impressive marksmanship, shooting the guns from their hands, as being redolent of the United States' threat of nuclear deterrence during the Cold War: "Unlimited power is celebrated as the ultimate defense because it presumably will never have to be used destructively. Magical silver missiles will keep the foe from aggression, thus bringing no blame on selfless redeemers."[28] In addition, Ariel Dorfman observes how strips from the mid-1950s responded to the public outrage toward juvenile delinquency, and another storyline from the 1960s engaged with growing concerns over the overexploitation of the natural environment.[29] However, Dorfman adds that it was not coincidental that the masked hero emerged "in the midst of the greatest crisis that capitalism had ever endured." He argues that when faced with the collapse of the market economy in the 1930s, "superbeings" from popular culture like the Lone Ranger became necessary to naturalize New Deal ideologies like "the cautious but decisive intervention of the State; . . . total participation in social benefits; fiscal assistance for technical progress and projects for public welfare" through his "two weapons. . . [:] persuasion and force," and paved the way for the "average citizen" to "dream a way out of crisis."[30]

Although Dorfman does not analyze any comics from the 1930s in his assessment of the character, a close reading of a sample of *The Lone*

Ranger strips from the era reveals how the series sticks to a familiar formula deployed in other Wild West adventure strips at the time. The Lone Ranger always rides to the rescue of good-natured Americans who are threatened by a range of crooked and greedy villains. In accentuation of the villain's dastardly deeds, the hapless people that they look to exploit are typically women, the elderly, and in one storyline from September 1939, a young orphan boy who is set to inherit a vast fortune if two crooks from the East cannot embezzle it from him first.[31] However, such fare is commonplace in the Lone Ranger's West. In 1939 more broadly, we see him foil a cattle-rustling plot, sabotage eastern gangsters who try to steal the map to a secret gold mine from a wholesome American family, and block a claim-jumper's attempts to swindle land from an elderly couple.[32] While working outside the remit of official law enforcement, the Lone Ranger does not employ bold vigilante justice and instead hands his captured foes into the correct authorities. For example, in the 1939 storyline where the Lone Ranger saves an elderly couple from having their land stolen, the masked hero constructs a cunning setup in which the villain admits to his guilt in front of law officials (fig. 3.5). With the villain's malicious plan foiled and the elderly couple's livelihood intact, we see the Lone Ranger, Tonto in tow, ride away in the final panel, calling out his famous parting catchphrase: "Hi-yo, Silver,

FIGURE 3.5. Fran Striker and Charles Flanders, *The Lone Ranger*, King Features Syndicate, December 31, 1939.

away!" The Lone Ranger's uplifting of the common American fallen victim to the corruption and greed of others made him the embodiment of
New Deal idealism, endorsing the support of public intervention.

Little Joe

One final example to consider is *Little Joe*, which was distributed by the
Chicago Tribune Syndicate from 1933 to 1972 and provides an interesting take on the Depression-era Western formula. The series follows Joe
Oak, a child who lives with his widowed mother on the family ranch that
is managed by a rugged former gunslinger, Utah. The strip follows the
many adventures of Joe and Utah and takes its setting in the contemporary American West of the 1930s—presented as a jarring mix of frontier
settings with modern-day trappings, as cowboys on horseback give way to
Native Americans driving automobiles. At other times storylines would
make so few references to the modern day that readers could be forgiven
for mistaking *Little Joe* for being a classic frontier-adventure strip.

Although presented in a simplistic cartoon style of drawing, the
series provides a captivating vision of the western range, capturing panoramic views of the rugged landscape, rendered in vivid colors. Moreover, the series offers some interesting subversions of the Western,
particularly when it takes aim at the racial imbalance at play within
the genre. The world of *Little Joe* is populated by clever and cunning
Native American characters who, although treated with condescen-
sion by the white folks that they meet, avoid becoming victims of
their trickery, often having the upper hand or emerging wealthier with
each encounter. For example, in one strip from November 12, 1939, the
grizzled rancher Utah attempts to swindle a Native American out of
his horse through a dodgy trade for a broken-down car (fig. 3.6). Thinking
his unfair trade is a success ("Heh! Heh! Jest wait'll th' illiterate cuss
tries drivin' it!"), Utah is left stunned and humiliated as the man hops
into the car, starts the engine, and drives away.[33] While the Native
American characters bear familiar hallmarks of racist caricature, such
as speaking in broken English, in the context of 1930s America, it's
striking how the Indigenous people presented in the strip transcend
these surface-level appearances and throughout the series bear admi-
rable traits like honor and justice, arguably adding a layer of complexity and nuance not often seen in contemporary Westerns.

Emerging at a time when the *Chicago Tribune* was expanding its
comics pages from eight to sixteen pages, *Little Joe* provided a perfect

FIGURE 3.6. Leffingwell, *Little Joe*, November 12, 1939.

FIGURE 3.7. Leffingwell, *Little Joe*, April 13, 1941.

mix of action, adventure, and comedy: at times its stories were imbued
with a melodramatic and dark tenor, where violence was displayed
frankly in a similar manner to the adventure comics from the decade;

at other times the strip employed cheerful burlesque humor, especially when documenting everyday life on the ranch. One illustrative example, printed April 13, 1941, opens with the characters "Ze General" and Utah reminiscing about what they had aspired to be when they were young (fig. 3.7). In the meantime, we see Joe traversing the perils of ranch life: bucked from his horse, chased by a bull, and narrowly avoiding being bitten by a rattlesnake. After surviving these ordeals, upon arriving back at the ranch house he's asked what he wants to be when he grows up: "When I grow up, I hope to be alive!" he responds.[34] These gag strips evoked content typical of domestic comedy strips of previous decades, providing humorous depictions of home life and the family, albeit with a Wild West twist. The splashes of comedy acted as a window into the day-to-day happenings on the ranch and provided readers with the opportunity to fall in love with the Oak family.

Moreover, this more tender comedic fare added a significant layer of tension when paired with those melodramatic storylines in which Joe and Utah's adventures threaten the livelihood of the family ranch. And the relationships that readers had built with the characters meant that they would naturally root for the Oak family and their success in trying times. This was most expressive in those storylines that were printed in the earlier years of the 1930s, when the hijinks and humor from the series were tempered with the bleak gloominess of the Depression years.

Take, for example, the inaugural storyline, in which the Oak family become aware of a gold mine situated on their land and must fend off numerous threats from the wicked former employee, Jack Russler, who looks to pilfer the mine's riches before a mining company can buy it from the Oaks. Along the way Russler hires fake mine inspectors, corrupt law officials, and threatening gangsters from big eastern cities to scare the family off their claim. This long-running saga lasted almost a year (from 1933 to late 1934) and followed a similar formula repeatedly articulated in Western adventure strips from the decade. For example, above we find a series of 1939 storylines from *The Lone Ranger* strips in which the archetypal hero helped the next interchangeable downtrodden family. However, *Little Joe* revises this common formula. Indeed, rather than following a wandering outsider who bravely staves off threats to troubled frontier families and communities, *Little Joe* takes its setting directly within the American home. Any troubles that the family face are resolved by their own efforts, and they do not require outside intervention from a lone hero. Moreover, the nuanced character development within the Oak family household allows the reader to really appreciate what is at stake. "Gold—millions—Little Joe can have everything—travel—college—it seems like a dream," Joe's mother effuses as they discover the mine.[35] Later, as the Oaks are misled by a fake mine inspector (hired by Russler) who informs them that the mine does not hold any gold, Joe's mother is found sobbing at the kitchen table—"We had such plans," she cries.[36] Mrs. Oak's dreams of wealth, success, and economic mobility rest on this mine, and the theme certainly resonated with a Depression-era readership. Nevertheless, printed amid the widespread poverty and misery that was a reality for many in early 1930s America, the Oak family's perseverance against the continued threats to their fortune and prosperity certainly reinforced assurance in the American Dream that hard work and tenacity would bring success. It may not be financial success, as is the case of *Little Joe*—it turns out that the family's mine does not hold a vast fortune, but merely fool's gold. Instead, the story reveals the moral that success can be attained through a stable and united household. Indeed, as Russler and his hired guns try to take the Oaks' ranch by force, the concluding scenes of the long-running saga see the family band together and defeat these villains in a deadly shootout, securing the sanctity of the ranch. Written during the Depression, *Little Joe* represented the value in struggling against injustice and adversity amid economic devastation.

Little Joe was a family drama at heart and was forged amid austere conditions as it focused on the humor and humanity within the Oak family ranch. But the politics of the series were certainly led by its writers. *Little Joe* is credited as being created by Ed Leffingwell, but research suggests that his cousin Harold Gray, who was well-known for another popular comic strip creation, *Little Orphan Annie* (from 1924), had a hand in designing, plotting, and dialoguing the strip from the start.[37] With Ed Leffingwell's untimely death in October 1936, the strip was taken over by his brother Bob Leffingwell and maintained its "Leffingwell" signature. However, Gray's point of view informed and shaped *Little Joe* into the next decade. Maurice Horn observes how "Gray never lost an opportunity of poking political fun" at various issues, from trade unions to politicians and the New Deal.[38] The banks were not free of this critique, and in a late-1934 storyline that sees some cattle stolen from the Oaks' ranch (therefore impacting the family's gain from their sale to a cattle buyer), Utah fails to gain a loan from the bank—whose officers are rendered as uncaring and untrusting of investment for honest and industrious American families.[39] With its repeated declarations of the family's misfortune in subsequent strips set on the ranch ("We work hard—why do we have to be poor?" Joe questions in one November strip), the storyline served to reinforce a common message that figures and institutions of wealth are the true cause of struggle during the Depression.[40]

Nevertheless, the weekly printing of *Little Joe* allowed the series to interact much more fluidly with current affairs and contemporary politics that were simultaneously being reported in the pages of the newspaper. And as times changed, new villains displaced old ones. For example, with the Japanese attack on Pearl Harbor in December 1941 and the subsequent entry of the United States into the global conflict, the villains of the Depression (greedy desperadoes, gangsters, and bankers) soon gave way to the Japanese. For example, in one July 1942 strip, as Joe and Utah wander through the wilderness, they notice a Japanese military plane land nearby and soldiers disembark. "Here we been big mouthin' bout how we wanted to go to war," Utah proclaims as he cocks his rifle and begins to fire on the enemy.[41] The storyline certainly serves as a cultural release in its timing with the nation's entry into World War II, but it also provides pleasing victories over a treacherous racial enemy. Alongside Joe's repeated insults about the physique and ability in battle of these devious invaders, the column of soldiers proves no match for Utah's gunfighting abilities, and they are rounded up and forced to work on the Oak ranch for free.

The strip captures the suppleness of the Western genre and illustrates how its narrative concerns could be realigned with shifts in politics and social change. In this instance, we can see how the rugged Westerner was refashioned to become a key asset in the fight against Axis powers. Moreover, it hints at the important potential of the Western hero in comics, and particularly how Western comics would play an important role both during and in the aftermath of World War II.

According to historian Walter Prescott Webb, part of the problem the Depression revealed was the crisis of a frontierless democracy. In his book *Divided We Stand* (1937) Webb argues that the frontier had provided conditions in which individualism, equality, and personal liberty could grow and flourish, and the existence of available land was like a safety valve for any pressures in society. However, the closing of the frontier allowed greater power to fall into the hands of big corporations, whose influence was crushing the little man. In a frontierless society big business was able to gain ascendancy, thus setting in place the conditions for the Wall Street crash in 1929. In a metaphor that can be read in the context of the end of Prohibition only a few years earlier in 1933, he wrote:

> For nearly three centuries Americans drank deep of the potent wine of the frontier, a wine which produced exhilarating experiences of freedom, adventure and boundless opportunity. It was a long, gay evening, but now America must face the morning after with its headache, moody introspection and pathetic glance at an empty bottle wherein only the tantalizing odor of wine remains.[42]

If Webb could use the loss of the frontier as a means by which to understand the internal order of the United States, arguably the Western was the logical cure for this societal hangover (if we stick with his alcohol-soaked metaphor), deploying the very exhilarating experiences of freedom and boundless adventure that Americans desired. Western comic strips posed as a nostalgic framework that allowed readers to look back to a romanticized rural past that could never be recaptured and speak to their collective hopes and fears. The hero did battle with villains—typically men in power who embodied the malfeasance that burdened the American psyche from the era (rampant capitalism, political corruption, financial greed)—and always triumphed. Likewise, the offer of recognizable and reassuring images of the mythic West helped remind readers of the nation's formative experiences—especially how Americans had always defeated threats to their prosperity in the past, reinforcing the idea that this was no different in a contemporary context. That is to say, Americans could overcome the austere conditions of the Great Depression if they remained true to the heroic impulses and traditional values that had helped the nation tame the Wild West.

The latter example from *Little Joe* hints at how Western comics continued to grapple with American concerns in the lead-up to World War II and offers an instance of how the cowboy hero could help combat the external threats to national interests posed by the developing war in Europe and the Pacific. The Western's supremacy was briefly challenged during the course of the global conflict as frontier heroism was supplanted by a rise in superheroism. Indeed, a diverse array of modern-day costumed avengers were deployed in the pages of comics as patriotic defenders of national interests against foreign enemies.[43] However, concurrent with the United States' newfound status as a world superpower in the aftermath of war, the Western reached new heights in popularity, and a spate of cowboy heroes rose up to further the cause. The following chapter examines the mythic potency of the burgeoning Western genre in postwar-era comics.

PART 2

A Golden Age of Western Comics, 1940s-1970s

CHAPTER 4

Cowboys, Crooks, and Comic Books

The Western Stands Tall

ONE ISSUE OF THE DC Comics anthology title *All-Star Comics* from 1949 included a story entitled "The Ghost of Billy the Kid." Set in the present day, the plot opens with a gang of cowboys who pull off a heist at a charity ball. The crime is orchestrated by a figure claiming to be Billy the Kid. The superhero team the Justice Society of America (or JSA) is called in to investigate. After following the trail that leads them to the gang's hideout (located in a nearby frontier ghost town), the JSA defeats these criminals and unravels Billy's claims of being the legendary outlaw from the Old West—he is in fact a former rodeo star who faked his own death so he could take on the Kid's identity.[1] While the ridiculousness of the story reflects the lighthearted fantasy that was commonplace in superhero comics of the postwar years, the cover image of this issue is particularly evocative. It depicts the superhero team bound to a stagecoach that is heading off the side of a cliff; meanwhile a cowboy figure looms large over the scene (fig. 4.1). The prominence of the Westerner in this image provides an arresting metaphor for the direction that comics storytelling (and popular culture more broadly) took in the postwar years. Indeed, with the United States' entry into World War II in 1941, the superhero genre experienced immense popularity in comic books, deployed as patriotic defenders of national interests against Axis powers. However, the superhero genre's dominance over the comic book market waned by the late 1940s and was replaced by a range of cowboy heroes and Western adventure titles (among other popular genres). *All-Star Comics* was itself emblematic of this transition—it was renamed *All-Star Western* in 1951 with issue #58.

Richard Slotkin describes the late 1940s as the starting point of the "Golden Age" of the Western genre: it was "a 25-year period . . . that saw the genre achieve its greatest popularity and that ended with its

FIGURE 4.1. Irwin Hasen (cover art). *All-Star Comics #47*, June–July 1949, DC Comics.

virtual disappearance from the genre map."[2] The late 1940s also ushered in a remarkable boom in comic book printing, which reached its
peak in 1954 when publishers issued one billion comic books (around
90 million a month) in service of the medium's widespread readership of around 70 million people (a mix of adults and children of all
genders), or roughly half of the US population.[3] Although the comic
book's remarkable breadth of reach was not sustained, and sales plum-
meted by the later 1950s (a situation I discuss in chapter 6), for a short
window at midcentury, comic books were among the most popular
media in America. Amid the diverse array of popular comic book
titles, the Western genre stood tall, and publishers offered a mix of
frontier-infused adventure, comedy, and romance series that appealed
to a wide range of readers. Paying considerable attention to those Western comic books printed in the first ten years of this Golden Age, this
chapter will discuss the Western's central positioning in the landscape
of postwar American popular culture.

The Postwar Transformation: Comic Books and the Popular West

On the eve of the nation's entry into World War II, the editor of *Life*
magazine, Henry Luce, announced that the twentieth century was in
fact "the American Century."[4] However, this observation resonated
more profoundly at the conclusion of this global conflict. The United
States was historically isolationist, but this stance was shattered by
the Japanese attack on Pearl Harbor in December 1941, throwing the
country into war. While the nation entered the conflict still reeling
from the effects of the Depression, the war effort dramatically revi-
talized the American economy. Above all, America's mainland had
not suffered any depredation from air raids or battles, while its army
held monopoly over a destructive new weapon, the atomic bomb,
which was dropped on the Japanese cities of Hiroshima and Nagasaki
at the close of the war. Cushioned by these factors, the United States
emerged as a world superpower in the aftermath of war, armed with a
weapon of catastrophic force and an industrial capacity that towered
above other nations.[5] As Maldwyn Jones concludes, Americans "could
be forgiven for supposing that their country was unassailable."[6]

A host of political and moral questions had arisen from Europe
across the 1930s and 1940s (such as the rise of fascism, the collapse of
Western liberal democracy, and grave atrocities like the Holocaust).

In light of these complications, historian Richard Hofstadter observed (with the benefit of hindsight) how "it was no longer possible [for the United States] to look to any foreign political system for moral or ideological illumination."[7] Indeed, after touring war-battered Europe in 1947, one cultural critic concluded that "the United States at the present time is politically more advanced than any other part of the world."[8] This self-concept lay in the renewed sense of American exceptionalism, conveying the euphoric mood of victory that permeated American public life. Popular culture encapsulated this zeitgeist, and this tenor of elation and superiority was most prominent in the Western genre. In particular, the thematic concerns regarding trailblazing and community building from the Western's narrative about settling the great nation reflected the public mood and strong sense of triumphalism from the immediate postwar years.

In theatre, the musical *Annie Get Your Gun* (1946) provided a unique "celebration of nationalism" through its retelling of Annie Oakley's shooting career in Buffalo Bill's Wild West show, drawing analogies to the American Dream of material success and individual liberty, as Timothy Donovan observes.[9] The theme was even more evident in film: Leonard Quart and Albert Auster observe how Howard Hawks's Western *Red River* (1948) best "conveyed [the] great confidence in the strength of the American character" in the postwar years; suggesting that John Wayne's character was an "exemplar of American individualism" who "easily masters the land, the cattle stampedes, and Indian attacks."[10] The film's cowboy hero embodied idealized national characteristics of courage, individuality, and dynamism.

But *Red River* was just one example of a larger framework of social discourse operating in Western films from the era. By exploiting the celebratory historical narrative of winning the West, the genre functioned as an affirmation of America both past and present. Likewise, any moral ambiguities regarding the atomic bomb were overwritten by the presentation of powerful and upstanding American heroes who conquered the West with rifle, six-shooter, and a whole lot of true grit. As Michael Coyne suggests, "In short, the Western was a safe vessel, its red-blooded Americanism beyond question."[11]

The genre's popularity in these years cannot be overstated. The production of big-budget, A-picture Westerns burgeoned as at no other time. Hollywood had been apprehensive about making large investments in producing Western films during the 1930s. However, between 1947 and 1950 Westerns made up 30 percent of the total output from major Hollywood studios. Douglas Pye states that "the last year in which over 50 Westerns [were] made was 1958 (with 54)."[12] This renaissance of the Western was not exclusive to cinema, and the postwar period saw a boom in Western-genre comic books, too.

The comic book medium had developed into a mass narrative form in the run-up to World War II. The tabloid-sized pulp magazines commonly understood as comic books made sporadic appearances across the 1920s and early 1930s and were a popular format for reprinting newspaper comic strips (for instance, *Comic Monthly* [1922], *Funnies on Parade* [1933], and *Famous Funnies* [1934]). However, these early forays into comic book publishing were just the beginning of a growing industry, and it did not take long for a variety of publishers to begin producing their own comic book titles after witnessing both the popularity and profitability of the form. Rather than continuing to reprint old comic strip material, the comic book medium was revolutionized when publishers began to offer original content to readers.[13]

In the 1940s and 1950s comic books were widely available in grocery stores, at newsstands, and in corner drugstores, and reading comics became a major leisure activity. While the primary reading demographic was children and teenagers, with most kids consuming at least a dozen comic books each month, nearly half of adults under the age of thirty enjoyed comic books as well.[14] Their popularity is best exemplified through monthly sales figures. Depending on the source, calculations of the monthly sales of comic books averaged anywhere between 60 and 100 million across the postwar decade (1945–1954).[15]

The massive readership of comic books was established in no small part due to the tremendous appeal of the superhero genre. This was led by the emergence of Superman in *Action Comics* (beginning in 1938) and was followed by a wealth of imitators across the war years.[16] With their appearance in the late 1930s, superheroes were positioned to promote America's entry into World War II in 1941, emboldening national interests through battle against threats from foreign enemies (the Nazis and, in particular, the Japanese). However, if the crusading spirit of the war had galvanized the superhero into action, making superhero comic books the flagship genre of the medium, their dominance over the market was decisively undermined by the climate of postwar America.[17]

In the wake of slumping sales figures of superhero comic books (many of the most popular superheroes titles were cancelled by the late 1940s), the comics industry resolved to diversify the market, bringing different genres to the fore to appeal to a wide readership:

choices ranged from crime to horror to romance to science fiction to teen humor. Nevertheless, comic book readers required a new type of hero who was separated from the contemporary ambiguities and grim realities of the global conflict and its aftermath. This gap was filled by the Western genre and the comfort of historical distance. Its righteous cowboy hero continued the brave and bold championing of the American way in the superhero's stead, only in stories set in the "glory days" of westward settlement.

Michelle Nolan suggests that as many as 3,472 different Western comic book titles had been printed by 1959.[18] Every comic book publisher, from Ace Magazines to Ziff-Davis Publications, offered a slew of Western titles that featured thrilling adventure tales about cowboys, gunfighters, outlaws, and historical frontier figures. Following earlier forays into the Western, such as Centaur Publications, *Western Picture Stories* (1937) and Chesler Publications, *Star Ranger* (1937–1939; fig. 4.2), Dell Publishing took the lead with its comic books *Red Ryder* (1941–1957) and *The Lone Ranger* (1948–1962), which reprinted the adventures of popular Western heroes from 1930s newspaper comic strips. Aside from that, Dell's output was chiefly defined by its licensed products, and the company's Western titles often tied in with singing cowboys of film, popular music, and later, television (e.g., *Gene Autry Comics* [1941–1959] and *Roy Rogers Comics* [1948–1961]). In addition, the comic book became an extension of merchandising ventures for a range of notable stars whose careers had been made in Western films, from Fawcett Publications' *Tom Mix Western* (1948–1953) to Toby Press's *John Wayne Adventure Comics* (1949–1955).

Other publishers elected to create fictional heroes. Atlas Comics (later known as Marvel Comics) stood out for its array of "Kid" characters, such as *Kid Colt Outlaw* (from 1948), *Two-Gun Kid* (from 1948), and *Rawhide Kid* (from 1955). DC Comics hosted a set of recurring Western heroes—like Johnny Thunder, Pow Wow Smith, and the Trigger Twins—through its anthology titles *Western Comics* (1948–1961) and *All-Star Western* (from 1951). Meanwhile, another strand of publishers used notable historical figures as the lead characters for their lines of fictitious action and adventure stories, such as Avon Periodicals' *Wild Bill Hickok* (1949–1955), *Jesse James* (1950–1956), and *Kit Carson* (1950–1955); Charlton's *Wyatt Earp Frontier Marshal* (1956–1967) and *Billy the Kid* (1957–1983); Magazine Enterprises' *Dan'l Boone* (1955–1957); and Youthful Magazines' *Buffalo Bill* (1950–1951), among many others.

Sometimes this type of Western comic would draw on the historical

FIGURE 4.2. W. M. Allison (cover art). *Star Ranger* #1, February 1937, Chesler Publications.

source material associated with its famous title hero, often in the form of an inflated origin story that served as a launchpad into a specific type of Western adventure. For example, "Kit Carson on the Santa Fe Trail" from *Kit Carson* #1, October 1950 (Avon Periodicals; fig. 4.3) recounts Carson's early life in the American Southwest and border regions to show how he became a prodigious scout and fearsome Indian fighter; subsequent issues in the series portrayed Carson's bravery in a variety of clashes against attacking Native Americans (fig. 4.3). Likewise, if a reader had an appetite for dramas involving cowboys versus crooks, it was a guarantee that any comic book cover that featured the famous lawman Wyatt Earp hosted a caper about crime-fighting on the pages within. However, more often than not the historical figures were easily interchangeable with the fictional heroes from other comic book titles: they were simply valiant protagonists who beat up the bad guys.

The bimonthly printing of each title meant that the hero would always ride off into the sunset at the close of the comic, only to return in the next issue for another bout of action, adventure, and crime-fighting on the frontier. However, Western comic books were not solely reserved for heroic fare centered on white males. A unique trend in this version of the genre was the conscious deviations publishers made from the Western formula in an attempt to appeal to the widest readership. The most common approach was crossing popular comics genres with Western themes. For instance, romance comics' avid readership made up of girls and young women could indulge in tales of love and lust set on the American frontier, in titles such as Ace Magazines' *Western Love Trails* (1949–1950), Fiction House's *Cowgirl Romances* (1950–1952; fig. 4.4), and Prize Publications' *Real West Romances* (1949–1950), among others.

Likewise, the growth in crime and gangster comics—owing primarily to Lev Gleason Publications' immensely popular *Crime Does Not Pay* (1942–1955) and its wealth of imitators—saw Fox Features Syndicate produce a wide variety of short-lived Western-inspired crime titles, including *Western Killers* (1948–1949), *Western Outlaws* (1949), *Western True Crime* (1948–1949), and *Women Outlaws* (1948–1949). Magazine Enterprises' *Ghost Rider* (1950–1954) was also representative of this trend in genre blending, crossing the Western with horror themes. However, its ghostly protagonist exemplifies the wide possibilities of who could be cast as the lead hero in a Western comic book, whether Native American (for instance, in Fiction House's *Indians* [1950–1953] and Dell's *Indian Chief* [1950–1959]), an action heroine

FIGURE 4.3. Everett Raymond Kinstler (cover art). *Kit Carson* #1, October 1950, Avon Periodicals.

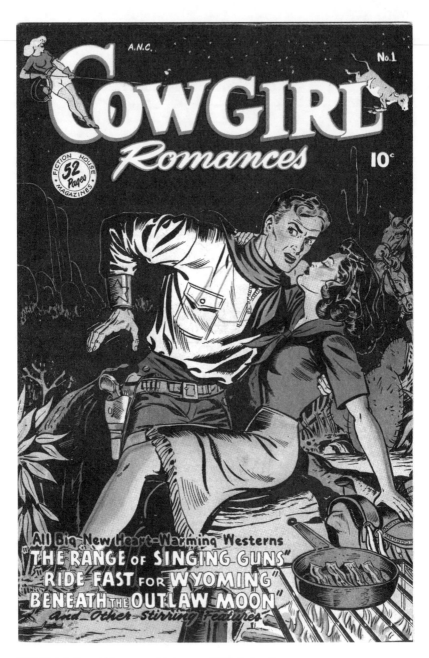

FIGURE 4.4. *Cowgirl Romances* #1, January 1950, Fiction House.

(such as Atlas's *Annie Oakley* [1948–1956] and Fiction House's *Fire-hair* [1945–1952]), or in a more bizarre twist, a crime-fighting horse (for example, Charlton's *Black Fury* [1955–1966]). The equine protagonist from the latter series was imbued with the same spirit of courage and zeal to uphold law and order on the Western range as any of the typical cowboy heroes who rode across the pages of comic books, indicating the suppleness of the Western's familiar themes and formulas and how they could be stretched, reshaped, and reimagined in comic books.

Lone Heroes and Dramatic Adventures

Genre fads governed the creative growth of the comic book medium for the first few decades of its history. The pattern remained largely unchanged: a new genre would arrive, and once it sold astronomically well, a torrent of imitators from rival publishers would appear. As one genre would rise and then subsequently fade into the background, another emerged to fill the void it left in the market. The above cross-genre blends, such as the short-lived spurt of romance Westerns, are indicative of this creative process, as publishers receptive to trends in the market tried to infuse the Western with other popular genres to catch the attention of new audiences. However, the content of comic books was incredibly heterogenous in the forties and fifties, and the Wild West was part of a rich fabric of exciting themes that contributed to the wonderment of comic book storytelling, transporting young readers to an array of exotic storyworlds from bustling high-rise cityscapes, dark and deadly jungles, to the far reaches of outer space. Nevertheless, in the crowded postwar comic book marketplace, in which a variety of genres experienced ebbs and flows in popularity, the Western long remained impervious to such shifts. The untrammeled and lasting success that the genre experienced may be owed to a number of different factors.

First, Western comic books featured a series of pleasing adventure stories to entice their readers—a set of tried-and-true formulaic narratives long-established in the wider canon of popular Western fiction. John Cawelti offered one of the first attempts to catalogue the formulaic plots and dramas of the Western genre. As he observes, the Western is set on a frontier at a time when forces of law and order are at odds with criminality and disorder, "a place where advancing civilization met declining savagery." At its center is a lone hero who must mediate between opposing forces of good and evil in a "narrative pattern [that] works out and resolves the tension between a strong need for aggression and a sense of ambiguity and guilt about violence." The landscape is an important component in this. The visual spectacle of an isolated town, ranch, or fort, set against untamed prairies or vast and foreboding desert vistas symbolizes "the thematic conflict between savagery and civilization and its resolution."[19] And it is these raw materials that coalesce to form a staging ground for a variety of recurring plots: the Journey (e.g., the stagecoach/railroad versus raiders/Indians), the Ranch (e.g., ranchers versus rustlers), the Empire (e.g., an epic ranch plot), the Revenge (e.g., a wronged man versus the truly guilty), the Cavalry (e.g., the cavalry versus Indians), the Outlaw (e.g., outlaws versus lawmen), and the Marshal (e.g., a story about law and order).

Such a list will always be reductive and cannot fully account for the boundless revisions and reinterpretations of the Western's mix of settings, situations, and narratives. However, it gives enough scope to broadly distill the content of midcentury Western comic books, which drew heavy inspiration from preestablished Western formulas and themes in their countless stories about lone heroes fighting against the odds in unsettled and contested frontier landscapes in the name of law, order, and the American way (or, conversely, how that balance is upset in those comics about the dastardly deeds of Western outlaws). Given the seemingly endless array of formulaic constructions made available to fans of the Western in the 1940s and 1950s, as the genre pervaded all forms of American popular culture, Robert Warshow suggests that the Western is in fact "an artform for connoisseurs" whereby "the spectator derives . . . pleasure from the appreciation of minor variations within the working out of a pre-established order."[20] While the comic book Western could satisfy the reader's appetite for formulaic action and adventure stories set on the rugged frontier, their lasting appeal lay in how they continuously delivered variations in heaps.

Take for example Ace Magazines' *Western Adventures* #1, printed in October 1948 (fig. 4.5). From the cover image alone, the reader can pick out key terms such as "injun," "justice," "outlaw," and "sheriff" which promise bold but formulaic stories of cowboys and Indians, despicable outlaws, and courageous individuals who uphold law and order that can be found within its pages. Nevertheless, on closer inspection the reader can see how the comic does not necessarily stick to the parameters of the Western's strict formulaic plots as outlined by Cawelti, but instead blends multiple elements in each story. For example, the storyline "Six-Gun Justice" ostensibly appears to be a Ranch story, as the opening page sees a town's law enforcement attempt to

FIGURE 4.5. Max Elkan (cover art). *Western Adventures* #1, October 1948, Ace Magazines.

bring the cattle rustler Patch-Eye to justice for his crimes. However, after Patch-Eye is let off by the judge and continues to terrorize the town, the plot shifts to something more in line with a typical Marshal story, as the wandering hero the Cross-Draw Kid must act as an unofficial agent of law enforcement and defeat the villains who look to cause harm to Silver Creek.

Likewise, the following Cross-Draw Kid story, "Injun Gun-Bait!," opens with an arresting Native American pursuit of a stagecoach, suggesting that this comic may resemble a Journey plot. However, as the Cross-Draw Kid arrives in Bluff City on a following page, the reader is introduced to the crooked gambler Blackie Dawson, who wants to have one of the townsfolk murdered so he can inherit their gold mine; the story then shifts to something more in line with an Empire story.[21] On the one hand, these rapid shifts between plot formulas in each comic indicate the limitations in attempting to place any given Western into a particular category. On the other hand, this fluid mixing of recognizable Western plots says more about the delivery on the genre in comic books.

Although comic book stories tended to be short (across just a handful of pages), each narrative has an impressive ability to incorporate numerous plot twists and additional complications that the hero must resolve. Likewise, any page that housed a segment of lengthy dialogue to establish plot was almost always tempered with an impressive action sequence on the following page, meaning that any one story could contain a multitude of thrilling episodes. Using *Western Adventures* #1 as an exemplar, the comic features a whole host of exciting sequences: ambush, kidnap, horseback pursuits, daring escapes, gunfights, a train heist, and cold-blooded murder, among other things. In short, midcentury comic books distill all the best bits about the Western into short and snappy, visually striking adventure stories. Their bright colors, arresting action sequences, and blending of gripping plot formulas all serve to capture readers' attention and appeal to their yearning for a slice of adventure in the Wild West.

The comic book Western's emphasis on heightened drama and extravagant action is amplified further when viewed in relation to the Westerns of other popular media. For example, Dell published a series of adaptations of popular Western novelists, including Zane Grey, Max Brand, Luke Short, and Ernest Haycox. Michael Barrier observes how most were illustrated by Everett Raymond Kinstler and quotes the artist's recollection about working on these adaptations: "[The publisher gave me] a degree of freedom to tell the story my way" and "allowed me to reinterpret the story if I thought I could make it more exciting."[22] The creative liberty afforded to this artist certainly connects with the uninhibited expressive freedom of the hand-drawn comics medium, which could exaggerate and extend the content of the Western in exuberant and marvelous ways.

If we look back to one Kinstler adaptation (discussed in the introduction)—"Western Marshal" (*Four Color* #534; fig. 0.1)—we can see how the artist not only incorporated visual film references into the original source material but gave dramatic life to the written word of the novel through his dynamic style of drawing, which encapsulated the hero's fluid movements: parrying, punching, and impressive gunplay, not to mention the spirited riding, roping, quick-fire shootouts, and ducking and diving found elsewhere in the comic. While just one example, it usefully highlights how comics art was integral to the storytelling and set Western comics apart from other versions of the genre. These adaptations also touch on the Western comic book's intersection with the wider genre canon.

Although providing their own unique brand of vibrant action and adventure stories, Western comic books, like their predecessors in the "funny pages" of American newspapers, were heavily shaped by, and shared similar thematic concerns with, the popular West of fiction and film. And it is this association with Westerns across popular media that is important here. As detailed above, the Western held the mantle for being one of the most popular genres of the 1940s and 1950s. Given that the creative content of comic books was largely driven by genre fads, so long as the Western held a prominent standing within the landscape of American popular culture—permeating fiction, film, radio, and television—the genre held a sturdy foothold in the comic book market. If we consider that each Wild West themed text (whether a comic book, novel, or film) contributed to the vitality of the Western genre as a whole in midcentury American popular culture, this helps us understand how the Western could persist in American comic books. Where other comic book genres experienced frequent ebbs and flows in popularity across the 1940s and 1950s, it could be argued that the unwavering popularity of the Western in comic books was sustained by the genre's continued success throughout American popular culture during this period. This self-sustaining cultural context, in which one version of the genre propped up the next, can be illustrated by the popular television and film tie-in Western comic books.

The Television and Film Western

In the inaugural issue of *John Wayne Adventure Comics*, the opening storyline has Wayne passing through the frontier town Gambler's Gulch and happening on the scene of a murder (fig. 4.6). Given the advanced age of the sheriff, the townsfolk wonder how they will bring the shooter Blackjack Wells to justice. Fortunately, "being a man of direct action" (as the sensational editorial just pages earlier describes the film star), Wayne does not need to think twice about pursuing the villain, pummeling him into submission, and locking him behind bars. The first issue of the series carries a couple of other short action stories about Wayne maintaining peace on the rugged Western range, and therefore the reader could be forgiven for thinking that the comic was a throwback to the actor's career as a B-Western star from years earlier, telling pleasing and simplistic fictive stories about conflict and justice in the Old West.

However, as the series progressed, issues began to pair Western adventure with stories about Wayne's present-day (fictional) escapades: for example, he joins the Marines to fight in the Korean War in #12 (December 1951) and foils a Communist plot to incite a workers' uprising while on vacation in a nameless South American country in #20 (May 1953). Moreover, stories such as "Tall Timber" from #13 (February 1952) made stronger links with the present day as the ostensible Old West adventure story about Wayne hunting for the wanted criminal Frank Staccy takes an erratic turn midway through the plot as the protagonist ditches his horse for a small airplane to pursue his bounty.[23] The ahistorical West of the series was in fact a present-day setting all along, and it becomes clear that the comic book was meant to document what John Wayne supposedly got up to in his free time when not on a film set for his next movie role. At once the comic book helps solidify the image of the actor in the minds of young readers as a brave and virile hero both on and off screen, but the series is also a useful exemplar that reveals the transmedial potential of comic books in midcentury popular culture.

Henry Jenkins defines a transmedial story as any that "unfolds across multiple media platforms, with each new text making a distinctive and valuable contribution to the whole."[24] Comic books had been primed for transmedial storytelling from the start, and a variety of characters born in other media (from literature, radio, television, and film) leapt onto the pages of comic books with relative ease

FIGURE 4.6. "The Cowboy and the Gambler," *John Wayne Adventure Comics* #1, December 1949, Toby Press.

and prosperous results. The success attained by Dell was chief among mainstream publishers. As Shawna Kidman describes, "Dell . . . built its business around exclusive licenses to publish comics based on a variety of copyrighted characters from film and other media. The company negotiated a deal with Disney first in 1940, but also secured the rights to titles from Warner Bros. and MGM. . . . By the 1950s, Dell was publishing seventy different comic book titles at a combined circulation of more than two hundred and forty million copies a year."[25] Moreover, the most popular titles could sell three million copies per issue, and even lesser-performing titles could achieve sales in excess of one million copies per issue. In fact, on the back of exclusive licenses, Dell's sales remained strong into the early 1970s.[26]

Amid a wide variety of genre types and recognizable characters from the realms of popular media that made the jump into comic books, the Western was the most prominent. Notwithstanding Toby's *John Wayne Adventure Comics*, by the 1950s there was an abundance of comic book titles devoted to the adventures of stars from a variety of film and television Westerns: Dell's *Gene Autry Comics* (1941–1959), *Rex Allen* (1951–1959), *Roy Rogers Comics* (1948–1961), and *Wild Bill Elliot* (1950–1955); Fawcett's *Hopalong Cassidy* (1943–1959), *Lash LaRue Western* (1949–1961), *Monte Hale Western* (1948–1956), *Rocky Lane Western* (1949–1959), *Rod Cameron Western* (1950–1953), and *Tex Ritter Western* (1950–1959), to list a few examples.

The film and television spin-off comic books were so popular that many of the best-known on-screen sidekicks also got their own titles, including *Dale Evans Comics* (DC, 1948–1952), one of few female-led titles; and *Gabby Hayes Western* (Fawcett, 1948–1957), which offered a humorous twist on the genre. Not to be outdone, some of the cowboys' trusty steeds got their own series, too, such as *Rocky Lane's Black Jack* (Charlton, 1957–1959), *Gene Autry's Champion* (Dell, 1951–1955), and *Roy Rogers' Trigger* (Dell, 1951–1955)—the latter of which was selling over 890,000 copies in 1952 "and outselling many non-equine actors," according to Davis.[27] Even cowboy stars who had passed away continued to live on in the pages of comic books: for example, *Tom Mix Western* (Fawcett, 1948–1953) featured the adventures of the silent-film actor who had died in 1940.

The success of the film and television Western comic books was often linked to the character's popularity in other media. For example, Barrier describes how "Dell's monthly cowboy comic book stars Gene

Autry and Roy Rogers were by the early 1950s stars of weekly television shows. [Dell's chief] George Delacorte wrote to Autry on January 4, 1951, a few months after the Autry show's debut, to tell him that television's power was making itself felt: the comic book's sales were about 5 percent higher in areas where the show was seen."[28] And the influence of the associated television shows certainly accounted for the swelling sales figures for the comic books. For example, by 1952 *Roy Rogers Comics* was selling 1.6 million copies per issue for Dell.[29]

However, there was money to be made through licensed comic books, and the stars themselves would earn their fair share of royalties. For example, *Business Weekly* reported that actor William Boyd's share from the *Hopalong Cassidy* comic books in 1951 was $55,000.[30] Likewise, Barrier recounts how Dell anticipated the success that television and film Western stars would attain in comic books, and "its contract with Autry provided that he would receive fifteen thousand dollars as a signing bonus, independent of his royalties on the comic books."[31]

The materiality of comics form set the film and television–inspired Western comic books apart from their on-screen counterparts. Unlike other popular media (like radio and film) comic books are a physical form that can be collected, read, reread, and shared with others. Therefore, while the on-screen adventures of certain film and television stars could only be enjoyed by audiences at one moment in time, there is a permanence to their adventures as they exist on the comics page, allowing fans of certain Western stars to keep coming back and experiencing their heroic exploits. For some series, like *John Wayne Adventure Comics*, these titles purported to capture the "true" off-screen adventures of the actors they featured, reinforcing their daring and zeal to do good as a means of boosting their star power. However, for others, the spin-off comic books served to extend a fan's enjoyment of a given star, adding to the fictive Western storyworlds the actors occupied in the minds of their young readers. This effect would continue into the 1960s as publishing of Western comic books remained strong and expanded to include tie-ins of many popular Western television series, including Dell's *Annie Oakley & Tagg* (1955–1959), *Gunsmoke* (1957–1961), *Have Gun—Will Travel* (1960–1962), and *Maverick* (1959–1962); and Gold Key's *Bonanza* (1962–1970), among many others.[32] In any case, the longevity of Western comic books was sustained by their popularity in different media across the 1950s and 1960s: as long as there were Western films playing at the cinemas and frontier drama series unfolding on television screens across the nation, Western comic books would continue to fly off the racks at American newsstands.

The Western was one of the central fantasies that captured the attention of readers during the Golden Age of American comic books. The violent history of the American West was lauded and mythologized in comic books about lone heroes who bravely resist and conquer the forces of evil in lawless and inhospitable landscapes. Particularly in the midcentury moment, as the United States emerged triumphant from World War II, the Western was propelled by the celebratory atmosphere of the time. The mythic West helped explain to young comic book readers how the nation's heroic character was shaped by the experience of claiming the frontier and how the country's will to triumph and prosper was forged through the inexorable westward movement of its people. However, the ongoing appeal of the comic book Western lay not only in how it encapsulated a jubilant moment in postwar American society. Indeed, comic books could bring together all the best bits that abounded in the Western genre (from its gripping plots to its arresting action sequences) and deliver them in a unique and fun way. The widespread creative production and printing of comic books meant that there was a rich diversity in the stories they could tell—Western adventure was not just promoted through cowboy heroics. Western comics were driven by a whole host of heroines, horses, Indigenous heroes, outlaws, vigilantes, and other champions of the oppressed. And their popularity was proven through sales figures—Western comic books sold in the millions.

This captive readership was not only enticed back to the newsstands time and time again because of the frenetic frontier adventure stories that comic books told; the Western genre's natural ability to address American society's desires, fears, and concerns gave comic book Westerns a mythic currency that kept readers coming back for more. Indeed, one aspect merely touched on in this chapter was how comic books were submerged in the political climate of their time and had the potential to engage with the pressing issues that encircled them. We can see this at play in those John Wayne comic books described above that feature his adventures in the Korean War and his standoff against some trifling Communist saboteurs in Latin America. However, as we shall see in the next chapter, the historical distance of the Old West allowed creators to engage with the backdrop of midcentury Cold War American politics in some innovative and unusual ways.

CHAPTER 5

Nuclear Showdown

Western Comic Books Ride through the Cold War

IN DECEMBER 1951 YOUTHFUL MAGAZINES' Western anthology title, *Buffalo Bill* (1950–1951), printed the comic "Swift Deer and the Russian Bear." The story takes its setting in early nineteenth-century California and focuses on Swift Deer and his fellow Ute tribe members who have been enslaved by a group of Russian settlers who recently arrived by boat. The Russians are a cruel invading force and exploit the Utes, using them as slave labor to build a fort. Wearied by this grueling work, one night Swift Deer is haunted by a nightmare about Joseph Stalin, the future Communist leader of Russia (fig. 5.1). Swift Deer consults the tribe's medicine man about his vision, who warns him: "Those men evil! I see heap trouble, many, many, moons in the future." Realizing the true danger of Russian presence on the continent, Swift Deer sees only one solution: "War!" He incites his fellow tribespeople to rise up against their oppressors and attack the Russian fort, driving the invaders to flee back to their native homeland.[1] The haunting presence of Joseph Stalin in this Old West story is emblematic of the zany narrative possibilities of Western comic books from the era. Moreover, Swift Deer's anxieties regarding Russian infiltration captures the dominant political rhetoric that surrounded the comic's publication.

On the surface, the postwar years gave the United States a renewed sense of exceptionalism as the nation emerged as a dominant global superpower in the aftermath of World War II. However, despite its nuclear monopoly, having unleashed the catastrophic power of the atomic bomb on the Japanese cities of Hiroshima and Nagasaki in 1945, the United States was not afforded the spirit of untouchable supremacy one might expect. And the implications of global dominance that history had delivered the nation in 1945 also heralded a spirit of anxiety and self-doubt. Indeed, it soon came to light that Soviet spies

FIGURE 5.1. Stephen Kirkel, "Swift Deer and the Russian Bear," *Buffalo Bill* #9, December 1951, Youthful Magazines.

had stolen nuclear secrets from the United States as early as 1942. (At least twenty-nine Soviet agents would penetrate the Manhattan Project.) Likewise, Stalin, the leader of the Soviet Union, threatened to fill the power vacuum in postwar Europe through his central geopolitical objective: expanding Soviet territory and domination across the war-ravaged continent. This was an affront to American international interests, which sought to export their own political and economic systems around the globe. Therefore, the incipient Cold War that had been building between the United States and Soviet Russia came to be defined by foreign policy excesses (the global anticommunist crusade) and domestic phobias (McCarthyism). This Cold War culture permeated every aspect of American life, from government to religion to cultural industries—even the family and home life were pervaded with anxieties about Communist infiltration.[2] As David Caute describes, the United States was "sweat drenched in fear," haunted by the specter of Communism.[3]

The comic "Swift Deer and the Russian Bear" certainly captures the atmosphere of the time, imagining, rather ridiculously, how even Native Americans from the nineteenth-century West could not escape the torment from the Communist menace. Notwithstanding this extremely quirky example, the Western genre in more broader terms provided an imaginative space in which consumers could explore and work through a variety of political and ideological problems posed by the Cold War, and Westerns garnered huge popularity across comic books, fiction, film, and television in this era. Although conventionally set in the nineteenth century (from post–Civil War to the 1890s), the thematic concerns of the Western could naturally address Cold War issues, such as reinforcing domestic imperatives through stories about cowboy heroes who settle lawless frontier towns or propagating unfettered American intervention in global politics through narratives about Western gunfighters intervening in affairs south of the border. Despite the comic book's stature as a popular form of youth reading material in this era, the ostensibly simplistic moral conflicts common to the vast range of Western adventure comics concealed a deep engagement with the culture of Cold War America.

Cold War Culture

The United States and the Soviet Union were uneasy allies in the aftermath of World War II, and any chance of true unity was doomed from the start. Neither country was able to agree on issues such as peace treaties and reparations; postwar Germany was ultimately split into capitalist West and Communist East; and plans for nuclear disarmament came to naught. After the war Stalin imposed dictatorships on Eastern European countries, which created the Eastern Bloc of Soviet Socialist Republics (including Poland, Czechoslovakia, Hungary, and neighboring countries), and he announced to the world a five-year plan to build up arms in anticipation of a military conflict with Western powers.[4]

However, antagonism soon intensified when it transpired that widespread espionage allowed the Soviet Union to develop a working atomic bomb by the summer of 1949.[5] This deprived the United States of the sense of military security it had possessed since 1945, and the nuclear arms race would come to define America's struggle with the Soviets. Indeed, with the prospect of mutual mass destruction a very real possibility, direct conflict became unthinkable; thus, this battle would be fought through economics, technology, politics, and ideology. For the United States, a key aim was to contain Communism in all of its manifestations.

At home, this era of containment saw a spectrum of American citizens, politicians, cultural industries, and corporations cling to a notion of consensus around a "vital center," casting society into a co-alition against the forces of Communism.[6] Generally, the vital center spoke of a community of white, middle-class families with faith in their great nation, united by a mission of progress, which was defined primarily as the export of their capitalist and individualist ideology across the globe: a mission that was sorely threatened by the forces of Communism. In counteracting this threat, stress was placed on strict cohesion and conformity within the domestic sphere.

This conformity led to a policy of containing and demonizing the parts of society that were breaking away from the vital center, includ-ing juvenile delinquents, homosexuals, Communist sympathizers, and other "undesirables."[7] Domestic containment culture appeared significantly more important as an ongoing series of high-profile cases pertaining to Soviet espionage forced the American public to invest credence in the conspiracy of an internal Communist threat. In 1949 the leaders of the US Communist Party were convicted under the Smith Act for conspiracy; Julius and Ethel Rosenberg were tried and sentenced to death for their part in passing on atomic secrets to the Russians in 1951; and the Hiss-Chambers affair (beginning in 1948) saw a government official, Alger Hiss, accused of being a Soviet spy and later charged with perjury. These successive revelations created an at-mosphere of suspicion and fear that Soviet Russia was as much a threat from inside as from outside the United States.[8]

The presumed domestic infiltration by Russian influences reached its paranoiac height as "subversives" were hunted down and rooted out in government, unions, and the film industry. Under the leader-ship of Republican senator Joseph McCarthy, a full-blown "Red Scare" paranoia (known as McCarthyism) took hold after 1950 and led to a scenario in which security checks and loyalty oaths became integral parts of Cold War American life.[9]

Beyond America's borders, the Truman administration (1945–1953) fully committed itself to resisting further expansion of Soviet power and influence. Described broadly as the Truman Doctrine, this princi-ple set the United States on what it saw as a global crusade on behalf of liberty, aiding any nation threatened by totalitarian aggression or

Communist subversion. This policy became increasingly imperative in the winter of 1949 with the news that China had become a Communist state. The Soviet-backed North Korean invasion of South Korea in June 1950 sparked the Korean War (1950–1953).[10] In this political climate, the Truman Doctrine shaped much of the United States' Cold War foreign policy for the next three decades. As American interests looked to contain Soviet influence abroad, the policies were expressed by a habit of intervention, both covert in developing countries such as the Philippines, Iran, and Guatemala; and overt with the United States' entry into the Korean War and later the Vietnam War (1964–1975).

Peter J. Kuznick and James Gilbert have described how "the principal effect of the Cold War may have been psychological," persuading "millions of Americans to interpret their world in terms of insidious enemies at home and abroad"; they add that this "dark, distorted lens" through which the American public viewed their condition was a product of the domestic and foreign imperatives of Cold War politics.[11] These popular fears surrounding internal and external Communist subversion manifested themselves in a number of ways through popular culture.[12] And the Western genre was directly caught up in this paranoiac atmosphere.

The Cold War Western

The Cold War provided creators of the Western genre with a renewed sense of purpose, and its prominence in American popular culture was not without motivation. Lary May observes how the wealth of Western and war films from the 1950s articulated the necessity of violence to resolve problems, presenting the theme of unity against a savage enemy (whether Native Americans, Japanese, Germans, or Communists).[13] The war film often provided its audiences distance from the violence, depicting battles against American enemies in far-flung regions of the globe. In contrast, the Western inculcated a sense of threat that was closer to home, weaving narratives of "savage" Indians roaming the American landscape and terrorizing wholesome white-settler communities.

As domestic and foreign imperatives of the Cold War instilled American culture with a sense of danger from "insidious enemies at home and abroad" (to repeat Kuznick and Gilbert), the Western arguably provided a rich thematic language in which Americans could conceptualize their struggle with Soviet Russia. The depiction of the heroic defense of the American way against attacking Native Americans provided the most basic of resolutions to pervasive Cold War anxieties, articulating former victories of American tradition over external enemies and projecting the United States as inviolable.

Comic books played an emphatic part in this cultural mythmaking, transforming historical frontier conflicts into powerful symbolic images of righteous American heroes repelling the attacks of menacing-looking Indigenous people. The cover from *Fighting Indians of the Wild West!* #2 is just one such example, featuring the crew and passengers of a stagecoach fending off attacking Native Americans coming at our heroes from all angles (fig. 5.2). Another cover, featured on Avon Periodical, one-shot *Custer's Last Fight* (see fig. 1.9), is emblematic of this context, recalling the iconic battle scene in which a heroic Custer stands undaunted, surrounded by attacking Indians, a theme that was first developed in the illustrated press from the late 1800s. This one-shot was indicative of Avon Periodicals' wider Western output.

Indeed, while many comic book publishers carried a wealth of thrilling cowboy and Indian stories in this era, Avon in particular was most prolific in its militaristic take on Western adventure, in an array of series (*Wild Bill Hickok* [1949–1956], *Geronimo* [1950–1951], *Kit Carson* [1950–1955]) and in short-lived titles and one-shots like *Chief Victorio's Apache Massacre* (1951), *Davy Crockett* (1951), *Fighting Indians of the Wild West!* (1952), and *Fighting Daniel Boone* (1953). Avon's Western comics figured heavily in tropes of Indian depredations such as murder, massacre, and treachery, and its stories often portrayed surprise attacks on military forts by Indians on the warpath for no reason other than to spill the blood of white soldiers and settlers. Such acts of unprovoked terror only helped to validate the subsequent retaliations from heroic white gunfighters and the righteous victories against these callous enemies.

One significant feature of Avon's Westerns, in their construction of Indian savagery, was the artists' reliance on aesthetics lifted from the cover art of horror comics. Indeed, in place of the stock monster (often an undead creature) looming large over its cowering victim—imagery found on the covers of many immensely popular horror titles from the period—Avon Westerns often featured grotesque, grimacing Indian figures menacing poor white settlers in fearsome scenes of murder and kidnap (see, for example, fig. 5.3).

To entice readers, these lurid images certainly played on the popularity of the horror titles in circulation at the time, but these Western comics stand out for how they deployed simulations of dominance in

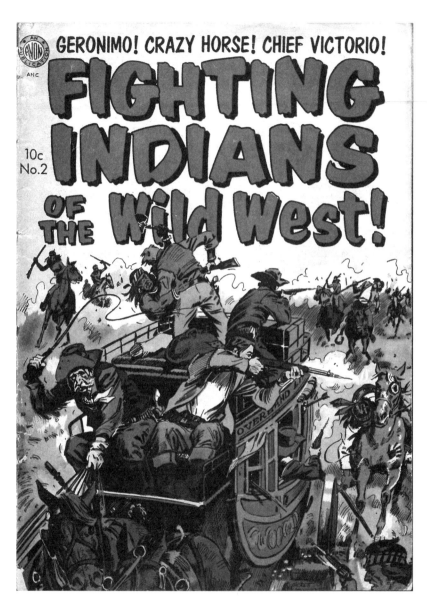

FIGURE 5.2. Everett Raymond Kinstler (cover art). *Fighting Indians of the Wild West* #2, November 1952, Avon Periodicals.

FIGURE 5.3. Everett Raymond Kinstler (cover art). *Chief Victorio's Apache Massacre*, Avon Periodicals, 1951.

response to threats to national security. At a time when pernicious Soviet influence sought to undermine the right of American expansion and hegemony on the global stage, the circulation of stories about a "savage," non-white threat looking to harm the American way can be read as a strong affirmation of contemporaneous Cold War rationales about the need for military action rather than diplomacy to support American interests. The construction of Native Americans as a type of monster in these cover images only added to this form of cultural mythmaking. By looking backward, to triumphal fables of taming the Wild West by freeing it from deadly native populations to make way for national progress, Western comics gave readers a way to envision the United States dominating a threatening new enemy.

The historical distance the genre provided meant that Westerns tended to engage with Cold War anxieties allegorically. However, this did not stop creators from encouraging audiences to draw parallels between Old West adventures and the contemporary milieu in increasingly emphatic ways. A direct example of this at work can be found in the film *Colt .45* (1950), which sees a killer, Zachary Scott, steal a pair of new Colt .45 repeating pistols before fleeing from the law. As regular guns are no match for this new advanced weaponry, Scott leaves a trail of dead bodies in his wake, calling out for a heroic gunslinger to put a stop to this dastardly killing spree. John H. Lenihan explains how publicists at Warner Bros. made sure that "audiences would not miss the contemporary point" of the film through advertisements: "In publicizing the Western *Colt .45* (1950), Warners highlighted the film's integral theme of keeping a new weapon 'out of hands of the wrong element—Indians and bandits in the Colt days, Russians and the Iron Curtain now.'"[14]

In contrast, the comic book version of the Western was not always so subtle, providing much more politically blunt framings of the same context. Through the stroke of a pen a comics artist could conjure imaginative Western storyworlds that forcefully brought the political undercurrents of the story to the fore. Rather than allegorical associations between the nineteenth-century Colt and the twentieth-century atom bomb (coding that in films relied on marketing material to make clear), for example, comics could be much more explicit in telling stories of cowboy heroes disrupting treacherous Russian spies from stealing top nuclear scientists for their own devious causes.

This was evident in a number of cowboy comics set in the mid-twentieth-century West. For instance, *Roy Rogers* (from 1948) comics regularly saw the titular cowboy deputized by local law enforcement to help uphold law and order on the present-day Western range. One comic tells of Dr. Roland Price, an atomic scientist developing a deadlier version of the H-bomb, who has gone missing in Colorado. As an unofficial authority figure who is familiar with the area, Roy Rogers is tasked by the FBI with finding the missing scientist. As the FBI agent reminds Rogers, spies from a "foreign power" may seek to capture Price. The cowboy eventually locates the scientist in an old mine shaft, and the FBI agent's suspicions regarding foreign enemies are realized, as Soviet spies are in pursuit of Dr. Price. These villains are no match for Rogers's sharpshooting, and the cowboy saves Price from his pursuers. In the closing scene of the comic, the scientist thanks Rogers: "If I were wounded and captured, and the enemy were to pick my mind of certain secrets—millions of persons would die horribly!"[15] The comic usefully illustrates how Russian saboteurs on American soil could naturally supplant the common villains found in the Western (from Native Americans to dastardly outlaws). It equally reveals the relevance of cowboy comics in this period as it underscores the ever-present danger from Communist subversion to its readers.

However, Roy Rogers was not alone in catching Soviet spies in the West. One comic from the *Gene Autry* series (1941–1959) features the titular cowboy on a search for an atomic scientist who was doing "super secret work vital to the security of the United States" before going missing on a mountain range (and feared to have been kidnapped by enemies of the United States).[16] Likewise, the comic series *Buster Crabbe* (1951–1953) regularly saw the film star clash with Soviets operating on American soil. In one instance, while on a bounty-hunting mission in Colorado's San Juan Hills, Crabbe does not find his fugitive but inadvertently stumbles on "Project U"—a secret Soviet military base that is mining uranium and exporting it back to Russia to be made into nuclear weaponry. In another story Crabbe disrupts a group of Communist saboteurs from blowing up an energy plant in the southwestern desert.[17]

The examples above begin to illustrate how Western comic books delivered their own unique pairing of frontier action and adventure with the pervasive culture of Cold War America.[18] While their presentations can be quite blunt—Native Americans haunted by the hammer and sickle and Soviet spies overrunning the Western range—this sample of comics serves as a compelling visual archive of Cold War America, bringing to the fore the tensions and fears of consensus America through simple conflicts pitting good against evil. However, comic books more broadly were integral to the fabric of Cold War culture.

Bradford W. Wright suggests that comic books of the late 1940s and 1950s were a crucial medium that "informed young readers about the Cold War and their role in it," adding that the "fear of communism gave the comic book industry an opportunity to . . . speak to the anxieties of its audience and boost its own patriotic image."[19]

This campaign was extended to the vast array of popular genre comics: romance comics (largely written by men) educated girls on their domestic responsibilities; spy comics narrated tales of Communist spies threatening American interests at home and abroad; war comics emphasized the villainy of the Soviet-backed North Korean army as the Korean War broke out.[20] Likewise, the vast range of postwar Western comic books facilitated the promotion of the vital center. William Savage describes how the comic book cowboys' efforts to stamp out threats to American prosperity, as unofficial agents of law enforcement, were crucial to the cause of fighting the Communist menace and encouraged readers to emulate the hero's sense of duty to his country and responsibility for his fellow Americans. As Savage writes, the cowboy hero "chased crooks, be they rustlers or despoilers of banks, railroads, stagecoaches, or other symbols of civilization, security, and economic development. He stood for law and order, peace and quiet, God and country, Mom and apple pie."[21] In addition, he suggests that in the "troubled times" of the 1950s, "the era produced nothing that the comic-book cowboy could not and would not speak."[22]

At face value, this assertion appears fairly broad, and Savage does not fully qualify it. However, with some unpicking, Savage's statement about how the comic book cowboy can speak to any contemporaneous concern proves quite useful. Indeed, by the start of the Cold War the Western had shed its original historical referents, as a result of continued repetition and expanded use in American popular culture. Instead, the genre was regarded as a form of fiction or fable. Its recognizable icons, symbols, themes, and conventions were therefore ideally suited to be reinscribed with contemporary meanings that were not associated with the Western's original historical source material.[23] The comic book in particular could readily participate in this cultural mythmaking. The creative freedom of this hand-drawn form could be exploited to its full by the comics creator, who could take the Western's familiar icons, symbols, and themes and manipulate and repackage them to speak of a range of different ideas, concerns, and meanings. By applying Charles Hatfield's thesis that "genre comic books can become vehicles of extended cultural argument," I suggest that an examination of the continued serialized publication of Western-genre comic books throughout the late 1940s and 1950s can unmask an ongoing dialogue with Cold War America.[24]

Take, for example, the law-and-order formula, which sees a zealous cowboy hero resolving a frontier community's problems or taming an unruly border town using regenerative violence to restructure and reinvigorate society. This quintessential narrative ran through many comics from the era, given the fact that large numbers of postwar Western comic books were geared toward cowboy heroism and crime fighting on the frontier. However, beneath their stories of rough and tough gunslinging heroes, these comics were inscribed with the dominant Cold War political rhetoric of the time, which spoke to juvenile readers about the virtues of supporting American superiority and hegemony.

Law and Order on the Western Range

The 1950s were marked by a trend of law-and-order Westerns, which broadly tell of a lone gunfighter who uses violence to set a crime-ridden frontier town on the path toward an idealized American way of life or to fend off a stock Western villain (the bandit, the crooked gambler, the greedy rancher, etc.) who threatens the sanctity of a wholesome community.[25] Specifically backed by the culture of the Cold War (as Americans clutched the notion of consensus around a vital center, uniting against the threat posed by the forces of Communism), certain tenets from the law-and-order Western story were ripe to be exploited, articulating an important commentary on the anticommunist crusade. The settings of small, emerging frontier townships, coded as American society at large, provided opportunities to show a community taking shape and to pose questions about the nature of this community and what values it should adopt. The Western gunfighter embodied the Cold Warrior who emerged as an agent and protector of American world dominance after World War II and was presented as a figure who creates security through violence. As Matthew Costello notes, the politically self-conscious law-and-order Westerns are important artifacts of the popular political culture of the Cold War, "treating the nature of the American community, the role of the individual within it, and the responsibilities of citizenship and of power, all within a tale of the lone lawman defending a town from a gang of cut-throats."[26]

Western comics from the era widely adopted this popular formula. The Western crime-fighter Johnny Thunder, in DC Comics' *All-American*

Western (1948–1952), is just one example; his bimonthly adventures encapsulate the recurring iterations of the formula for comic books. Each issue saw Thunder, an unofficial agent of authority, uphold law and order in Mesa City, a frontier town continually threatened by all manner of villains, ranging from crooked law enforcement to bank and train robbers to roving outlaw gangs to aggressive Apache Indians.[27] Thunder's zeal for upholding peace and prosperity is driven by his alter ego, John Tane, the local schoolteacher of Mesa City, who is duty bound to teach the youth of the town about the importance of American values, like freedom, democracy, and the necessity of law and order. For example, in one lesson that cannot be read without the steer of the contemporaneous political atmosphere, Tane instructs that his class must strive to "keep democracy strong—here in our country—and thus in the whole world!" (fig. 5.4).[28] Thunder's defense of the American way of life, opposing all threats to societal prosperity, offers its readers cultural reassurance, reinforcing the idea that the American way was undefeated throughout history and doing so at a time when the nation was trapped in a troubled conflict with the Soviet Union. Through numerous stories in which the hero champions downtrodden frontier settlers (including the elderly and disadvantaged, innocent children, the lonesome widower, the hapless ranch owner, and the pretty schoolmarm), the comics creator was afforded the space to emphasize a virtuous American community worth saving. The villains were always extremely evil, often driven by greed and personal gain, and were set on damaging the livelihood of hard-working Americans. However, the comic books' illustrated storyworld allowed for the set boundaries of this formula to be stretched in some unusual directions, with particular regard to who was cast as the villain.

Alongside the regular miscreants that threaten Mesa City (outlaws, Native Americans, and other stock wrongdoers), in one issue of *All-American Western* Johnny Thunder must fend off a band of marauding Arabs astride camels, who rampage across the desert, murdering all they find, after arriving aboard a boat from the Middle East.[29] This peculiar take on the formula was common in a wider set of Western series. For example, one *Hopalong Cassidy* comic sees an evil sheep rancher, Mack Gowan, mail order crates of wolves to be delivered to neighboring sheep ranches, causing the value of his own livestock to increase as his competitors' sheep are slaughtered by the released wolves.[30] Only the titular sheriff's investigation skills in rooting out the source of this carnivorous danger can restore the tranquility of the town of Twin River.

FIGURE 5.4. Robert Kanigher and Alex Toth, "Double Danger!," *All-American Western* #112, February 1950, DC Comics.

Aside from mail-order wolves and menacing Arabs, other threats posed to frontier communities include a man who transforms into a werewolf and a vampire bat that feeds on the blood of cowboys and livestock alike; a Roman emperor, Nero, who lures gunslingers to fight in his Colosseum in the Western desert; a baron who kidnaps townsfolk from a frontier settlement, forcing them to mine radium below his medieval castle; a man disguised as Death, who delivers skulls to his victims before murdering them. Of course, his victims are industrious ranchers who look to tame the West (in this case, by introducing an irrigation system).[31] The Western comic books' particular novel brand of frontier adventure provided clear alternatives to the more common law-and-order formula Western films from the era.

However, beneath these quirky Western adventure stories, the dominant ideological thrust remains the same: the right of American conquest and the obligation to fructify untended natural resources and civilize unruly regions, ridding them of undesirable elements. The *Ghost Rider* extract in figure 5.5 illustrates this context. It introduces the story of four "honest and good" ranchers who, "using their wisdom and wealth to spread prosperity throughout their ranchland," clearly seek to bring richness and civility to this once-barren expanse. While the mysterious stagecoach driver dressed as Death threatens this ambition, the heroic Ghost Rider puts a stop to this villain at the end of the comic, and American progress can continue to allow the region to prosper.[32]

The Western typically takes its setting in the latter half of the nineteenth century and the twilight years of the frontier. These decades represent a triumphal moment in which certain values and traditions that comprise American national identity were forged. John Lenihan observes an epochal quality in this type of Western story: "In its classic form the Western depicted the heroic interlude that ushered in the good society."[33] The genre often captures this point of transition, showing a moment of social upheaval (such as subduing an unruly border town or removing a tribe of Native Americans) whose resolution marks the coming of civilization and the values and mores of American nationalism taking a strong hold in a formerly unsettled frontier locale. Therefore, in focusing on the results of the conflict that they depict, the Western naturally promotes the terms of American superiority and expansionism.

Stanley Corkin observes that the postwar Westerns built on these antecedents and "provided a conceptual bridge between frontier mythology and Cold War imperatives."[34] In particular, Corkin contends that the economic rationales behind postwar US expansion could be addressed and promoted through the structural connections with the Western story of nineteenth-century American imperialism. We begin to see this in practice in comics in the above stories about Western heroes who quell threats to the spread of order and prosperity on the nineteenth-century frontier. These tales encouraged readers to forge links between the Western individual who uses violence to allow American society to flourish in its Old West setting and the core terms of postwar foreign policy, which shifted notions of American hegemony from a local context onto a broader global stage. However, a certain set of Westerns that took their setting south of the border in Mexico could be much more explicit in articulating this concept.

FIGURE 5.5. Dick Ayers, "Death's Stagecoach!," *The Ghost Rider* #2, December 1950, Magazine Enterprise.

Trouble South of the Border: Comic Books
and the Mexico Western

In "Aztec Gold Brings Hot-Lead Justice!" from *Two-Gun Kid* #4 (1948), the title hero becomes embroiled in local affairs as he passes through a small Mexican border town. Bandits have been looting from an Aztec temple sacred to the local inhabitants, driving them into a bitter rage. The Two-Gun Kid takes it upon himself to stop these thieves and restore order. After tracking the bandits down, pummeling them into submission, and bringing them back to the town to be served with a punishment, the campesinos cheer, "Viva! Viva el Americano!" The local priest confirms, "You have brought peace to our territory! Bless you, my son!"[35] The short space of the comic book narrative (across several pages) forces the ideological tenets to be condensed into their most basic meaning: the hapless nature of the local people necessitates American assistance to bring order and structure to a subordinate locale. All the elements of the familiar law-and-order formula are here: an unruly town, abused locals, and an American hero who selflessly defeats obstacles to usher in "the good society" (to take Lenihan's phrasing). However, by placing this familiar storyline within the politically troubled Mexican frontier, the comic showcases an alternative use of the law-and-order formula. Indeed, studies by Carlos E. Cortés and Camilla Fojas have developed the idea that American popular culture of the 1950s increasingly utilized Mexico as a backdrop from which to reaffirm US presence in the affairs of developing nations and to portray the positives of American intervention in foreign lands.[36]

The nuclear balance of terror and the Korean War stalemate proved that direct conflict yielded little advantage for the American mission to effectively limit Communist expansion. Therefore, the Cold War competition was increasingly transferred to developing nations in the mid-1950s, where underdevelopment and the disorders of decolonization provided a potent environment for anti-American ideas and local Communist movements to ferment. In counteracting this, the United States sought to institute American-inspired reform, but this meant that native political conditions needed to be changed first. Such change generally involved defeating radical attempts at controlling the political order or coercing the downfall of a regime ostensibly receptive to Communist influence.[37] Early instances included the CIA's orchestration of Mohammad Mosaddegh's downfall in Iran in 1953 and the overthrow of the democratically elected leader Jacobo

Árbenz in Guatemala in 1954. In both cases, the CIA engineered coups to replace these progressive reformers with "friendly" dictatorships that were ideologically open to American interests (which included procapitalism, openness to penetration from international corporations, anti-unionism, and antileftism). Likewise, in the Philippines, American military advisors assisted nationalist leader Ramon Magsaysay in his successful campaign against the Communist Hukbalahap insurgents (1949–1953).[38] These early forays into foreign intervention mapped out different methods of dealing with an ostensible Communist threat in developing nations around the globe—from training local militias, to sabotage and subvert the current dispensation that opposed US interests (as in Iran and Guatemala), to assisting nations in their own counter-insurgency operations (as in the Philippines).

The Western genre's confidence in American westward expansion and its stories of righteous heroes who go forth to tame inhospitable and unruly landscapes in preparation for settlement and commerce was, according to Stanley Corkin, "well suited to convey important ideological rationales for postwar US foreign policy, including the inevitability of American expansion and the strategies for hegemony that guided the Truman administration's foreign policy."[39] This was most expressive in a thematic cluster of Westerns from the 1950s described by Slotkin as "Mexico Westerns," which followed American heroes who head south of the border and intervene in Mexican affairs. They included films such as *Vera Cruz* (1954), *The Treasure of Pancho Villa* (1955), *The Last of the Fast Guns* (1958), *The Wonderful Country* (1959), and *The Magnificent Seven* (1960). Slotkin argues that these films envisioned the Western gunfighter "as an American 'freedom-fighter' battling the forces of oppression and 'alien ideologies' in the Third World."[40] This type of plot normalized US foreign policy, promoting geopolitical objectives to contain Communism overseas.[41] The political stance is clear: the Westerner, driven by his strict heroic moral code, must be prepared to use violence against treacherous enemies that pose threats to the American way of life outside of the nation's borders.

The use of the Mexico Western formula in comic books was frequent and indeed predated many of the films listed above. Therefore, we can read Mexico Western comic book stories, which emerged much earlier than their cinematic counterparts, as laying the ideological groundwork for these later Western films, helping readers to assimilate much of the ongoing US foreign intervention of the 1950s. One storyline from the Western comics anthology *Death Valley* (1953–1954) is useful in elaborating upon the problems of those countries that did not have the privilege of American assistance. "Trouble in Mexico" dramatizes a criminal's ascent to power in nineteenth-century Mexico. It tells of El Toro, a cruel bandit who wins the presidential election through buying votes and violently crushing his enemies. One page from the comic details this corrupt electoral process of bribery and murder (fig. 5.6). Likewise, in another sequence, El Toro's henchmen torture a competing presidential candidate, El Lopez, described as a "statesman" and a "democrat." El Toro is assassinated at the end of the comic, closing this nightmare scenario of political subversion. However, the comic highlights the perils of self-rule, presenting the weaknesses in foreign political systems where cutthroats can easily rise to power.[42]

While the plot of "Trouble in Mexico" does not explicitly stress the need for American intervention south of the border, the comic usefully provides a context that affirms the importance of cowboy heroes involved in Mexican affairs and is a theme present in a range of other stories. For instance, when the Two-Gun Kid returns to Mexico in one comic from 1954, the gunfighter actively targets those criminals in positions of power. The story opens with the Two-Gun Kid discovering that his friend Don Estaban Rodriquez, a respected Mexican government official, has been murdered by revolutionaries led by the bloated renegade Colonel Verduga. The comic in no unclear terms spells out how these revolutionaries are regressive to progress and order: by murdering official agents of power and authority and making political gains through treachery and deceit. As the opening panel articulates, the revolutionaries are no more than bandits: Verduga's title, "Colonel," is placed inside quotation marks to further undermine the authority of his cause (fig. 5.7). Likewise, the enemy clearly fights by unfair means (we see that the Two-Gun Kid is beaten while his hands are tied behind his back), which adds to the hero's mission to halt the expansion of this rebellious faction in a foreign land. Biding his time, the Two-Gun Kid is able to stop Verduga and his army by the end of the comic. Indeed, the Kid thwarts an illegal weapons transaction, keeping the firepower out of the hands of these criminals, and uses dynamite to wipe out Verduga's entire army.[43]

The Two-Gun Kid was not alone in his quest to actively address injustices across the border, and many other cowboy comics would tread these same thematic concerns. For instance, *Cowboy Action* (1955–1956) continued the basic narratives of downtrodden campesinos and ineffectual law enforcement in far-flung lands south of border; unable

FIGURE 5.6. A crude imagining of the corrupt electoral process in South America. Don Heck, "Trouble in Mexico," *Death Valley* #6, August 1954, Comic Media.

FIGURE 5.7. Chuck Miller, artwork. *Two-Gun Kid* #17, October 1954, Atlas Comics.

to control their own condition, they require the guidance of American gunfighters to resolve their problems. Indeed, in the story "Mission of Murder!," we see the Prairie Kid travel to the small Mexican town of Tortilla, where his search for the outlaw Snake Benson becomes an aside to a plot about a thieving padre who steals from local businesses and villagers alike. Only the Prairie Kid, with his intelligence, quick-draw shooting, and honed investigation skills, can single-handedly crack the case, ridding Tortilla of this corruption. Likewise, in one story from *Black Rider* (1950–1955), the masked gunfighter heads to Mexico to assist Captain Garcia and his soldiers in the capture of the bandit The Spider, who has been rampaging across the countryside.

In an episode of *The Gunhawk* (1950–1951), the titular hero decides to take a break from crime fighting on the American frontier and heads to Mexico to enjoy some fine wine. Upon arrival at the once-peaceful village, San Juan del Rio, the Gunhawk realizes the town is now being terrorized by Manuel Ramon Juarez del Oro and his gang of thugs. Driven by a selfless need for justice, the Gunhawk stands up to these villains. When questioned by del Oro about why he is meddling in foreign affairs, the gunfighter replies: "It's an old American custom, I reckon, fightin' fer the underdog!"[44] The latter example presents an explicit endorsement of foreign intervention outlined in the Truman Doctrine, which promised to "support free peoples who are resisting attempted subjugation by armed minorities or by outside pressures" (or, as the comic suggests, to fight "fer the underdog"). But more broadly, this range of comic book stories fits into a framework that highlights the perils of self-government in foreign lands and the requirement of American assistance, underscoring the contemporaneous arguments for US intervention in international affairs. However, as this chapter has reaffirmed, comics are not always so subtle in their toying with the surrounding political atmosphere.

One example can be found in American Comics Group's *The Hooded Horseman* #27 (1953) and the story "Cowboy Sahib" (fig. 5.8). The plot follows the adventures of the Wyoming cowboy Joe King, better known as Cowboy Sahib. After acquiring a sultan's ring, Cowboy Sahib is named ruler of a small kingdom called Larijuna and wastes little time in setting out a civil society with a distinctly American vision. Cowboy Sahib's leadership is vital for the kingdom to thrive. At one point he is found training his soldiers "Wyoming style," readying them for any upsets to the established order. Indeed, the reader soon finds out that the Soviet agent Konchak the Cossack has embedded himself within some local tribes and has incited them to rise up against Cowboy Sahib's rule. Konchak has been sent from Russia to create an atmosphere of disorder from which Communism can subvert the current regime. However, the Cossack is no match for the cowboy's fighting skills, which have been toughened on the Western range, and Sahib soon manages to crush this uprising and restore order to the Indian kingdom of Larijuna.[45]

At face value, the common framing of the Western hero who goes forth and tames unruly territories is present. But here it has been extracted from the familiar nineteenth-century American frontier context and placed within a far-flung exotic locale in which American expansion is not threatened by "savage" Native Americans but by Communist guerrillas. Comics form is ideally suited to this purpose, as it naturally works with visually codified representations. In his

FIGURE 5.8. Leonard Starr (cover art). *The Hooded Horseman* #27, January–February 1953, American Comics Group.

discussion of icons in comics, Scott McCloud suggests: "By stripping down an image to its essential 'meaning,' an artist can amplify that meaning in a way that realistic art can't."[46] In this instance, the comics artist's line allows for an unlikely setup whereby a righteous American cowboy can clash with a Russian Cossack, with the plot offering a pleasing resolution as frontier courage and dedication trump Russian treachery. However, the key aspect here is how the comic reimagines the Western's imperial story of settling the Wild West by placing it in a contemporary kingdom in India ruled by an American hero. To maintain peace and prosperity in his South Asian domain, Cowboy Sahib must fructify the resources at his disposal (in this case, training his primitive military forces), while undermining threats to the kingdom's harmonious existence (that is, the Russian spy who ignites a guerrilla insurgency). In this instance, we can see how the comic emphasizes the dominant ideological thrust of the Western formula, which is unquestioning in its assertions of the American right to penetrate and dominate foreign affairs for personal gains.

Collectively, the range of examples from Western comic books discussed above indicates how frontier mythology surrounding westward expansion was adopted to speak to the terms of these international affairs. As noted, the American ethos of the righteous individual who forcibly changes conditions to create a moral order was based on postwar assumptions regarding American exceptionalism and hegemony. This could be introduced on an implicit level. For instance, if we return to the schoolteacher alter ego of Johnny Thunder, the character John Tane from *All-American Western*, his teachings were laced with Cold War didacticism (see fig. 5.4). In one of his classes, as he writes out the names of the Founding Fathers on the blackboard, he lectures his pupils: "These men fought for justice and the rights of man! In so doing, they helped create the United States! We must follow their example to keep democracy strong—here in our country—and thus in the whole world!"[47] This lesson certainly encapsulates its publication context, and Tane's outward-looking viewpoint is redolent of contemporaneous arguments in support of US interests on the world stage. However, the latter examples of Western cowboys in Mexico were particularly apposite in acting on these assumptions, which shifted the terms of the law-and-order formula onto foreign locales. The foreign setting made a strong case for how the American hero served to oust subversive threats to the established order, making the world safe and ready for the American way to thrive. By introducing the concepts behind contemporary imperialist rationales—grafting them onto assertions of the cowboy hero's right to go forth and settle inhospitable landscapes and reorder lawless expanses—this helps illustrate the symbolic power of Western comic books in the Cold War era. Western comics had the potential to transform the more repugnant aspects of American cultural and economic hegemony into palatable concepts.

Stanley Corkin suggests that "imperialism is one key phenomenon that Cold War Western [films] helped their audiences assimilate."[48] Comic book Westerns certainly fall into a similar framework, evidenced through their diverse array of stories about advancing the frontier and extending the borders of civilization—from the heroic adventurer embattled with native populations in an inhospitable landscape to the gunfighter setting a lawless frontier town on a righteous path. However, comic books stand out precisely for how they play with the raw materials of both the familiar Western space and the surrounding political atmosphere in ways unimagined by the Westerns of other media: from Native American nightmares about Stalin in the nineteenth-century West to Russian subversion threatening an American cowboy's kingdom in a distant region in India. Nevertheless, these comics were aimed at children, making their political dialogue ever more fascinating. The quite politically blunt comics about cowboys fighting Soviet spies in the contemporary West are perhaps most indicative of this trend, talking down to their young readers about the contemporaneous Cold War antagonisms through simplistic battles between good (American cowboys) and evil (Soviet spies). However, examples like the Mexico Western comics added nuance to this context through storylines that conveyed and naturalized American interference in foreign lands under the cover of exciting adventure tales about cowboy heroes south of the border. Returning to a quote I used earlier from Bradford Wright's cultural history of American comic books, the medium "informed young readers about the Cold War and their role in it." It is puzzling that few histories about the midcentury American Western or the comic book medium have sought to consider the significance of Western adventure comics in their accounts of Cold War culture. Nevertheless, close readings of the thrilling stories of vengeance and justice reveal a compelling rationale for how postwar Western comic books could instruct readers on pressing foreign and domestic Cold War imperatives, and these texts exist as a vibrant document of consensus America.

CHAPTER 6

"I Know It's Not in the Romantic Western Spirit"

Subverting the Mythic West in Postwar Comics

IN OCTOBER 1953 THE STORY "The Yella Lawman!" was printed in Atlas Comics' Western anthology title *Wild Western*. In the story the retired lawman Slade Hardy arrives at the crime-ridden town of Gulch Falls (fig. 6.1). The ex-lawman's reputation precedes him, and it is not long before Hardy is elected as the new sheriff in an attempt to tame the town's rough inhabitants. However, it soon comes to light that Hardy is a pacifist and has never actually killed a man. This only encourages Bat Blackburn and his gang of criminals to terrorize the town in a more unrestrained manner, knowing that Hardy won't react to their reign of terror. As the opening panel depicts, the gang's brazenness leaves the sheriff gripped in fear but also indicates the direction that the story will take as the hero must question the efficacy of violence to bring about order on the rugged frontier.

From both a formal and mythological perspective, violence is central to the Western and its countless stories about heroic individuals who conquer and subjugate the untamed wilderness and its unruly populations. Indeed, nearly all cowboy comic books from the postwar era feature an array of stories in which zealous heroes use violence to civilize inhospitable landscapes. Examples like "The Yella Lawman" stand in contrast: it depicts a lone hero who lacks assuredness, and it raises larger questions about the use of violence in the Western.[1] The comic intersects with a wider set of critical and demythologized Western films from the era, such as Delmer Daves's *Broken Arrow* (1950), Anthony Mann's *Devil's Doorway* (1950), Henry King's *The Gunfighter* (1950), and Fred Zinnemann's *High Noon* (1952).[2] Particularly regarding the latter two films, Stanley Corkin describes how they "dwell explicitly on whether violence is an appropriate means of resolving various crises defined in their plots . . . questioning whether violence should

FIGURE 6.1. Bob Fujitani, "The Yella Lawman!," *Wild Western* #30, October 1953, Atlas Comics.

be employed to kill those who are typically, elsewhere in the genre, disposed of without a second thought." The ambivalent depiction of violence, he suggests, "show[s] sensitivity on the part of producers, directors, and screenwriters to issues that were coalescing around the war with Korea and the extremes of domestic anticommunism."[3]

Despite the Allied victory in World War II and the revived sense of American exceptionalism (which the popularity of the Western genre mirrored and boosted), in some quarters audiences grew steadily more disillusioned by the traditional myths of unfettered progress and triumphant heroic figures that cultural vehicles iterated; such consumers required a much more complex type of story. This irreverent tenor certainly imbued the above examples, but comics more generally had a habit of presenting critical reinterpretations of the Western genre, appealing directly to readers by offering alternatives to the grand narratives and mainstream values and traditions from the high Cold War years (1948–1962). This critical space could employ cartoon-style artwork in comics to lampoon and satirize the resonant images from the Western, or it could complicate and subvert the genre's dominant myths through frank retellings of the story of frontier conquest, giving a skewed view of American heroism. Where the previous chapter highlighted the aspirational and guiding spirit of midcentury Western adventure comic books, this chapter illustrates how some comics from the era directly challenged the myths of the popular Western by toying with the underlying sense of unease and disillusionment that marred Cold War American life.

Affluence and Anxiety in Cold War America

Paul Levine and Harry Papasotiriou suggest that "the post-war period brought Americans a dual legacy of unprecedented affluence and unparalleled anxiety."[4] Affluence was fueled by a postwar economic boom, driven by the rise in private consumerism and public military spending, a world-leading and expansive industrial capacity, and a population who received double the per capita income of the next-richest countries. This prosperity was visible in all walks of American life: from the construction of new suburbs and the Interstate Highway System (developed to accommodate the increase in car ownership), to the ubiquitous television set, which hosted programming that spoke to the American public about the virtues of suburban middle-class living. Nevertheless, cracks began to appear in this façade. Indeed, despite a sense of exceptionalism and unassailability that victory in 1945 afforded, the Soviet Union's development of a working atomic bomb by 1949 fed into a growing anxiety surrounding the profound sense of vulnerability that afflicted the nation. As the theologian Reinhold Niebuhr observed in 1952, the Cold War placed Americans in "an historic situation in which the paradise of our domestic security is suspended in a hell of global insecurity."[5]

Culture captured these tensions in the slow decomposition of what Tom Engelhardt describes as "victory culture": the national myth developed across centuries that justified Euro-American acts of Indigenous extermination in the name of settling the nation. That myth certified the American character as embodying traits of heroism, triumphalism, and communal progress through the crushing of a savage enemy. Victory culture and the spirit of American triumph permeated popular culture more widely (evident in Hollywood war and Western films, for instance). However, Engelhardt makes a compelling case for the collapse of the nation's heroic war ethos amidst this age of affluence and anxiety. Overshadowed by the atomic bombs that leveled the Japanese cities of Hiroshima and Nagasaki, the narrative of triumph that had helped shape the nation's sense of history for almost three hundred years no longer proved sustainable. Indeed, American victory culture became entangled with the complexities and grave horrors of nuclear culture and the developing Cold War with the Soviet Union. Engelhardt instead describes a growing sense of "triumphalist despair" that was enacted through a contradictory experience of pride in the American victory of 1945 and the feelings of an anxiety and fear that the war's most "wondrous weapon" would subsequently engender.[6]

A number of psychological Western films from the midcentury evoke these contradictions. As mentioned above, Daves's *Broken Arrow* and Mann's *Devil's Doorway* challenged American complacency over the standardized, yet problematic, frontier story of white subjugation of Native Americans. These films distanced themselves from the heroic myths that arose in the American experience of "winning" the West, while simultaneously offering a much more sympathetic handling of Native Americans by accentuating acts of terror and greed perpetuated by Euro-Americans as they usurped Indigenous lands.

Western newspaper comic strips added further complexity and nuance. For example, Warren Tufts's *Lance* (1955–1960) stands out for continuing the trend of upending racist tropes from the Western genre, following the adventure of Lance St. Lorne, a lieutenant with the US Cavalry charged with policing the untamed territories west of Missouri. Tufts's strip was heavily influenced by the artwork of comics artist Hal Foster, and his painstakingly detailed and grandiose natural landscapes stood just as tall as his captivating and socially and psychologically charged frontier saga. Tufts describes the Indian campaigns with historical accuracy but makes clear that Native American aggression was a consequence of white settlers' unprecedented advances into their homelands, starkly presenting how this impacted the picturesque natural environment. Furthermore, Tufts was adept in dealing with taboo themes, such as miscegenation. (Fig. 6.2 is taken from a story in which the character Eliza Hackett leaves her abusive husband for a tribal chief.) He also tricks his readers by playing on their assumptions about Native Americans. In one story Lance stumbles on a scene of slaughter, and readers are encouraged to infer it is the result of an

FIGURE 6.2. Warren Tufts, *Lance*, Warren Tufts Enterprises, March 4, 1956.

Indian attack: the child quivering under an overturned wagon recalls "Bad mens with feathers," while another character surmises that the massacre was perpetrated by "Injuns, most likely." But in the following Sunday's strip, Lance and his group meet a couple of trappers, and it becomes apparent that these white men (their coats and hats embellished with decorative feathers) murdered and pillaged the young child's pioneer family.[7]

Tufts's Western embraced the spirit of what Engelhardt describes as "triumphalist despair" through its engagement with the ambiguities about Manifest Destiny and the settling of the Wild West. However, the challenging subject matter of *Lance* would be matched by other Western strips from the period. For example, Stan Lynde's *Rick O'Shay* (1958–1981) poked fun at the reverence for the Western in contemporary American culture. Humor was not foreign to the comic strip version of the Western, and gag-filled frontier adventures found an avid readership in long-running strips like *Little Joe* (1933–1972) and *Texas Slim* (1925–1928; 1940–1958). But *Rick O'Shay* stands out for its continuation of the theme of modern America's interactions with the mythic West (a theme discussed in chapter 2), which allowed Lynde to use the Western to comment on contemporary society and culture. The series opened with two characters, the gambler Deuces Wilde and the naive Rick O'Shay, stumbling upon a frontier ghost town, Conniption, and immediately appointing themselves as mayor and marshal, respectively. As the series progressed, a wider set of offbeat characters chose to make Conniption their home, including Hipshot Percussion, the rugged gunslinger; Gaye Abandon, the saloon singer; and Chief Horses Neck, who turned the trope of noble Indian on its head, outwitting any would-be white oppressors.

The series paired typical Western adventure with humor and stands out for its unique setting in the present day (although the series would eventually be relocated in the nineteenth-century West). Storylines regularly satirized popular culture from the era (such as the abundance of detective shows and spy films from the 1960s), but it most commonly spoofed film and TV Westerns. Indeed, in one storyline from 1962 a group of characters from the fictional Kyute tribe descend on Hollywood after becoming disgruntled by the lack of fair representation for Native American characters in Western movies: "Why doesn't Hollywood use real Indians to play Indian roles? Aren't we authentic enough?" questions Chief Horses Neck.[8]

Lynde was a resident of Montana (and owner of a 160-acre ranch), which not only afforded the artist a certain precision in depicting the Western scenery and livestock, but also informed his comic strip's openly affectionate yet satirical handling of the Western and its clichés. Reflecting on the strip's creation, Lynde said: "Instead of wanting to do a serious adventure strip, I had decided to produce a feature which would satirize the fictional Western, the TV Western, from the standpoint of the authentic West in which I'd grown up, taking the Western conventions and stereotypes of fiction and standing them on their heads."[9]

The Western dominated American television, and for an hour each evening cowboys and Indians, gunfighters and dastardly desperados galloped across the nation's television screens in shows such as *Bonanza* (1959–1973), *Cheyenne* (1955–1962), *Colt .45* (1957–1960), *Gunsmoke* (1955–1975), and *Maverick* (1957–1962), among many others. David Reynolds suggests that these historical dramas resonated so strongly with audiences during this period because they encouraged "a confidently American-centred view of the world"; whereas Neil Campbell and Alasdair Kean observe how Western shows struck at the heart of consensus-culture America, portraying a sanguine image of domestic stability through masculine heroes who led successful lives filled with adventure while the female characters were contained within the parameters of the ranch house.[10]

Lynde regularly took aim at the romanticized nature of television's synthetic West in *Rick O'Shay*. For example, in one storyline from 1959 an aged gunfighter from the Old West, Tom Foolery, sees his life on the rugged frontier recounted on a Western-themed television show, *Tom Foolery, U.S. Marshal*. Outraged by the fictionalized saga, Foolery heads to Los Angeles to confront the show's producers. The storyline is conspicuous as a document of the American obsession with Western adventure shows from the period—captured best in one strip in which Rick hastily rides to the chief's tent to catch the latest installment of *Tom Foolery*. The heightened melodramatic absurdities of the show's plot ("I've got t' face him, Miss Lucy. . . . I'm Tom Foolery, U.S. Marshal"; fig. 6.3) undermine the show's seemingly serious nature. However, the effect of the sequence is amplified further by the closing punch line of the strip, as Rick confesses, "Ah jes' love these true-to-life drammers!" Meanwhile, Chief Horses Neck breaks the fourth wall to deliver a knowing look directly to the reader.[11]

Lance and *Rick O'Shay* present just two examples of the inroads made by midcentury Western newspaper strips, deconstructing and stretching the boundaries of the genre (whether through heavy-hitting content or overtly comedic fare), but both signal to the potential for an imaginative Western space in comics that was more self-consciously parodic or subversive than other forms of the genre. Indeed, Christine Bold describes how Western comics' "pronounced foregrounding

FIGURE 6.3. Stan Lynde, *Rick O'Shay*, Chicago Tribune Syndicate, August 1959.

of parody is largely foreign" to wider forms of popular Western fiction, while the "subversive gestures" from some of its adventure stories "offer readers the opportunity to challenge the codes and hierarchies of the Western genre (and the society that it represents)."[12] Interestingly, in this era of "triumphalist despair" (to borrow Engelhardt's wording), as some quarters of American popular culture captured the slow dissolve of the nation's victory culture, the fears and anxieties of the coming nuclear age and the ensuing Cold War held unexpected thrills for some. Engelhardt suggests that in this period when adults were steeped in doubts about their guiding national mythos and haunted by fear of an omnipresent nuclear culture, "many children instinctively grasped the corrosiveness of the postwar transformation, gravitating toward new forms of storytelling [such as comic books]."[13] Engelhardt observes how comic books made visible the underlying tensions and anxieties within postwar American culture as the medium "drew on the horrors of the bomb, the Holocaust, and the Communist menace." Other media also triggered these tensions: "Juvenile delinquency movies . . . drew on fears of a missing underclass; rock and roll and hipsterism . . . fed off fears of racial and sexual otherness; and *MAD* magazine . . . drew on a mocking, dismantling voice lodged deep in the culture." He argues that American youth's consumption of comic books that contravened cultural norms was an instinctive response: "In those years, some children embraced with gusto the secret despair of adults who claimed to be living happily in the freest, richest, most generous country on Earth."[14]

The popularity of crime and horror comic books in the postwar years testifies to this context, offering a macabre and perverse vision of what critic Irving Howe had declared in 1954 as "This Age of Conformity."[15] Crime comics deconstructed the American Dream through tales of characters who achieve material success not through hard work but via a glorified life of crime and murder. For instance, Entertaining Comics (or EC) developed its own brand of domestic horror in storylines that were often set within the American household, telling of murderous and conniving wives and abusive and vengeful husbands. As David Hajdu concludes, "In EC's horror paradigm, the true graveyard was the living room of the American home."[16] Typically consumed by a younger reading demographic, popular genre comics had the potential to contravene mainstream ideals and values and provide violent and subversive content that was largely out of reach to their young readers in other forms of popular media.

The implications were the same for the comic book Western too. Within the early Cold War milieu, comic books offered a fertile setting for creators to present young readers with an overtly iconoclastic take on the Western, which not only dismantled the genre's conventions but also critiqued Cold War America and the surrounding principles of consensus culture that had colored many Western films and television shows from the midcentury. The output of EC exemplifies this context: a variety of stories utilized caricature, irreverent humor, and countermythic retellings of the Old West.

EC's Challenge to the Cold War Western

The robust comic book market had reached its zenith by the early 1950s in both readership numbers and sales figures. In 1950 it was estimated that some three hundred different comic book titles were published that year—a figure that doubled to over six hundred titles by 1953. Surveys suggested that 90 percent of young people under the age of eighteen read comic books. And while average monthly circulation figures for comic books rolled into the millions, *Publishers Weekly* reported that the American public spent $1 billion on comic books in 1953.[17] Sales and readership figures help to convey the mass appeal of mainstream comic books for a captivated young audience by the 1950s—a success that was propelled by an amazingly diverse set of popular genres, from funny animals to crime, Western, war, romance, and teen comics. Given that most titles were marketed toward a juvenile readership, comics books typically toed the line of prevailing ideals and values from the postwar era and affirmed the basic principles of Cold War culture. Few would challenge the aspirational idealism of America's dominant middle-class suburban existence and its prescribed social roles. Likewise, few would question the underlying problems of the prevailing US mission to export American values and virtues throughout the world.

However, as a fairly new narrative medium, the comic book industry remained largely unregulated in the postwar decade (1945–1954), meaning that content could be imbued with a strong critical component that went unchecked. This feature came naturally to comic book publishers like EC, who took pride in confronting, not endorsing, Cold War imperatives from the era. As one of the more notorious publishers from the midcentury moment in US comics publishing history, known for graphic content and a rebellious spirit, EC's handling of the Western genre is worth deeper consideration.

EC is most widely remembered for producing crime, horror, humor, science fiction, and war comic books throughout the late 1940s and early 1950s. Starting out as a midlevel New York–based comic book publisher in 1944, EC was originally known as Educational Comics and delivered a series of morally upright comic books about science, history, and the Bible. However, when owner Max Gaines died in 1947, the company was handed over to his son, William Gaines, who had little interest in the industry nor in the ailing publishing house (which he inherited encumbered with $100,000 worth of debt). Gaines sought to reorient EC to turn a profit. Observing the popularity of genres like crime, romance, and Westerns at the time, Gaines dropped "Educational" from the company name, rebranded it Entertaining Comics, and began promoting a series of new, popular genre comic books for both readerly pleasure and financial gain.

EC's line of grisly crime and horror titles (such as *Crime Suspen-Stories* [1950–1955] and *Tales from the Crypt* [1950–1955], to name two notorious examples) openly attacked the façade of consensus culture America through stories of murder in suburbia. Likewise, its popular antiwar comic books (*Two-Fisted Tales* [1950–1955] and *Frontline Combat* [1951–1954]) deglamorized the triumphal war story.[18] Despite the politically charged undertones and graphic content, EC's creative team tempered this subject matter with humor, which Matthew J. Pustz suggests heightened their appeal to readers: "Although the stories could be very grim, the puns gave readers the idea that nothing should be taken too seriously, that they were involved in a secret, inside joke that non-readers or those not devoted to EC Comics simply could not understand."[19]

With its well-plotted stories and quality artwork in the pages of a range of its genre comics, EC set a new standard of creativity in the comic book industry. The publisher's success showed in its sales figures, and despite having a relatively small distribution network, sales of EC's horror titles averaged almost half a million copies per issue, and *MAD* attracted even higher numbers.[20]

EC's *MAD* magazine (from 1952) provided a stark counterpoint to its range of genre comics by focusing on humorous content. The first target for the title's satire was pinned squarely upon comic books, and early strips comedically reinterpreted popular characters, including "Superduperman" and "Bat Boy and Rubin." Before long, however, *MAD* turned its critical lens on film, music, and politics, and more broadly began to attack capitalism, consumerism, and authority. The magazine's blend of strips, cartoons, and fake advertisements lampooned the status quo of everyday American life. This iconoclastic fervor extended to the title's handling of national myths, too, and the historically resonant images of the Western were fair game in this pursuit. Harvey Kurtzman, *MAD*'s creator, perhaps best described the magazine's approach to the Western when discussing the title's brand of humor: "Satire and parody," he suggested, "work only when you reveal a fundamental flaw or untruth in your subject. . . . The satirist/parodist tries not just to entertain his audience, but to remind it of what the real world is like."[21]

This approach is exemplified through the strip "Cowboy!" from *MAD* #20 (February 1955), which was written and drawn by artist Jack Davis (fig. 6.4). In its opening page the comic questions: "Did you ever read any authentic stuff on the old Wild West? . . . Next, did you ever compare it with the movie and television version of the old Wild West? Ain't it a howl?"[22] The comic then continues to deconstruct the fallacies inherent in the heroic cowboy of film, accentuating this by placing the immaculately dressed and rugged fictional hero, Lance Sterling, next to a cowboy of the real Old West, John Smurd. This brand of satirical humor, which plays on the tensions between the real and the fictive West, is well served by comics form, and particularly by the juxtaposition of images within the space of the page. Indeed, the comic throughout portrays the parallel lives of Sterling and Smurd. Sterling is the typical squeaky-clean protagonist who beats up the bad guy in a saloon showdown through his superior fighting skills and wins the heart of the beautiful girl. Smurd, on the other hand, has a constant ring of flies buzzing around his head from general ranch life, and when he does happen to get into a shootout with one of his neighbors, his gun jams ("as often happens in real life") and he gets beaten up. Only through treacherous and unfair means does he finally beat his adversary one month later, by sneaking up and shooting him in the back.

Karin Kukkonen describes how comics make meaning through a reader's "inferences" from "the layout of the entire page and the details of the individual panels [which] feed into a larger whole."[23] In this case, the comic operates on a system of co-presence. It requires the reader to flit between the interrelated images on each page of this comparative breakdown of the cowboy hero and invites a resistant reading of the mythical West.

However, MAD's cartoonists not only highlighted the deceptions that lay beneath the mythic West; their undermining of the Western also took aim at popular Hollywood films. For example, in "Vera's Cruz" (a take on Robert Aldrich's 1954 film Vera Cruz), Kurtzman and Jack Davis take the premise of the Mexico Western plot and turn it on its head. Instead of promoting US intrusion in the affairs of developing nations (as does the film's plot about American mercenaries who seek adventure south of the border), the comic highlights the problems of American interference in foreign affairs by emphasizing how these Western gunfighters create chaos while in Mexico. As one caption reminds the reader, "No wonder they don't like Americans in other countries! No wonder they say 'Yankee go home!' "[24]

Another example is their parody of the film High Noon, which tells of the town marshal, Will Kane, who awaits the arrival of the vicious outlaw Frank Miller and his gang. Unable to gain assistance from the disobliging townsfolk, who want no hand in the imminent violence, Kane must stand alone to anxiously await the gang's arrival on the noon train. MAD's "Hah! Noon!" extrapolates the film's complex psychological nuance and the social critique underpinning the disobliging American township and the zealous American individual who defends it, condensing the lone hero into a neurotic and cowardly sheriff, Marshall [sic] Kane (fig. 6.5). With news that Killer Diller Miller (a play on the film's antagonist Frank Miller) will arrive on the

COWBOY!

FIRST OF ALL, IN MOVIES AND TELEVISION, THE COWBOY IS USUALLY NAMED SOME-THING LIKE... *LANCE STERLING!*... NOT THAT YOU'D MEET ONE GUY IN A HUNDRED WITH SUCH A NAME!...MAINLY PEOPLE HAVE NAMES LIKE... GEORGE FREEBLE... IGGY SIEDENHAM ...MELVIN POZNOWSKI...! COULD YOU EVER PICTURE A COWBOY HERO CALLED MELVIN POZNOWSKI?... SO HIS NAME IS LANCE STERLING!... AND HIS CLOTHES... OH BROTHER!... HAND TAILORED!... WITH GLOVES!... IN THE HOT SUN ALL DAY LONG, WITH GLOVES!...ANYBODY HERE EVER WEAR GLOVES IN THE HOT SUN ALL DAY LONG?... YOU BETCHA YOU DIDN'T! YOU'D GET A RASH AND YOUR HANDS WOULD ROT OFF!

NOW IN REAL LIFE... THE 100% GENUINE COWBOY HAD AN ORDINARY OLD NAME LIKE MAYBE...*JOHN SMURD!*...THEY'D HANG ANYBODY WITH A NAME LIKE LANCE STERLING! AND IF THEY COULD GROW THEM, MOST GENU-INE COWBOYS HAD BIG WALRUS MUS-TACHES WHICH WERE THE CUSTOM OF THE TIMES! CAN YOU IMAGINE ANYTHING MORE NAUSEATING THAN THE HOLLYWOOD COWBOY WITH SUCH A NAUSEATING MUSTACHE, GOING INTO A CLINCH WITH THE LEADING LADY?... NAUSEATING MAINLY SINCE THESE MUSTACHES OFTEN HAD TOBACCO JUICE SOAKED IN!... AS FOR CLOTHES ... LET'S FACE IT! WHAT DO YOU HAVE TO WEAR TO TEND COWS BESIDE A GOOD PAIR OF BOOTS?

FIGURE 6.4. Jack Davis, "Cowboy!," MAD #20, February 1955, EC.

FIGURE 6.5. Harvey Kurtzman and Jack Davis, "Hah! Noon!," *MAD* #9, March 1954, EC.

noon train, Kane's wife implores him: "If you meet that 12:00 o'clock train, Killer Diller Miller willer killer you . . ." Kane replies, "12:00 o'clock train? Who said anything about a twelve o'clock train! I gotta meet the 11:45 o'clock train an' git the heck outta hyar!"[25]

Alongside the raucous humor, wordplay, and textual winks to the reader, the artwork is an equal partner in *MAD*'s subversive display of the Western. Joseph Witek identifies two distinct traditions of visual representation in comics, or "comics modes": the "naturalistic mode" (relying on the recreation of physical appearance in a realistic art style), and the "cartoon mode" (growing from caricature, with its basic principles of simplification and exaggeration, and associations with verbal humor and slapstick comedy).[26] The cartoon mode was a fundamental part of *MAD*'s take on the Western, which could represent its subject with some verisimilitude (whether a particular Western character or film), but the representation was simplified and stretched through the artist's line. This lay open the Western to emphatic ridicule and visual satire far beyond the realms of what was achieved in the Western comedies of the photorealistic film world (for instance, *Ruggles of Red Gap* [1935], *Cat Ballou* [1965], and *Blazing Saddles* [1974]).

Taking "Hah! Noon!" as its example, the extract featured in fig. 6.5 illustrates this point, with the cartoon mode accentuating the subversive content of the comic. As noted, the strip takes the traits of the film's unhelpful community and imbues these perceivably un-American traits onto the cowardly Western hero, Marshall Kane. Kane's features shift to match the emotive logic of each scene: the sheriff is depicted as hunched over and grimacing as he refuses to help the pleading mustachioed local only to switch to extroverted and passionate as he encounters Ramona (his eye bulge in desire and he sports a lustful grin as he decides to stay in town). As Scott McCloud has identified, an important feature of comics' storytelling is in its "amplification through simplification": an artist's cartoon style of drawing, while simplifying abstractions from reality, can carry more important meanings than a naturalistic or realistic art style through its emphasis on specific details.[27] In "Hah! Noon!" this is achieved through an unstable and ever-changing physical reality, which dismantles the boundaries of the Western space to make its point. Indeed, to counteract the threat from Killer Diller Miller and his gang, Kane ultimately decides to bring in the National Guard, shooting the outlaws while their backs are turned. This departs from any relationship with the understood order of the classic Western's setting (including featuring anachronisms like a military tank that rolls in with the National Guard), while it also accentuates Kurtzman and Davis's breakdown of the Western hero: as Marshall Kane admits about his deceitful action of creeping up and shooting the villains while their backs are turned, "I know it's not in the romantic Western spirit."[28]

It is the departure from the "romantic Western spirit" that I want to stick with. In the pages of *MAD* this is articulated through overt, irreverent humor that takes aim at popular Western films and franchises from the era.[29] By using cartoon lines in the artwork, the artists could accentuate the iconoclastic intent of their work, stretching the fixed boundaries of the mythic West. The previous chapter illustrated how the fearless cowboy hero's confidence and zeal for uplifting American society and trampling threats to prosperity had a didactic quality that helped reinforce foreign and domestic Cold War policies for young readers. Beneath the eccentric and wacky humor of *MAD*'s Western spoofs, these comics counteracted this coding and provided a series of interpretations of overtly flawed Western heroes. In *MAD*'s world the cowboy could be unremarkable, smelly, and rough-hewn, as was the case in "Cowboy!," or neurotic and cowardly like Marshall Kane from "Hah! Noon!" *MAD* stands out as a stark example of how comics artists employed this critical Western space, precisely because of its brash illustrated caricatures of Western icons, settings, and stars alike, as well as for its crude and jocular humor. However, the critical space developed in EC's Westerns could be much more subtle and yet still provide potent political critique, as illustrated by the Western adventure stories featured in the publisher's line of war comic books.

EC's war comics like *Two-Fisted Tales* and *Frontline Combat* divorced retellings of war and conflict from the triumphalism of American victory culture. Instead of being imbued with lofty ideals and a zealous crusading spirit, each issue warned about the grave consequences of war, particularly as the tensions of the Cold War hung heavy over the nation. While generally focused on more contemporary conflicts like the Korean War and World War II, both *Two-Fisted Tales* and *Frontline Combat* often incorporated historical narratives into each issue, from the American Civil War to battles in ancient Rome to pirate adventure to Western action on the contested frontier.

The overtly antiwar coding of these comics can be added to Qiana Whitted's hypothesis about EC's printing of certain types of stories that she describes as "preachies." The preachies refer to a set of stand-out storylines that often ran in the pages of EC's popular genre comic books and tackled controversial social and political issues like race, violence, and environmentalism. Whitted suggests that these "social protest" or "message" stories served to "underscore the deep moral failings of the status quo through acts of violence and depravity that reflect the contradictions of the post–World War II era."[30] The contradictions to which Whitted refers are the unprecedented affluence and unparalleled anxiety that Americans faced in the postwar years. Indeed, despite America's military supremacy, Russia developed hydrogen bombs that threatened nuclear annihilation. Likewise, while Americans experienced remarkable progresses in industry and technology, such prosperity encouraged white, middle-class, American families to become more insular and complacent about the need for social change. EC's oeuvre served to shake up the status quo, reflecting a deep fragmentation at the heart of consensus America through its stories that emphatically portrayed the racial inequalities, violence, and unquestioned conformity in society. Whitted's analysis of the preachies is largely restricted to EC's line of horror and science fiction comic books but could arguably be located in the publisher's printing of Western stories, too, as the genre was regularly deployed as an argument against the destructive and futile acts of war and conflict.

One example of this in practice can be found in John Severin's story, "Justice!," from *Two-Fisted Tales* #36 (1954). The previous chapter observed how the Indian Wars narrative naturally asserted a sense of threat on American soil, accentuating Native Americans' armed and deadly resistance against white encroachment at a time when Communist infiltration in all walks of American life seemed palpable. "Justice!" departs from this basic formula and creates a much more mediated view of the conflict between cowboys and Indians by highlighting the common misunderstanding of the Native American's peaceable nature. As the opening page details, "the American Indian . . . was simple, straightforward, gentle with his loved ones . . . but harsh with his enemies! Trouble was, most white men didn't understand him! They were terrified by what really was only the red man's direct, uncompromising sense of justice!" This detail sets up the opening page, where we see how three sneering, gap-toothed cowboys have hung a Pawnee Indian for refusing to give up his horse to them (fig. 6.6). Watching from a distance, the chieftain Shon-Ton-Ga vows to avenge his tribesman. Hunting the three murderers down to a nearby fort, the Pawnees infiltrate the stronghold using an arriving steam train as cover, capture the three cowboys, and drag them off into the wilderness. As the Pawnee Indians ride into the distance with their captives, one of the fort's defenders observes: "Now how do you figure that one? They bust in here and kill half the people in the fort—then, just when everything's going their way, they pull out!" The other replies, "And they didn't lay a finger on anyone in the train! You sure can't figure them redskins!"

This knowing prompt to readers encourages a more objective view of racial conflict on the frontier, in this case showing how casual (white) observers were ignorant of the murder of a Pawnee man (by white men) that had precipitated the Indians' retaliatory aggression. In general, popular Westerns from this era accentuated Native American "savagery," often showing unmotivated attacks on hard-working Americans, but here the comic openly signals its attempt to rewrite this portrayal of racial conflict from the genre, offering a more balanced outlook.[31]

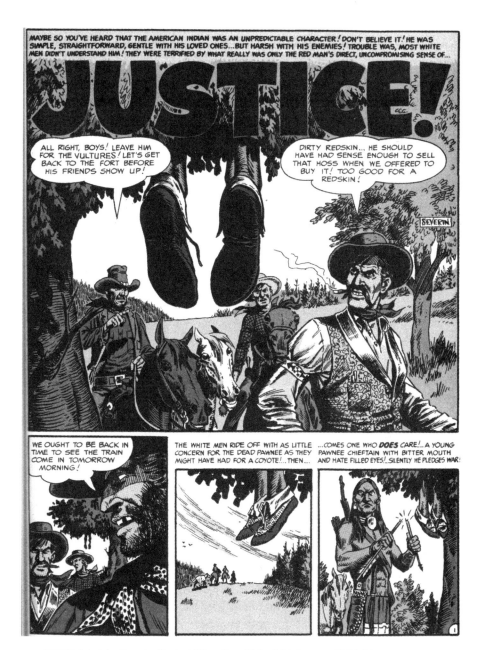

FIGURE 6.6. John Severin, "Justice!," *Two-Fisted Tales* #36, January 1954, EC.

The "Justice!" storyline is useful in highlighting how EC Comics debunked myths that shaped the American understanding of national history: the stories emphasized the needless war of attrition fought against Native Americans and minimized the sense of pride engendered by the American experience of nation building. This antiwar sentiment was emphatically underscored in "Custer's Last Stand," a retelling of the Battle of the Little Bighorn (1876) told from the unusual perspective of an enlisted soldier. Narrated as an internal monologue, the central character casts Custer as an egotistical maniac who was willing to risk the lives of his men to kill Indians for his own greater glory ("so's he can be president of the United States!"). But there is no glory in this conflict, as the soldier reflects: "God forgive me for the sinning I'll do today! We've got no God-given right to kill the poor redmen! We've broke their treaties. . . . We've chased them out of their hunting grounds and killed their women and children!" As the battle quickly turns in the favor of the united Lakota, Cheyenne, and Arapaho tribes and they surround Custer's regiment, the soldier-narrator witnesses Custer's demise: "Ha! Custer's hit! He's killed! I'm glad! I'm glad!"[32]

The unusual celebration of American defeat was matched by other stories that accentuated the adverse effects of US imperialism. In terms of the Western genre, this was the human cost of white conquest of Native American land. For instance, "Geronimo!" narrates the life story of the titular Apache leader. The comic condenses Geronimo's life into several pages, following his campaigns against Mexican soldiers and later the US Army. After being constantly pursued by soldiers on both sides of the border, and as the number of people within his group slowly dwindles through continued skirmishes, Geronimo is eventually worn down and surrenders. However, on the final page of the comic, Kurtzman and Severin reveal their powerful statement. The story jumps to the turn of the twentieth century and a time when the American West has been settled. We see a well-to-do family at the World's Fair in St. Louis excitedly seeking the chance to catch a glimpse of the legendary warrior who is on display (fig. 6.7). However, to their dismay they find an elderly Geronimo selling photographs: "I guess he's adopted the ways of the white man," the gentleman disappointedly concludes.[33]

Severin's artwork plants the seed to this end scene much earlier, contradicting the assumption that Geronimo *chose* "the ways of the white man," by including pages devoted to the US Cavalry's incessant hunt for him and his people and the slaughter that finally subdues them. In this respect, the final page presents a harsh commentary on a

FIGURE 6.7. Harvey Kurtzman and John Severin, "Geronimo!," *Frontline Combat* #10, January 1953, EC.

nation that has become arrogant and distant from the American ideals that the Western story of conquest typically espoused—a myth that downplayed social conflict and foregrounded the triumphal American experience of forging the proud nation. Here, in this final panel, we see a noble warrior humbled and downtrodden by an invading force, a stark representative of the genocidal nature of American imperialism.

Bradford Wright observes how EC's comics "stand as some of the most nationally self-critical documents in American entertainment at the time."[34] In regard to their Western stories, from "Justice!" to "Geronimo!," these comics offered starkly radical retellings of frontier politics from the era, matched only by the previously mentioned psychological Western films of the 1950s like *Broken Arrow* and *Devil's Doorway*. However, the critical rendition of the Western myth and the society that it represents in EC's comics looms large in comparison to

the demythologized Western films from the midcentury precisely because of the audience who consumed them. Indeed, these comic books
were not targeted at a wide-ranging demographic but were primarily
aimed at a juvenile readership.

The implications of this alternative Western content being targeted at a youthful audience are made more compelling when viewed
in parallel to the mainstream idioms that commonly imbued the Western genre of the time. Indeed, during the late 1940s and 1950s, the
Western was the preeminent cultural expression of the nation's claim
to power—a historic validation of the progress of the American way
and Manifest Destiny. In the context of comic books, this was most
readily expressed by the evocative covers that framed the historical
narratives of struggle into resonant symbolic images of triumphant
American heroes forcing back waves of threatening Indians. (See, for
example, fig. 5.2 from the previous chapter.) While Cold War rhetoric of the period instilled an omnipresent sense of threat from Soviet
subversion, these Western stories about great Americans who quelled
threats from "savage" Native Americans allegorically sought to foster
a sense of ideological cohesion around US superiority and the will to
triumph over despoilers of national interests.

In this respect, EC Comics made an important contribution in
challenging this problematic mythology, accentuating the barbarous
aspects of extermination within the stories set during the Indian Wars.
In an interview regarding the content of his war comics, writer Harvey Kurtzman claimed, "Everything that went before *Two-Fisted Tales*
[and *Frontline Combat*] had glamorized war. Nobody had done anything on the depressing aspects . . . and this, to me, . . . was a terrible
disservice to the children."[35] To this end, EC offered its young readers a vital alternative to what was on offer at the time, demolishing
the myths, empty triumphalism, and fallacies that equally informed
consensus-culture America and the Cold War Western.

Whitted suggests that the financial success of EC allowed for the
publisher's "message stories to accumulate over an extended period."[36]
Granted, with the promise of violent action, monsters, and gruesome
murder on their lurid cover images, it seems unlikely that readers came
to EC comic books just for their moralistic tales about the consequences
of racism (among other social issues). Nevertheless, as Gerald Early
points out, EC's major contribution to the culture was how their comics
"effectively combined pulp with liberal politics, and . . . offered a more
challenging moral vision than usually directed toward adolescents."[37]

Extrapolating from this hypothesis, I would argue that this observation could be extended to a wider sample of Western comic books, which had the ability to be much more subversive toward and critical of the genre and the society that they represented. Indeed, despite a general standardization of mass-produced literature during this era, comic books had the ability to fly under the critical radar and question and complicate the grand narratives from the era. This may be due to the small creative teams that were involved in the creation of comics (typically a writer, artist, and editor), which sometimes allowed for subversive content to be slipped into the pages. This sleight of hand was never particularly subtle in EC's take on the Western: from its caricatured rendering of the frontier and irreverent humor in strips from *MAD*, to its Western adventure stories that diverged from the common formula, EC used the Western genre in a much more critical manner. However, a wider sample of publishers also made subversive breaks from the formulas of Western stories about conquest and justice, undermining the seriousness and reverence for the mythic West through stories of rebellious kids, violent cowgirls, and heroic Native Americans.

Kids, Cowgirls, and Indians: Undermining Myths in Comic Book Westerns

EC's comics are exemplary in showcasing an active attempt at reframing and critiquing the status quo and the prevailing grand narratives from the era through their use of the Western. However, a consistent trend of more progressive versions of the genre can be found in a wider sample of comic books in this time frame. For example, a number of comic books ran a type of cowboys and Indians story that emphasized peace and understanding over confrontation with Native Americans. These comics often feature white heroes who, upon realizing the dangers of military confrontation with local American Indians, look to find peaceful resolutions to avoid conflict and create harmony for both races. For instance, in one story from *Hopalong Cassidy*, as white settlers and a group of Native Americans prepare to fight over disputed land, Cassidy intervenes to try and stop these two warring parties. Eventually realizing the grave human cost the conflict would bring, one of the Indigenous characters thanks Hopalong: "We all die if paleface sheriff not come along and save us!" Likewise, in one episode from *Two-Gun Western*, the Apache Kid attempts to stop the cavalry from attacking a neighboring Apache tribe: "Why should the Apaches give up land they've always owned? You've both got to compromise," he implores the general. After successfully stopping the cavalry's march, the Apache Kid rides into the sunset vowing: "I must ride alone . . . till I can bring peace to the border . . . to all men . . . pale-face or red!"[38]

During the ongoing ideological conflict with the Soviet Union, these comics speak of peaceful coexistence. More importantly, as Cold War imperatives had been slotted neatly into the contours of the troubling Western story of Native American extermination, reflecting the American way as inviolable, these instances also indicate how comics could offer a deviation from the Western myth of conquest. In contrast, some comics dropped the guiding presence of a cowboy in favor of a Native American hero, and a range of stories told of protagonists who attempt to heal tensions between Native Americans and white settlers.[39] For example, in "The Duel of the Devil Knives" from *Indians* #15 (1952), the story's protagonist Manzar foils the plot of a wicked traveling performer, the Flasher, who intends to turn a once-peaceful tribe against the white settlers from a nearby fort. When one of the soldiers from the fort appears bewildered that a Native American would try to mediate and resolve the conflict, Manzar reveals the egalitarian message that drives his sense of justice: "Indians, like white men, also fight evil where they see it."[40]

Comic books such as Fiction House's *Indians: Picture Stories of the First Americans* (1950–1953) sit alongside other titles from the era such as Magazine Enterprises' *Straight Arrow* (1950–1956) and Dell's *Indian Chief* (1951–1959), which were remarkable for their unique focus on Native American adventure stories. For example, unlike the common theme of white heroics on the contested frontier, comic books like *Indians* featured the recurring adventures of a series of Native American characters like Manzar, the Blackfoot orphan Longbow, and the Indian maiden Star Light. The title's Western adventure stories emphasized the peaceable and egalitarian nature of their protagonists and could be considered sympathetic of the Native American's plight in the nineteenth-century West. Indeed, quite like the white heroes of other Western comic book anthologies, the heroes from *Indians* also reflect positive qualities such as courage, bravery, and an unwavering sense of duty to promote order in the West. In terms of representation, these comic books as cultural products would be deemed wholly unacceptable by today's standards: their wide cast of Native American characters often speak broken English, and Indigenous people in the stories are often depicted as members of a primitive and directionless racial group who are easy to rile up and always require the guidance of a lone hero to resolve their problems. Nevertheless, at the time of publication, the stories of peaceful coexistence found in titles like *Indians* provided a remarkable counternarrative in popular culture, signaling the conscious deviations that publishers made from the Western formula.

In addition, David Huxley has identified further layers of dissent in the letters page of the comic, which provided a platform for Native American readers who regularly submitted comments and criticisms about Indigenous representation in Westerns.[41] Comic books like *Indians* opened up a space for readers to contest content and to demythologize narrative tropes, allowing a critical reworking of the Western's central myth of conquest; still, they could produce content starkly different than the Westerns of film (and other media) from the era, and in particular who could be cast as the hero.

As I have said elsewhere about the hero from postwar Western comics: "The squeaky-clean image of the comic book cowboy (a primary symbol of national identity), and his function to uphold law and order against despoilers of prosperity on the American frontier, can be read as a fundamental product of consensus America."[42] This framing of the Western individual in comics was certainly fashioned from the perspective of its adult creators, imparting values and morals that they believed young people should aspire to in the Cold War era. In this respect, the cowboy hero provided a deliberately virtuous model for young readers. Many of the cowboy adventures analyzed in the previous chapter exemplified this. However, the postwar milieu was more complex and nuanced, and some Western comic books overturned this notion through alternative gunslinging protagonists. We can see how titles such as *Indians* deviated from this mold through a set of Native American heroes.

However, titles like Jack Kirby and Joe Simon's *Boys' Ranch* (1950–1951), subverted the common framing of an Old West that was won by adult gunslingers through portraying the adventures of a group of orphaned boys (Angel, Wabash, and Dandy), who, under the guidance of frontiersman Clay Duncan, live a life of freedom and liberty on a Western ranch devoid of adult authority.[43] The dichotomy between young and old runs throughout the series, which typically sees the youthful heroes undermine, outwit, and outdraw the adult gunfighters, as evidenced through fig. 6.8.[44] The stories from the series often featured the juvenile adventurers tangling with exaggeratedly obnoxious adult antagonists, inviting young readers to empathize with the protagonists in their fight against the unfair and mean-spirited adult figures who look to undermine the boys' autonomy. Instances that encouraged participation in this resistant reading include the inaugural story from the series, "The Man Who Hated Boys," which tells of Jason Harper, a rancher who, having been betrayed by his own son, refers to "all children" as "hateful little savages" and "young devils" who are "at the bottom of all troubles." Another story, "Mother Delilah," sees the young Angel deceived by the cruel and vengeful saloon owner, Delilah, who steals his guns. As illustrated in the image from "Lead Will Fly at Sunset!," Angel is known for his quick wit and sharp-shooting abilities (fig. 6.8), but without his guns he is emasculated, and the tough-talking shooter reverts to being a harmless child. He is subsequently subjected to a humiliating experience of ridicule and beatings by adult gunslingers in the local town.[45]

In the postwar years the Western largely drew from historically resonant images of a West won by monomythic heroes. Kirby and Simon's comic instead points to a new imaginative Western space that encourages a specifically adolescent readership to identify with its rebellious and youthful protagonists and engage with the dismantling of the genre's traditions. As mentioned earlier, Engelhardt suggests that through American youth's consumption of convention-defying comic books, "children embraced with gusto the secret despair of adults who claimed to be living happily in the freest, richest, most generous country on Earth." The liberal rethinking of the cowboy and Indians story in the array of comics discussed above engaged with this paradigm by offering its young readers a demythologized Western space that challenged the aspirational idealism and sense of triumphalism that equally informed consensus-culture America and the Cold War Western. Nevertheless, comics did not need to be so political in producing convention-defying material. Indeed, the iconoclasm of Kirby and Simon's *Boys' Ranch* entered this exchange through its noticeable encouragement of resistant readings of any semblance of adult authority in the comic, which was certainly directed at a distinctly adolescent readership. However, *Boys' Ranch* provides a useful starting point in illustrating a type of irreverent and rebellious Western story that serviced young readers of comic books in the postwar years.

The theme of resistance to authority found its most outrageous expression in crime-inspired Western comic books, which completely dismantled the idealistic virtues of "law and order, peace and quiet, God and country, Mom and apple pie" that William W. Savage suggests

FIGURE 6.8. Jack Kirby and Joe Simon, "Lead Will Fly at Sunset!," *Boys' Ranch* #2, December 1950, Harvey Comics.

imbued Western comic books from the postwar decade.[46] Crime was a popular genre in comic books from the early Cold War years, influenced by the surrounding popularity of gangster and detective pulp fiction and films. Crime comics deconstructed the American Dream through stories of crooked characters who achieve material success through a life of crime and violence. Beneath the façade of a moral cautionary tale (the criminal always gets brought to justice at the close of the comic), the comics glamorized the lavish yet sadistic lifestyle that the protagonist leads. The Western's recognizably formulaic tales of law and order were open for reworking in this paradigm, focusing not on the lawman's capacity to protect the frontier community from the threat of banditry (as was most common in comic books from the era) but on the thrills Western outlaws enjoyed during a life of crime.

Fox Features Syndicate's output was emblematic of this context, producing a wide variety of short-lived Western-inspired crime titles (*Western Killers* [1948–1949], *Western Outlaws* [1949], *Western True Crime* [1948–1949], and *Women Outlaws* [1948–1949]). For instance, one story from *Western True Crime* tells of John Ringo, a young easterner who struggles to find work after graduating from a university and heads west in search of his fortune. After a chance meeting with Curly Bill, a cattle rustler who educates John in the tricks of the trade, it is not long before the young graduate embarks upon a life of robbery and murder. At one point John confesses to Bill, "Easiest money I ever heard of!" as the payout from their cattle-rustling operation makes them extremely wealthy. While the courts repeatedly fail to convict John and Bill for their misdeeds, the local law enforcement is not so ineffectual. The legendary Western lawman Wyatt Earp ambushes the pair at the close of the comic, leaving them in a bloody, bullet-riddled mess in its final panel, underscoring that a life of crime always ends in a gruesome death.[47]

Another story, "Cattle Kate: The Queen of the Rustlers," from *Women Outlaws* #1, July 1948 (fig. 6.9), tells of Kate Maxwell, who settles in Carbonville and quickly becomes the proprietor of a new saloon in the town. However, it is not long before Kate sets up a cattle rustling operation, stealing livestock from local ranches and selling the animals for profit. As she and her fellow conspirators become more successful in their misdeeds, they take bigger risks by stealing from larger, better-guarded cattle ranches. Soon Kate's trail of theft and murder attracts the attention of the local authorities. In the final page of the story, law officials lynch "Cattle Kate" and her gang of cutthroats for their crimes.[48] The story appears to be a fairly standard reworking

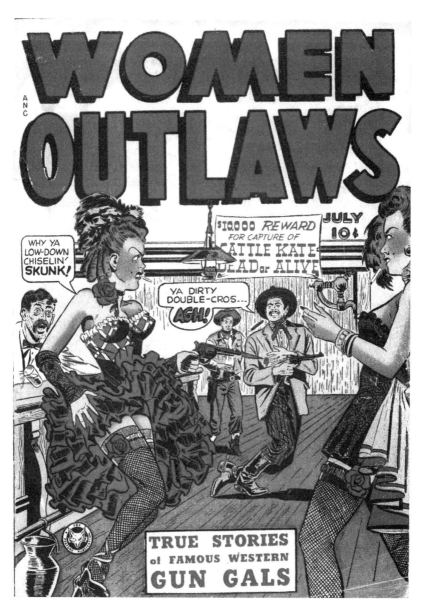

FIGURE 6.9. Cover of *Women Outlaws* #1, July 1948, Fox Features Syndicate.

of the crime-comics formula, depicting a thrilling tale of banditry on the Western range in which a violent criminal meets a bloody end at the hands of law enforcement. The comic matches the rebellious tenor of other comics such as *Boys' Ranch* (albeit with a heightened focus upon the thrills of lawless behavior), delivering an alternative to the familiar stories about advancing the frontier and extending the borders of civilization. However, like *Boys' Ranch*, *Women Outlaws* represented new spaces for who could play the protagonist in the Western, even children and women.

Regardless of what women's lives were actually like during the high Cold War years, most media from the time portrayed an idealized representation of an American woman whose interests lay in the domestic sphere. Elaine Tyler May maintains that women were seen as a potential security risk during the Cold War and were blamed for "weakening the nation's moral fiber at a time when the country had to be strong."[49] Women were thus expected to stay home and become a strong foundation for the household by supporting their husbands and children. As Betty Friedan lamented in *The Feminine Mystique*, "The suburban housewife—she was the dream image of the young American women and the envy, it was said, of women all over the world. . . . She was healthy, beautiful, educated, concerned only about her husband, her children, her home."[50] This idiom was reflected across a variety of popular media: on domestic television sitcoms; in romance comic books (written by men), which educated girls on the virtues of marriage and their domestic responsibilities; and in an abundance of advertising for household goods, which presented a fantasy world of the ideal white, middle-class, American family.

The Western genre was no exception to this zeitgeist, and women characters across Western fiction and films from this period were typically confined to marginalized roles such as the mother figure, rancher, schoolmarm, and saloon girl. In this regard, *Women Outlaws* provided a break in this stereotyping and represented the unrestrained Western woman, although her freedom served as a cautionary tale about the perils of women who remain uncontained outside of the domestic sphere, rather than as a symbol of liberation. The protagonists in these comics were often smart and quick-witted, morally corrupt, and always ready to manipulate and undermine the unsuspecting cowboys of the American West. However, this type of character was matched by a wider set of frontier-action heroines in comic books.

Fiction House's *Firehair* (1945–1952) follows the adventures of an amnesiac young woman who is raised by Native Americans and fights off the various threats (whether from rival tribes or villainous white settlers) to her adoptive tribe in each issue. Likewise, the sharpshooter Annie Oakley, who rose to fame as a member of Buffalo Bill Cody's Wild West Show in the 1880s, provided enough historical eminence to feature as a fictionalized title heroine in a variety of comic books. For example, Dell's *Annie Oakley & Tagg* (1955–1959) paid great attention to Oakley's shooting prowess, and each adventure often saw the plucky sharpshooter become an unofficial agent of law enforcement, foiling the misdeeds of a host of desperadoes through quick thinking and impressive gunplay. Atlas Comics' *Annie Oakley* #1–4 (1948) dropped the narrative of a successful sharpshooter in a man's world, and Oakley is instead characterized as a successful cowgirl on a man's ranch. A continued tension marks this short-lived comic series between showcasing Oakley's impeccable roping, riding, and shooting skills—which are unmatched by the other men on the ranch—with her need to settle down with a man. Her free spirit is corralled in *Annie Oakley* #4 as the heroine finally decides to marry her lover, the cowboy Tex.[51]

While providing a marked break from the gentler roles of women in Western fiction and films, these comics sometimes present troubled representations of the frontier-action heroine by virtue of being written and drawn by male creators: from a successful cowgirl, in the case of Atlas Comics *Annie Oakley*, who will give up all her aspirations in service of her male love interest, to the hypersexualized imagining of a female gunslinger in *Women Outlaws* #1 (fig. 6.9).

However, I want to further explore the artwork from *Women Outlaws* #1, as it stands out for the critical attention it would later garner. Indeed, the image of the aggressive and scantily clad character Cattle Kate was sarcastically read as "giving children an image of American womanhood" by the psychiatrist Fredric Wertham in his 1954 book *Seduction of the Innocent*.[52] Wertham's focus on specific images, alongside close readings of selected violent and licentious material found in comic books from the era (particularly from the pages of crime and horror comics), helped inform his conclusion that the "chronic stimulation, temptation and seduction by comic books . . . are contributing factors to many children's maladjustment."[53] Taking the above crime-inspired Western stories as one example, Wertham argued that such content could incite disobedience, as young readers took delight in these rebellious frontier tales of crime and resistance to authority. His rhetorical arguments against comic books were articulate and gave critics a credible rationale to claim the pernicious effects of the medium on American youth. Furthermore, Wertham's theories about the perils of reading comic books shaped many of the beliefs that underpinned the "comics scare" of the mid-1950s, which fundamentally changed the way that the comic book industry operated and what popular genres were published.

The 1950s "Comics Scare" and Its Aftermath

Mass entertainment has sometimes acted as an easy scapegoat when attempting to understand the dissenting behavior of American youth. For example, in the late nineteenth century attention turned toward the violence of Western-themed dime novels as a possible culprit in the ostensible immorality and corruption of young boys and girls.[54] Nevertheless, Daniel Worden describes how the "dime novel panic" soon dissipated, and "in the face of more graphic and seductively illustrated pulp magazines and comic books" that emerged in the early twentieth century, "critics viewed dime novels as evidence of an innocent past rather than a chronicle of insipid and dangerous mass culture."[55]

This attitude was evident in a later editorial published in the *Chicago Daily News* in May 1940, titled "A National Disgrace." In it, the literary critic Sterling North describes comic books as "badly drawn, badly written and badly printed—a strain on young eyes and young nervous systems," and he suggests that the medium's "hypodermic injection of sex and murder make the child impatient with better, though quieter stories." Next to the earlier Western dime novels, "in which an occasional redskin bit the dust," North argues that these texts could be considered "classic literature compared to the sadistic drivel pouring out" of the comic books.[56] Cultural critics, teachers, and librarians alike had remained ambivalent toward, if not deeply critical of, the comics medium, dating back to the rise of newspaper strips at the turn of the century. For these bastions of high culture, comics were crude, unsophisticated, and subliterate and could diminish a child's reading ability.[57] However, the concern over the medium reached new heights in the postwar decade.

James Gilbert observes how in the postwar years "a large proportion of the public thought there was a delinquency crime wave, and they clamored to understand how and why this was happening."[58] The paranoiac atmosphere of the Cold War left the American public fearful of the effects from corrupting propaganda and subversion. As Gilbert describes, a popular theory took hold in the public imagination in the early 1950s: mass culture aimed at youth markets had "misshaped a generation of American boys and girls."[59] Much of the comic books' material that defied traditional values and notions of middle-class morality had made the medium into an easy target for blame. Various articles appeared in popular magazines (including the *Saturday Review of Literature*, the *New York Times*, *Parents Magazine*, and the *Journal of Educational Sociology*, among others) that gave a national platform to the debate about the harmful content and effects of comic books.[60] Although some of these articles invoked a similar vitriolic approach to North's earlier diatribe, the most publicized and vigorous assault came from the psychiatrist Fredric Wertham, whose writing on the subject made explicit connections between comic books and juvenile delinquency.

Alongside Wertham's critical reading of crime-inspired Western comics like *Women Outlaws*, the psychiatrist examined a variety of popular comic book genres, homing in on the medium's deplorable content and influence. For example, he suggested that the superhero was essentially a representation of fascism; romance comics were morally bereft; and crime and horror comic books could lead to delinquency. The psychiatrist connected the influence of comic book content and certain case histories of juvenile crimes.[61] Ultimately, Wertham's observations offered adults a palpable causality for the ostensible change in youth behavior.

The commercial success of *Seduction of the Innocent* and the increasing visibility of its subject matter made Wertham a primary witness for the US Senate Subcommittee on Juvenile Delinquency. Its hearings investigating the effects of comic books and their role in the development of youth crime became a nationally televised event that took place between April and June 1954. During the hearings the subcommittee was presented with testimony from experts in the field, and material from comic books was exhibited to help assess the appropriateness and decency of the medium for children. EC's line of comic books bore the brunt of the attack in these proceedings, primarily for their overtly violent content and politically subversive themes, but comic books more broadly were described as "perverted magazines" in testimony to the subcommittee and presented as "instruction[al] in crime, narcotic uses, and sex perversions, and moral degradation."[62] The primary conclusion from these hearings was that comic books had the power to influence and corrupt young minds.

The highly publicized backlash against the largely unchecked comic book medium forced the industry to establish a self-regulatory body in 1954, the Comics Code Authority (CCA), to protect itself from further condemnation. The strict code stipulated numerous rules to sanitize comic book content. For instance, comic books could no longer present particularly violent imagery and subject matter (which had defined the horror comics), and stories could not show sympathy to criminals. While some rules were progressive—the Code strictly forbade content that attacked religious or racial groups and prohibited overtly sexual content (women in particular could no longer be rendered in a salacious or sexually suggestive manner)—these regulations helped terminate some of the more distasteful comic book genres (namely crime and horror comics).[63] Indeed, if a comic did not meet the CCA's standards, it would not receive an approval logo on its cover. This effectively quashed its chances of publication, since most major distributors, printers, and wholesalers backed the Comics Code, giving the authority considerable industry-wide enforcement power.

Wright details the adverse effects that the CCA had on the comic book industry: "Between 1954 and 1956, eighteen publishers exited the field, and none entered. The number of comic book titles published annually fell from about 650 in 1954 to just over 300 in 1956. . . . Never again would the comic book industry enjoy the kind of mass circulation and readership that it had commanded before the code."[64] Publishers like EC, which had built its success in the early 1950s on violent horror comic books and politically subversive war and Western stories, struggled to adapt to the newly regulated landscape of comics publishing. After some attempts to conform, the publisher completely dropped its line of genre comic books and instead focused its energies on a newly rebranded *MAD* magazine. Other publishers best adapted to the new conditions of the industry through rejuvenating the superhero genre, which tapped into currents of mainstream culture while appeasing CCA regulations.[65]

In terms of the comic book Western, the majority of frontier action and adventure titles were hardly emasculated by the CCA's guidelines. Indeed, the Cold War Western comic book predominantly underscored the values and mores of consensus culture and naturally conformed to CCA regulations through formulaic tales of wholesome cowboy heroes who uphold law and order on the Western range. This was expressed in Atlas Comics' continued investment in publishing Western genre titles. For instance, the *Rawhide Kid* emerged in 1955, riding to

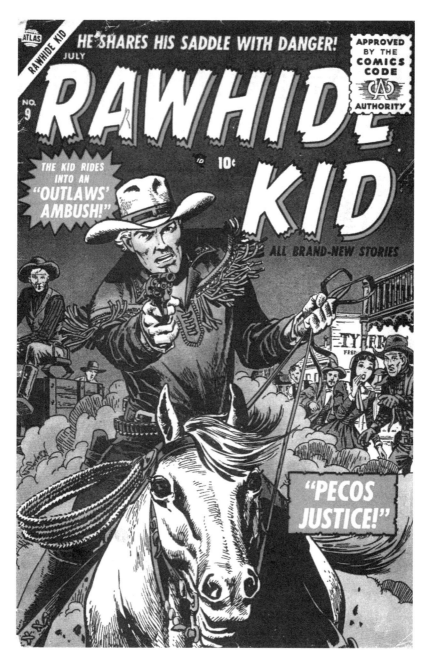

FIGURE 6.10. John Severin (cover art). *Rawhide Kid* #9, July 1956, Atlas Comics.

the rescue of hapless frontier communities as an unofficial agent of law enforcement, fighting for social justice and the American way just as the comic book cowboy always had, but with the addition of the CCA's seal of approval in the top right-hand corner (fig. 6.10).

Although largely unscathed in the immediate aftermath of the Comics Code, many of the most popular and longest-running Western comics titles had folded by the end of the 1950s or the early 1960s: Dell's *Red Ryder* (1941–1957), *Gene Autry Comics* (1941–1959), *Roy Rogers Comics* (1948–1961), and *The Lone Ranger* (1948–1962); Fawcett's *Hopalong Cassidy* (1943–1959); and DC's anthology titles like *Western Comics* (1948–1961). This had less to do with shifts in the comic book publishing industry, however, and perhaps reflected how the Western genre was in a state of flux. Indeed, the 1960s witnessed the pronounced development of youth culture, which found a powerful social force centered on the medium of rock music. A significant generation's rebellious voice was forged through this genre, and its potency was amplified as the young men who were part of this new autonomous youth demographic were steadily being drafted to serve in the United States' fight against Communist guerillas in Vietnam. The thematic concerns of the classic Western failed to resonate with younger audiences by the 1960s. As Leonard Quart and Albert Auster observe, "No longer could . . . the old patriotic and macho certainties and clichés about decent, freedom-loving Americans and brutal [Indians] capture and dominate the moral center of the American imagination as it once had."[66]

Although these darker ambiguities had begun to be addressed in subversive Western comics from the 1950s—from the demythologized take on the Western found in Tufts's newspaper strip *Lance* to the raucous cartoon West of *MAD* magazine—by the 1960s there was a growing need to emphatically reshape the genre to reflect the profound changes in American society. It is precisely these tensions that will be the focus of the following chapter, which discusses Western comics in the context of the fractious 1960s and 1970s.

CHAPTER 7

Blood on the Borders

*Mixing the Wild West with Political Unrest in
Comics from the Troubled 1960s and 1970s*

"COLD-BLOODED KILLER, VICIOUS, UNMERCIFUL HELLION without feeling, without conscience . . . A man consumed by hate, a man
who boded evil . . . that was . . . Jonah Hex."[1] The disfigured antihero
burst onto the pages of DC Comics *All-Star Western* in 1972 and offered
readers a new vision of the West that was in sync with the troubled
times. By the late 1960s the United States had been rocked by violent
upheaval on all fronts. The decade was punctuated by a series of high-
profile political assassinations, from John F. Kennedy to Martin Luther
King Jr., which brought to the fore the issue of American violence both
at home and abroad. Indeed, the losing war fought against North Vietnam shattered the illusion of American omnipotence and horrified the
nation as violent images from the conflict unfolded daily on television
screens. Moreover, the development of youth movements and the
counterculture in the 1960s led to a tumultuous rebellion that spilled
onto American streets and campuses. A new militancy among Black
Americans and other disenfranchised groups produced violent confrontations in their fight for change within the current dispensation.
This widespread trauma led to a deep cultural malaise within society
as prevailing assurances about American exceptionalism eroded.[2] The
classic Western and its expansionist mythologies about Manifest Destiny were out of touch with current times. However, the dark vision of
the West found in Jonah Hex comics resonated with readers.

The opening page from Hex's inaugural storyline encapsulates this
new spirit, as we see the bounty hunter dragging two corpses across the
comics page (fig. 7.1). Meanwhile, a young child shrugs off his mother's attempts to shield him from the scene: "Ah, shucks, Ma—I wanna see who
Jonah killed!" Children were conventionally representative of innocence
and progress in the classic Western, but here they have become a tool in

FIGURE 7.1. John Albano and Tony De Zuñiga, "Welcome to Paradise," *All-Star Western* #10, March 1972, DC Comics.

the genre's revision: they became as much a symbol of the bloodthirsty and mean-spirited frontier space that the Western now occupied as a comment on how contemporaneous society had become desensitized to the spectacle of violence, which adorned newspapers and evening news broadcasts throughout long stretches of the sixties and seventies.

Jonah Hex comics offer just one example of many revisionist Westerns that emerged in this era. In the age of the Vietnam War, political protests, and widespread civic unrest, the myths and ideals of the Western had become deeply problematized, and a backlash ensued in various popular texts such as Thomas Berger's novel *Little Big Man* (1964), the violent Spaghetti Western films of Sergio Leone (and others), and in Hollywood movies like Sam Peckinpah's *The Wild Bunch* (1969) and Ralph Nelson's *Soldier Blue* (1970). Likewise, Godfrey Hodgson suggests that the "new awareness of the predatory side of the frontier tradition" was evident in the extraordinary sales of Dee Brown's book *Bury My Heart at Wounded Knee* (1970), which provided a nuanced rethinking of the history of the American West and reminded readers how the settling of the region was achieved through fraud and genocide.[3]

Western comics gave dramatic life to the dissident politics of the era. Stories about white-Indian conflict became thinly veiled critiques of US involvement in Vietnam through a comparable look at genocidal warfare by whites against Native Americans (for instance, in the underground comix of Jaxon). More broadly, specific codes and conventions of the genre were broken down and subverted, either through irreverent humor like that found in the nationally syndicated anti-Western newspaper strip *Tumbleweeds* (1965–2007), or tonally darker and grittier Western comic books like DC's *Weird Western Tales* (1972–1980), which did away with virtuous frontier communities and wholesome cowboy heroes in favor of cold-hearted gun-slinging protagonists who must fend for themselves within a corrupt and calloused American West.

The jaundiced reimagining of the Old West in such texts was an emphatic reaction against the conservative mythology of the Western and reflected how the triumphant tenets and chauvinistic optimism that characterized the mythic West had become sour illusions in the eyes of many. Nevertheless, the Western's fixture at the forefront of the American cultural landscape illustrates how the genre, even in revisionist form, remained a powerful narrative mode with which to make sense of unfolding events in an era that Leo Braudy would later describe as "a nightmare, an allegory of good and evil, a metaphysical comic book."[4]

New Frontiers in Western Comics

On July 15, 1960, John F. Kennedy made his acceptance speech in Los Angeles for the Democratic Party's nomination as candidate for president of the United States. In his speech, entitled "The New Frontier," Kennedy invoked the resonant symbols of the Western as metaphors to describe the spirit of his campaign: "We stand today on the edge of a New Frontier—the frontier of the 1960s, a frontier of unknown opportunities and perils, a frontier of unfulfilled hopes and threats. . . . For the harsh facts of the matter are that we stand on this frontier at a turning point of history."[5] The New Frontier slogan combined the promise of rugged adventure with the reassurance of American tradition and became a shorthand label for a variety of Kennedy's domestic and foreign programs that would define the decade. For example, invoking the resonant images of the contested frontier helped Americans conceptualize the continuation of Cold War foreign policy from the 1950s, as the Kennedy administration committed the United States to further intervention in developing nations (most notably in the prolonged military confrontation with Vietnam [1964–1975]). Likewise, Kennedy's emphasis on a New Frontier advanced a promise of youthful vigor and an innovative approach to politics (he would soon become the first president born and raised in the twentieth century) and presaged the significant role young people would play within the political culture of the new decade.

The landscape of youth culture was dramatically changing by the 1960s, and the decade saw a major reevaluation of American youth as an economic, social, and political force. Advertisers became increasingly aware of adolescents as independent consumers and bypassed parents to focus their marketing directly at young people. Record companies reorientated their output to rock-and-roll music and simultaneously brought to the fore a series of teen idols for mass consumption. For example, the irreverence and nonconformity of bands such as the Beatles struck a pleasing chord with millions of young people—a demographic described as "growing up absurd" by the intellectual Paul Goodman. Goodman's book *Growing Up Absurd* (1960) was an attack on contemporary American society, which he observed as being out of touch and offering no good reason for the younger generation to be a part of it. He argued that increasing numbers of American youths were becoming alienated by the impossible demands imposed on them by society. This divide would only deepen, and by the middle of the 1960s millions of young Americans were taking an increasingly active role in trying to change the current dispensation, either through political activism or social protest.[6]

Despite being aimed at a distinctly adolescent readership, the comic book industry had not kept pace with changes in youth culture by the dawn of the 1960s. Bradford Wright describes how comic books by and large continued "presenting a world that conformed to a restrictive code and a bland consensus vision."[7] The industry was in a grave state of uncertainty fed by several contributing factors: the arrival of the CCA in the previous decade, which had made comic book content stale and homogenized; problems with distribution, which forced some already struggling publishers out of the industry entirely; and the rise of television as the nation's primary source of entertainment, which ate into the public's leisure time formerly reserved for comic book reading (among other things). While sales and readership figures would never bounce back to levels witnessed in the early 1950s, one remedy for this recession in the industry was through the reinvention of the superhero genre. Marvel Comics (previously Atlas) best reflected this change when it dropped a range of its genre titles in favor of a new lineup of superheroes (such as *The Fantastic Four* [from 1961], *Spider-Man* [from 1962], and *The Incredible Hulk* [from 1962], among others). Under the direction of editor Stan Lee, Marvel's superhero stories were imbued with real-life problems, such as Spider-Man's teen angst and the Hulk's hero/monster dilemma. Young readers could identify with this new set of complicated heroes, who were misunderstood by the public and persecuted by the authorities. Likewise, artist Jack Kirby's cosmic themes and imagery added a psychedelic and hip visual aesthetic that captivated teenage readers and college students alike.[8]

Marvel's set of reluctant superheroes successfully tapped into adolescents' sense of alienation and disorientation, producing a compelling narrative formula that was relevant to a generation that was "growing up absurd" (to borrow Goodman's phrase). Nevertheless, this popular formula found traction earlier on in Marvel's Western comics. For example, since 1955 *Rawhide Kid* had been providing formulaic stories of law and order on the Western range, led by an adult rancher with a zeal for justice. However, in issue #17 (August 1960) the series was revamped under the direction of writer Stan Lee and artist Jack Kirby, and the lead character was recast as the eighteen-year-old Johnny Bart. Johnny was an orphan adopted and raised by his uncle Ben Bart, a former Texas Ranger. Living in the rough-and-tumble Texas town Rawhide, the elder Bart teaches Johnny skills in quick-drawing and marksmanship that are necessary to survive in this wild and rugged border town. After Ben is gunned down by bandits, Johnny avenges his uncle's murder and thus becomes an outlaw himself, taking up the moniker the Rawhide Kid.[9]

From this point onward storylines revolve around how this misunderstood teen cowboy is forced to live a life on the run after being marked as an outlaw, simultaneously grappling with the incessant pursuit by law enforcement, all the while trying to atone for his previous misdeeds by helping hapless frontier communities. The Rawhide Kid's fearsome reputation as a gunfighter and a criminal is his greatest vulnerability, ensuring that the character will always be a social outcast that society fears, despite his best efforts to help and uplift them. The frenzied scene from the opening page of the inaugural storyline, "Beware! The Rawhide Kid," perhaps best encapsulates this theme (fig. 7.2). We see a frowning and nonthreatening-looking Rawhide Kid in the foreground and a hysterical crowd of townsfolk running away in fear upon catching sight of this teenage social pariah. The Rawhide Kid fits into a similar framework of Marvel superheroes from the decade and is indicative of the publisher's efforts to incorporate a teenage subtext into its output to curry favor with its adolescent readership.

Elsewhere, the Western genre was experiencing an identity crisis. This is perhaps most expressive in Sam Peckinpah's 1962 film *Ride the High Country*, which grappled with themes of the passing of the Old West and the gunslinger's struggle to adapt to changing times. In the 1940s and 1950s the Cold War had given the Western a tremendous sense of purpose, with triumphal retellings of taming the West reinforcing American exceptionalism in a time of conflict and consensus. However, this driving force had slowed by the new decade, and a sense of ambiguity about the genre's direction began to creep in, in films such as *The Misfits* (1961), *Lonely Are the Brave* (1962), and *Hud* (1963). Edward Gallafent describes how Western films from the early 1960s intensified the elegiac tone of the genre through stories about westerners on the brink of decrepitude; they presented a sense of loss or contraction within the West itself, which became "a natural world that is strangely diminished and unable to sustain itself."[10]

In contrast, Western comics avoided engaging with similar themes about receding frontiers. Given the medium's specific market reach, publishers instead put their efforts into rejuvenating the genre for a younger generation. For example, *Rawhide Kid* was reshaped into an

FIGURE 7.2. Stan Lee, Jack Kirby, and Dick Ayers, "Beware! The Rawhide Kid," *Rawhide Kid* #17, August 1960, Marvel Comics.

Old West adolescent fantasy by the 1960s, led by an ostracized teen gunfighter that young readers, who were struggling with their own sense of place within contemporary society, could readily identify with. The adventure stories about crime fighting on the frontier were short and pacey, and any conflict always required the Rawhide Kid's impressive shooting skills to resolve. The action was enhanced by the dynamic artistry of some standout talent from the era (such as Dick Ayers, Jack Davis, and Jack Kirby). Moreover, Marvel continued to playfully reinterpret the genre across its range of long-running Western series (including *Two-Gun Kid* and *Kid Colt, Outlaw*).

Amid the generic ensemble of Western villains that Marvel's "Kid" gunfighters fought (from outlaws to corrupt law enforcement), writers began to confront their heroes with a series of costumed supervillains. The antagonists sometimes came disguised in animal-inspired attire that matched the acrobatic edge they brought to their criminal operations (such as the circus performer turned bank robber the Rattler or the criminal gang leader the Panther). Sometimes their costumes offered a super-powered upper hand in combat, such as the flying capabilities of Red Raven or Iron Mask—a villain encased in bulletproof metal who takes on Kid Colt (fig. 7.3).[11] This zany take on the genre may have been a conscious effort to align the title with Marvel's wider superhero output. Nevertheless, where some Western films reflected the struggle to acclimatize to the changing tastes of American audiences at the dawn of the 1960s, Western comics appeared to be more receptive and negotiated the shifts in youth culture and market demand in a number of different ways.

In newspaper comic strips, T. K. Ryan's *Tumbleweeds* (from 1965) stands out for how it deconstructed the Western through irreverent humor. The series took place in Grimy Gulch, a ramshackle town populated with a wide variety of buffoonish character types from the Western (from the inept sheriff, the cowboy that cannot shoot straight, the shady outlaw, the fast-shuffling gambler, and so on). *Tumbleweeds* both sustained genre expectations and subverted them, with Ryan's simplistic lines abstracting the familiar codes and conventions of the Western while simultaneously shattering the entire framework of clichés and myths for comedic purposes. In fig. 7.4 we see the dim-witted lawman assist the outlaw Snake-Eyes McFoul in a bank heist: "They was right. . . . He's one smoo-ooth talkin' dude!" he reflects as he helpfully carries one of the money bags.[12]

The previous chapter's exploration of subversive Western comics

FIGURE 7.3. Stan Lee and Jack Keller, "The Return of Iron Mask," *Kid Colt, Outlaw* #114, January 1964, Marvel Comics.

FIGURE 7.4. T. K. Ryan, *Tumbleweeds*. From *Presenting the Best of "Tumbleweeds"* (Boca Raton, FL: Cool Hand Communications, 1993), 59.

from the 1950s indicates how the genre was supple enough to encourage satire and parody of its familiar plots, themes, and characters. However, Ryan described the comedic spirit of *Tumbleweeds* as combining "the Old West with a hip approach," which suggests that his delightfully flippant take on the Western was a means by which to entice a specifically younger (hipper) reading demographic to the genre.[13] This was indicative of a wider trend of Western comedies from the 1960s.[14] Indeed, Michael Coyne's close reading of the Western spoof film *Cat Ballou* (1965) connects the appeal of the film's band of happy-go-lucky outlaws with the emerging countercultural sensibilities of the decade.[15]

If themes of comedy, nonconformity, and resistance to authority were gaining a specific currency in popular Westerns of the 1960s, they found clear expression in DC Comics' *Bat Lash* (from 1968), which crossed Western adventure with running humor, following an antiheroic and dandified gunfighter who has an atypical concern for the finer things in life, such as style, quality food, and flowers (fig. 7.5). Bat Lash's interests in gambling, scams, and beautiful women always placed him on the wrong side of the law, evident in one storyline in his failed attempt to romance a bathing woman who turns out to be the local sheriff's wife.[16] However, these self-inflicted scrapes with the authorities often took a back seat to broader storylines about justice and revenge.[17]

The development of the CCA in the previous decade had severely limited the political bite of the comic book medium, and to earn the seal of approval publishers cautiously toed a fine line in appealing to the nonconformist sentiments of youth culture. However, the rebellious spirit that permeated comics such as *Bat Lash* and its focus on a loveable rogue and his scrapes with the law allowed publishers to break with the CCA's enforced restrictions and strike an antiestablishment pose without appearing political. Publishers continued to seek

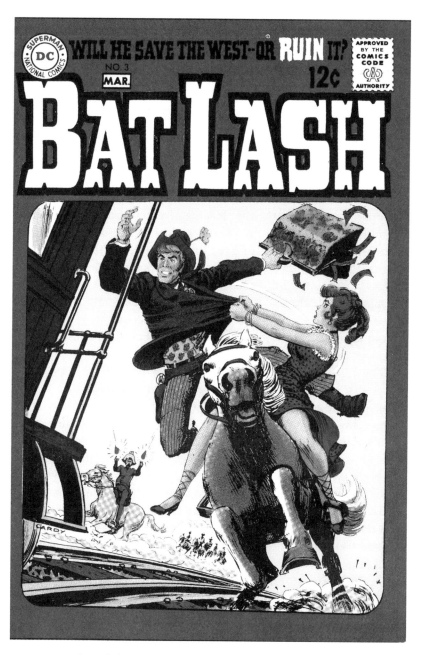

FIGURE 7.5. Nick Cardy (cover art), *Bat Lash* #3, March 1969, DC Comics.

out ways to address readers' concerns by subtly infusing their comics with the surrounding social climate, although their efforts found varying success.

For instance, the rise of the civil rights and Black Power movements caused entertainment industries to take tentative steps toward exploring racial issues through Western stories and settings.[18] One standout title was Dell's *Lobo* (1965–1966), which told of a Black gunslinger who fights for justice after being accused of crimes he did not commit. Granted, the title only ran for two issues, due to poor sales (selling only 15,000 issues out of a standard 200,000 copy print run).[19] However, *Lobo* broke new ground for its positive portrayal of a Black westerner, not least as the first leading Black character amid a sea of Western comics led by white cowboy heroes, but also as the first African American character to have his own series with his name on the cover (fig. 7.6).[20] *Lobo* emphatically pushes back against the Black cowboy's omission from the history of the Western. As Lobo rides into the sunset at the close of the first issue, a caption reminds the reader of the many great people who opened the American West and whose legends have since been forgotten: "Men like Lobo don't deserve to be forgotten. . . . For they were there!"[21]

The historical distance of the Western naturally equipped the genre with an ability to address the concerns and issues of modern society. While the above examples trace the divergent paths down which comics could take the Western—from the camp absurdity of the superhero-infused Marvel Western to DC's rebellious vogues—they make clear how the genre was being regeared for a specifically adolescent readership in the New Frontier of the 1960s. This placed the comic book Western in a prime position to react and adapt to the currents of change. Indeed, at the center of the upheaval from the 1960s—the push for civil rights, Black Power, and feminism; the rise of the New Left and the counterculture; and the growing antiwar movement protesting the escalating Vietnam War—were angry and idealistic young people determined to transform society.

The Turbulent 1960s

According to Morris Dickstein, the postwar period can be simplified into a set of characteristics: "A beaming president presiding over a stagnant government, small-town morality, racial segregation, political and sexual repression, Cold War mobilization, nuclear standoff,

FIGURE 7.6. Tony Tallarico (cover art), *Lobo* #1, December 1965, Dell Publishing Co.

. . . the domestic confinement of women, and the reign of the nuclear family."[22] However, the tumultuous events of the 1960s suggest that this age of uniformity and Cold War consensus was in fact dead. For example, despite a continuation of 1950s foreign policy as the United States ramped up its efforts to combat Soviet influence abroad—both covertly, through the failed CIA operation to overthrow Cuban leader Fidel Castro at the Bay of Pigs in 1961, and overtly, with the US entry into the Vietnam War—the highly publicized antiwar marches that flooded through American streets and college campuses revealed a growing ideological divide between the Cold War politics of the previous decade and the youth culture of the 1960s.

The Vietnam War started as a proxy war in which the Kennedy administration sent American military advisors to assist South Vietnam's fight against the Communist North Vietnamese. This troubled foreign intervention dramatically escalated under Kennedy's successor, Lyndon B. Johnson (1963–1969). By the end of 1967 the United States had committed over half a million troops to combat in Vietnam, without decisive results. Their woeful attrition strategy, in which American success in combat was measured by a body count, meant that civilians killed in the crossfire were added to the total. The consequences of this type of operation were encapsulated in horrific atrocities such as the My Lai Massacre, in which the US military attacked a small village and murdered hundreds of unarmed civilians. The gruesome photographs of screaming Vietnamese children and piles of dead bodies, alongside distressing reportage that documented the horrors of the conflict, swayed public opinion irrevocably against the war.[23]

The antiwar movement was closely aligned with youth movements and the New Left and underscored greater chasms between government and citizen. The hippie culture of sexual liberation, drugs, and psychedelic rock music certainly challenged conventional sensibilities, and the various ideological persuasions (such as women's liberation and Black Power) disrupted the status quo. On college campuses and city streets students protested domestic problems (such as misogyny and racism) and foreign issues (such as the escalating war in Southeast Asia), which drew national attention. Such events indicated a growing generation gap, but the distrust of authority and sense of disillusionment with politics spread across other divides.

For example, the fight for civil rights had become an ever more visible and pressing issue by the early 1960s. The movement was a reaction to both the disparities of wealth between white and Black

Americans and the conditions of racial segregation characterized by Jim Crow laws. The civil rights movement utilized a variety of nonviolent methods of disruption such as sit-ins and marches. Nevertheless, nonviolence soon gave way to violent confrontation as appalling acts of brutality committed by the Ku Klux Klan marred the 1960s, while militant Black groups like the Black Panthers advocated violent action to meet its goals of Black liberation.[24]

The excessive violence that local and federal authorities used to suppress political protest and unrest at home, alongside the continued influx of harrowing news reportage pertaining to the Vietnam War, fueled what Paul Levine and Harry Papasotiriou describe as "a widespread sense of crisis in American society."[25] This atmosphere only deepened with the political assassinations of civil rights activist Martin Luther King Jr. in April 1968 and the Democratic presidential candidate Robert F. Kennedy in June of the same year. Levine and Papasotiriou suggest that many Americans, faced by these further revelations, "saw their world crumbling around them."[26] The fractious discord from these unfolding events could hardly be ignored by popular culture. Amid the increasingly visible social disorder of the 1960s, creators began to immerse their comic books in the pressing social injustices and political concerns of the time—and the historically distant setting of the comic book Western was no exception.

Coupled with earlier efforts such as Dell's *Lobo*, mainstream publishers made gestures toward equal racial representation with a new set of heroes of color in the early 1970s. Alongside the Black hero Luke Cage in 1972 and the Asian kung fu master Shang-Chi in 1974, Marvel produced the nine-issue series *Red Wolf* from 1972 to 1973 (fig. 7.7). The series tells the story of Johnny Wakely, a Cheyenne Indian who fights for justice for all people on the frontier, whether they are white settlers or Native Americans. The egalitarian quality of the story spread to other emerging series, such as the *The Gunhawks* (1972–1973), which follows the adventures of Reno Jones, a former African American slave, and Kid Cassidy, a son of a plantation owner, whose interracial friendship had flourished long before the American Civil War. In the war's aftermath, the two reunite and embark upon an adventure out west, putting their skills as gunfighters to good use in a search for Jones's fiancée Rachel, who was kidnapped by soldiers during the war.

Likewise, despite the *Rawhide Kid* having been devoid of Black characters previously, Marvel's long-running Western series could not avoid the surrounding political atmosphere. In the storyline "Day of

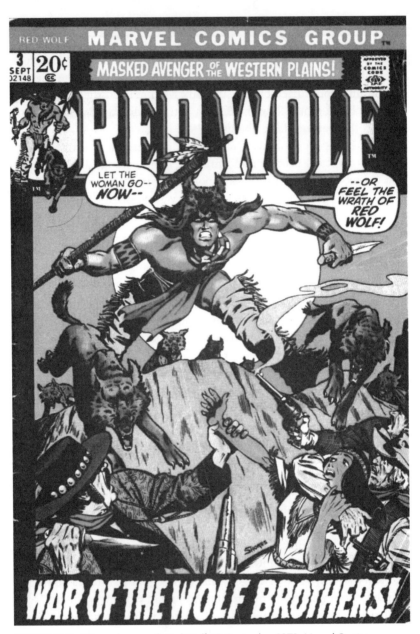

FIGURE 7.7. Syd Shores (cover art), *Red Wolf* #3, September 1972, Marvel Comics.

the Outcast" from 1971, the Rawhide Kid meets Rafe Larsen, a Black gunslinger who distrusts white people. At their first meeting, the Kid questions why Larsen is so aggressive toward him, to which the westerner responds, "Because yore white—and I'm black!" Larsen then details the struggle he has faced in life on the Western range since the end of the Civil War: "The war ended slavery—but not oppression! You whites still treat us like we're less than human! I've been freed—but not from hate, bigotry, and cruelty!"

Sympathizing with the man, the Kid follows Larsen into Paradise Flats, where he witnesses firsthand the injustices that Larsen faces: upon their arrival, townsfolk instantly pick a fight with him; he is refused a room at the local hotel; and later he is accused of a theft he did not commit and locked up in a jail cell. Before Larsen can be lynched by a rowdy mob, the Rawhide Kid springs into action to bring the real thieves to justice. With the case resolved, Larsen is freed from jail. The Kid promises him, "It won't always be like this! Times will change!" To which Larsen responds, "Sure they will! Long after I'm dead!" As Larsen rides into the sunset, the Kid is seen with his head hung low, deep in thought: "He's right! Bigotry and hate will end. . . . But not in our lifetime!"[27]

While the above examples present the merits of an egalitarian spirit during a time when conversations about racial inequality loomed large, the concluding scene from the *Rawhide Kid* storyline reflects the limitations of this type of cultural work: even as these comics acknowledge the racial injustice that persists in the United States, the narratives feel critically impotent because their protagonists take a middle ground in mediating the conflict rather than joining the fight against inequality.

This tentative engagement with contemporaneous issues such as race and political violence was evident in other genre comic books too. Indeed, Spider-Man would take time out from fighting supervillains to mediate student unrest on a university campus in one storyline, whereas Captain America and the Green Lantern grappled with their proestablishment stance in a world full of racial injustice and political corruption.[28] Such fare did not go unnoticed, and news media began to take note of the comic book industry's interaction with the political climate. The *New York Times* (among other outlets) heralded the importance of this age of "relevance and social commentary" in comics at the dawn of the 1970s, observing how their stories played out as "a reflection of both real society and personal fantasy."[29] However, as a counterpoint, Jean-Paul Gabilliet suggests that while mainstream comic books may have become socially relevant, they were certainly not radical: "At best they cracked the armor of decorum in which they had been straitlaced since the 1950s."[30] Ultimately, the baby-boomer generation constituted the largest market demographic by the late 1960s. Therefore, subjects that resonated to this broad audience, such as social rebellion and dissident politics, were increasingly rendered into a marketable commodity rather than any serious contribution to the critical discourse associated with the era.

A similar type of cultural work was at play in other forms of popular media. For instance, cinema engaged with a variety of themes such as alienation from society (*The Graduate* [1967]), race (*Guess Who's Coming to Dinner* [1967]), youth activism (*The Strawberry Statement* [1970]), and sexual liberation (*Barbarella* [1968]). However, as John Belton observes, "The majority of films that tried to deal with the 1960s youth culture, the civil rights movement, the student protest movement, or the women's movement depoliticized their agendas or disguised them in such a way that they no longer possessed any confrontational power."[31] In these terms, mainstream popular culture that broached the subject of contemporary America generally presented a sterile version of the disorder that did little to unpack the complex problems associated with radical politics from the era. Nevertheless, this issue was not without remedy. As Belton states, "It was through the disguised medium of genre pictures that the counterculture got its message into the mainstream."[32]

The Western instantly springs to mind. The historical distance of the genre made it a significant narrative vehicle to critique and dissect the contemporaneous milieu while allowing creators to embed contemporary concerns within the Western's familiar plot structures. Simultaneously, this historical basis made the genre one of the greatest casualties of the era. The triumphalist myths surrounding the American West's history of conquest had become unpalatable for audiences in the age of murder and My Lai and had to be increasingly rethought and revised. By the 1970s a much more cohesive and defined ethos dominated the Western: one that characterized the genre with cynicism, pessimism, and brutality.

Revising the Western in Troubled Times

The gory scenes from the Vietnam War, featured every evening on television screens across the United States, the violence and unrest on the city streets, growing antiwar protests, and the damaging political assassinations that rocked the nation meant that cultural industries could not blithely produce the self-congratulatory Westerns that had entertained previous decades. This sense of unease with the genre was encapsulated in an article from *Time* magazine in June 1968, published three weeks after Robert Kennedy was assassinated. As the author observes, "All too widely, the country is regarded as a blood-drenched, continent-wide shooting range." They hasten to add, "The image, of course, is widely overblown, but America's own mythmakers are to blame. In U.S. folklore, nothing has been more romanticized than guns and the larger-than-life men who wielded them. From the nation's beginnings, in fact and fiction, the gun has been the provider and protector."[33] *Time*'s lament about the national love affair with guns and glorified violence in popular culture naturally implicated the Western—a genre built on quick-draw shootouts and explosive action.

However, this growing sense of disillusionment with tropes intrinsic to the Western was matched by a much deeper disenchantment with the ideological myths that undergirded the genre. Maldwyn A. Jones declares that the values and traditions associated with American national identity (which equally informed the Western) were damaged, and that society had entered a "chastened, puzzled, and introspective frame of mind" by the 1970s:

> They were no longer sure that the country had lived up to the aspirations of the Founding Fathers or that the traditional national goals of freedom and economic abundance were attainable, still less that the United States could reshape the world according to its heart's desire. Vietnam had demonstrated that the United States was not omnipotent [nor] uniquely virtuous. . . . In short, the old sense of boundlessness had gone. . . . Americans were painfully aware of the limits of liberty and of power.[34]

The tensions and contradictions from within American society were fragmenting the Western genre. Indeed, the internal conflict that called into question the aspirational idealism of the American experience and its underlying violent impetus placed the genre at odds with shifting societal values. But rather than fading into obscurity, by the late 1960s the Western was rethought, keeping pace with a nation that, according to *Time* magazine, had fast become a "blood-drenched, continent-wide shooting range."

Interestingly, this shift first took shape abroad, most explicitly through the Spaghetti Western films that were popularized by Italian director Sergio Leone's successful Dollars Trilogy (*A Fistful of Dollars* [1964], *For a Few Dollars More* [1965], *The Good, the Bad, and the Ugly* [1966]). Leone's brand of "foreign" Western adventure was remarkably popular with American audiences when the trilogy was released in US cinemas in 1967 (despite initially being dismissed by film critics). Leone's first Western opus, *A Fistful of Dollars*, opens with an avenging gunslinger entering a Mexican border town and closes with the protagonist riding away, leaving a mass of bullet-riddled corpses in his wake. In Leone's hands, the violence of the American hero is starkly foregrounded, and the director's stylistic camerawork made a nightmarish spectacle out of the killing. As Engelhardt observes: "For this vision of a West transformed into a landscape of torture and atrocity, [American] audiences offered up fistfuls of dollars."[35] As death was served daily to the nation on news broadcasts, no longer could the ritualistic violence of the Western be held disconnected from reality. Leone's nihilistic American West—described as a locale "where life has no value" in his film *For a Few Dollars More*—held an intense poignancy for US cinemagoers. The impact of the Italian Western is best measured by how it reverberated through the American version of the genre.

Sam Peckinpah's film *The Wild Bunch* (1969) is often considered to be the benchmark of American Westerns of the period: its fierce break from tradition inaugurated a flourish of innovation in the early 1970s. *The Wild Bunch* tells of an aging outlaw gang in the modern world of 1913. Faced with receding frontiers and an intense pursuit by deputized bounty hunters, the Bunch head south of the border into Mexico in search of new opportunities. They offer their services to the corrupt General Mapache in his fight against local revolutionaries. Arguably the most glaring element of the film was its fervent depiction of bloodletting. For example, the Bunch are betrayed by General Mapache in the closing scene, leading to a blood-drenched final shootout between the outlaws and Mexican soldiers that few survive. To accentuate the Western's violence, Peckinpah intercut slow-motion shots with normal-speed footage to show bloodied bodies falling to the ground in hails of gunfire, exposing his audience to a deeper absorption of the nightmarish spectacle of death than what conventional editing could afford.

The sense of disillusionment with the genre and its mythos blatantly manifested itself in *The Wild Bunch*. Peckinpah's film was an explicit realization that the Western's triumphalism was dead, as was the romanticized frontier experience, and the genre now occupied a deglamorized and vicious space. In its wake further revisionist Westerns came to the fore to tackle the benevolent myth of the West. Michael Coyne provides a useful summary that traces how various character types were revised to reinforce the unremittingly pessimistic framing that now dominated the genre.[36] Indeed, Westerns began to reveal the cruel machinations of power that underscored the settling of the American West: from the broken promises made to Native Americans in Arthur Penn's adaptation of *Little Big Man* (1970) to the explicit corruption within law enforcement and authority found in John Huston's *The Life and Times of Judge Roy Bean* (1972), a loose retelling of a historical figure who appointed himself as a judge in a small frontier town. The asymmetry of power was often exercised at the expense of the protagonists, as found in George Roy Hill's *Butch Cassidy and the Sundance Kid* (1969) and Peckinpah's *Pat Garrett and Billy the Kid* (1973), which outlined a crooked system that drove legendary outlaws into the grave. Moreover, the Western gunfighter was now being graphically murdered on screen, a bloody spectacle found in Robert Altman's *McCabe & Mrs. Miller* (1971) and Robert Aldrich's *Ulzana's Raid* (1972). It reached its most iconoclastic moment with the slaying of John Wayne's character in Don Siegel's *The Shootist* (1976).

The traumatic events of the 1960s certainly tarnished the sanguine veneer that the Western genre had propagated about the American way. In mainstream comic books this was explicitly realized in the scathing vision of the Western delivered by DC Comics' *Weird Western Tales* (1972–1980)—a title that rebranded the former anthology series *All-Star Western*. *Weird Western Tales* hosted an array of standout characters, from El Diablo, a supernatural masked gunslinger who stalks the night fighting for justice after being raised from the dead by an Apache shaman; to Scalphunter, a white man raised by Kiowa Indians who stands outside both ways of life. In a West dominated by racial hatred, greed, and corruption, Scalphunter matches the cruelty inflicted on him with equally violent savagery. For example, in *Weird Western Tales* #43 (1977) the artist blurs the line between good and evil. The story portrays an outlaw gang who massacre the occupants of a bank during a heist in the opening of the comic; they subsequently meet a grisly end at the hands of Scalphunter, who butchers them with a knife (fig. 7.8). The artist collapses the boundaries that separate the virtuous Western hero and the reprehensible antagonists, underlining

FIGURE 7.8. Michael Fleisher and Dick Ayers, "Feather for a Savage!," *Weird Western Tales* #43, December 1977, DC Comics.

the shared violent impulses of both character types. The hero's violent actions had traditionally been depicted as morally justifiable in the Western, but here it becomes a necessary, vicious fight for survival within this nihilistic Old West setting.

This merciless and cruel atmosphere was a uniting thematic for many of the characters from *Weird Western Tales*, including the bounty hunter Jonah Hex. Described in one comic as a "killer of killers . . . A vicious executioner meting out swift and final justice to law-breakers . . . for a fee . . . ," Hex is driven by money, and in each issue he is found wandering the frontier in search of a new repugnant criminal with a price on his head.[37] Hex's heavily scarred face matches his taciturn amorality; he often kills his foe in shocking reversals of their cruelty. For instance, one storyline sees a treacherous town leader, Craig, sell blankets tainted by smallpox to Native Americans in order to rid the area of this neighboring tribe. However, in a twist of fate, Craig contracts the disease. The closing page sees Hex hand Craig the only available bottle of smallpox antidote before quickly shooting it out of his hand, guaranteeing the wicked town leader's slow demise from the disease.

Likewise, in another comic Hex is captured, tied up, and left for dead under the blazing desert sun by the bandit the Butcher—this cruel torture an act of vengeance for the bounty hunter killing the Butcher's brother. Hex manages to escape, however, and repays this courtesy at the end of the story. The Butcher is bitten by a rabid wild cat, and rather than mercifully shooting him, Hex opts to leave the Butcher alone in the middle of the desert to suffer from the fatal effects of the bite.[38]

In a manner similar to the Scalphunter stories, this shocking type of frontier justice has an equalizing effect, in that the mean-spirited nature of Hex's foes serves to cancel out the abhorrent deaths they suffer. However, the harsh Western setting that the *Weird Western Tales* antiheroes occupy is arguably a condition of their publication context. Indeed, in the opening to *Weird Western Tales* #17, a group of "savage desperadoes" violently rob a bank, and in an act of complete overkill, before they make their getaway they use a stick of dynamite to blow up the bank and its occupants. A caption describes this act as an "unconscionable atrocity."[39] This can perhaps be read as a statement about the American condition of the late 1960s and 1970s. The ease with which these bandits brazenly kill a group of innocent people reflects a disconnection from or desensitization to the act of killing, and certainly mirrors the atmosphere of senseless murder that marred the contemporaneous publication context.

However, the nihilistic Western setting, where murder and mutilation are graphically visualized in the form of serialized Western genre fiction, may serve to reinforce to its readers what Jones observed as a growing realization by the 1970s—"that the United States was not omnipotent [nor] uniquely virtuous." The serial repetition of a darker and grittier take on the Western mythos may be one of comics' defining features in articulating how the tumultuous events of the era were subverting the genre; the strategies of visual representation afforded by the comics form were an important partner in this work.

Take, for example, the Jonah Hex storyline "Promise to a Princess" from *Weird Western Tales* #12. It opens with Hex having to flee from a small frontier town, pursued by those townsfolk who resent morally dubious figures like bounty hunters. However, the spirit of this community is revealed to be much more cold-hearted when Hex comes across the neighboring encampment of peaceful Native Americans

FIGURE 7.9. John Albano and Tony De Zuñiga, "Promise to a Princess!," *Weird Western Tales* #12, July 1972, DC Comics.

who have been massacred by these white settlers (fig. 7.9). The caption reveals the page's intent, showing "the depths to which the animal known as man can sink": a stark reminder to the reader of appalling historic acts of American genocide.[40] The following page further accentuates this horrific scene, as Hex rummages among the dead to find a small Native American child he had befriended, murdered alongside her family. Formal elements of comics composition afford a stronger potency to the image: the splash page breaks from the regular grid-based panel layout, a switch in narrative pace that forces the reader to pay close attention to the image of atrocity, while its delivery on the page-turn adds to the shock value. Nevertheless, the page cannot be divorced from its publication context. Artist Tony De Zuñiga's positioning of the corpses in a disarrayed mass deliberately mirrors the recognizable images from the My Lai Massacre.

This suturing of the present onto the past points to rhetorical metaleptic trickery. Rhetorical metalepsis, broadly a process of narratological interplay between the realms of fiction and reality, comes in many forms in comics.[41] In this case the artist's line grafts the familiar images of contemporary American violence onto a historic scene of slaughter, effectively defamiliarizing and alienating readers and their experience with the Western. The Western's Indian Wars narrative commonly celebrated the American experience of victory over a "savage" racial Other, but here the accentuation of the dubious exterminatory instincts from the myth of the West serve both to appall its reader and to symbolically condemn contemporaneous acts of imperialism. The sequence fits into a framework of Westerns from the era that repeatedly appropriated the recognizable Indian Wars narrative as a metaphor to productively engage with the moral ambiguities of American atrocities from the ongoing Vietnam War.

The Indian Wars

Native American studies scholar Gerald Vizenor observes how Westerns were never invested in representing tribal cultures. He suggests that as a consequence of the Vietnam War, "the Indian [became] a new contrivance." The "invented savage," formerly a bankable character construction to justify and promote American imperial desires, had fallen into "the ruins of representation." The tragic cost of settler colonialism, which was once denied proper exploration in the Western, was now "a new invention," and "the tribal others [were] now embraced."[42]

Indeed, in the wake of the Vietnam War and the visibility of American savagery in modern combat, the myth of the West was sullied in the American imagination. Western adventure stories about righteous pioneers who fought and defeated aggressive Indigenous populations that blocked their mission of progress did not hold the same allure. Creative industries had certainly taken note, and it became commonplace to invert those components from the Western's myth of conquest that struck most evocatively with this contemporaneous war. Whites were now the savage aggressors, committing acts of murder and terror against a peaceful Indigenous people, and the slaughter of Native Americans became a haunting spectacle that resonated with the surrounding milieu.

As we can see above, the tragic massacre of Native Americans was threaded into the bleak and foreboding fabric of the Western universe established in DC Comics *Weird Western Tales*. Likewise, Marvel began to increasingly incorporate a similar storyline into its titles. For instance, *Rawhide Kid* #91 (1971) took aim at the infamous Indian fighter George Armstrong Custer, casting him as a megalomaniac and the machinations of the army as a political excuse for murder (fig. 7.10). Marvel titles in general grew more accustomed to featuring rampaging US cavalrymen with a single-minded intent on killing innocent Native American women and children, matching the contemporaneous press coverage of American war crimes abroad.

For example, in *The Gunhawks* #3 (1973) Reno Jones and Kid Cassidy are captured by US soldiers who fear they may warn a nearby Native American tribe about a plan to attack their village at dawn (fig. 7.11). Bound and helpless, Jones and Cassidy can only look on from a distance as the soldiers descend upon the sleeping village. The ensuing massacre is largely left in the gutters of the comics page, leaving it up to the reader's imagination to envisage the cruel acts of murder from the scene. In place of gruesome images of slaughter, captions describe atrocities indiscriminately committed against unarmed men, women, and children, the horrors of which lead Cassidy to break down in tears: "It makes me . . . ashamed to be . . . an American!"[43]

The emphasis placed on atrocities enacted against Native Americans had largely been overlooked in the Western up until this point, but it was beginning to be foregrounded in historical narratives about the settling of the American West. Dee Brown's *Bury My Heart at Wounded Knee* (1970), a victim's history of westward expansion, details the injustices faced by the Plains Indians in the late nineteenth

FIGURE 7.10. Dick Ayers (cover art), *Rawhide Kid* #91, September 1971, Marvel Comics.

FIGURE 7.11. Syd Shores (cover art), *The Gunhawks* #3, February 1973, Marvel Comics.

century. However, according to the historian Hampton Sides, the re-markable sales of Brown's revisionary history were owed to the pow-erful impact of My Lai: "*Bury My Heart* landed on America's doorstep in the anguished midst of the Vietnam War, shortly after revelations of the My Lai massacre had plunged the nation into gnawing self-doubt. Here was a book filled with a hundred My Lais, a book that explored the dark roots of American arrogance."[44]

Elsewhere, Arthur Penn's Western *Little Big Man* (1970), a film adaptation of Berger's 1964 book of the same name, documents the life of Jack Crabb (played by Dustin Hoffman), a white boy who is raised as a Cheyenne Indian, and tells of his experiences growing up amid the heightened tensions between Native Americans and white pioneers in the late nineteenth century.[45] Crabb's upbringing among the Chey-ennes emphasizes their paradisal, communal way of life, described as a "countercultural idyll" by Coyne.[46] This depiction may have served to appeal to a young cinema-going audience of the period, humanizing a racial group often demonized in the Western, but it also helped to maximize the impact of the horrific attack that the Cheyenne village suffers at the hands of the US Cavalry during the film's finale.

This mélange culminated in one of the most brutal visualizations of American conquest in the nineteenth century—Ralph Nelson's *Sol-dier Blue* (1970). The film reimagines the events of the Sand Creek Mas-sacre of 1864, in which a regiment from the Third Colorado Cavalry (composed of volunteers) slaughtered a peaceful encampment of Chey-enne and Arapaho Indians (made up mainly of women and children). A year before the film's release, horrific images depicting the mass mur-der of unarmed Vietnamese civilians at the hands of US troops in My Lai had flooded American media. *Soldier Blue's* final massacre scene cannot be divorced from this context, and camera shots of screaming women and children and piles of dead bodies deliberately mirror the war photography that emanated from Vietnam. The film presented cinemagoers with some of the most graphic scenes of slaughter yet portrayed in a Western—scenes that had previously been omitted if they were mentioned at all.

In depicting the 1864 massacre, Nelson overloads his cinematic images, challenging and disturbing the viewer with expressive camera-work. Close-up shots of US soldiers dismembering, raping, and shoot-ing Native Americans are crosscut with reaction shots from horrified onlookers to this debauchery. The intercutting of slow motion and normal speed, utilized in Peckinpah's *The Wild Bunch*, is noticeable here. It exposes the viewer to a greater absorption of information than conventional editing can afford. In addition, the soldiers' mocking of their victims and laughter as they enjoy their actions create a certain jarring and discomforting aural experience. One review, from the *New York Times*, praised the fervent condemnation of the American past: "I think we need to face our violence more openly within its historical context; we need to face it as it was and is if we are ever to overcome it."[47] If the embracing of historic violence was a necessary ritual for the American psyche, then the underground comix of Jack Jackson were fundamental to this healing process.

Nits Make Lice

The development of underground comix in the 1960s grew out of the decade's hippie culture and drew inspiration from precursors such as *MAD*'s iconoclastic and subversive response to a conservative and conformist society. However, underground comix provided a much more radically profane mode of expression for their creators, capturing the mood of the time in content that explicitly dealt with drug culture, sex, politics, and rock music. Their positioning outside of the mainstream (they were generally self-published or released through small presses and sold in "head shops" [drug paraphernalia stores]) meant that they could evade censorship.[48] Amid a variety of notable creators, the Texan Jack Jackson, better known by his pen name, Jaxon, is regarded as a pioneer of the form, producing the underground comic *God Nose* in 1964. Moving to San Francisco in 1966, he established himself as a key member of the scene that saw the founding of the comix publisher Rip-Off Press alongside several other creators. In these formative years of his career, Jackson honed his skills as a storyteller through a variety of genre comics, but these were distinct from the historical comics he began to produce in the 1970s and onwards.

Indeed, after moving back to Texas in the mid-1970s, Jackson began to devote his work almost entirely to the history of Texas, and his storytelling shifted with it. Joshua Kopin describes his work as becoming "heavily textual, visually stiff, and weighted down with detail."[49] Jackson's history comics were narrated through dense narrative captions, scrupulously researched (often coming with a comprehensive bibliography at the end that encouraged further research from the reader), and made wide-ranging reference to and reuse of American Western art.[50] Some of his standout works include *Comanche Moon* (1979), which documents the life of Cynthia Ann Parker, an Anglo-Texan child who was taken captive and raised by Comanches, and her son, Quanah Parker, who became a key Native American political figure; *Los Tejanos* (1982) retells the story of Texas-Mexican Juan Seguín, who fought at the Alamo.

Jackson's look backward offered a marked break from the typical contemporaneous concerns on display in underground comix, but his work appealed to the counterculture sensibilities of its readership through his use of gratuitous aspects from comix like graphic violence and his iconoclastic handling of American history. Indeed, Kopin writes that although Jackson's historical comics "looked like Westerns, they showed disdain for Western heroes and challenged received notions of the ends of American history."[51] They intersected with the anti-Westerns from the era, showing a complete lack of respect for the resonant images of the genre, and offered readers a countermythic interpretation of the history of the West through a sympathetic handling of Native Americans.

One standout example is his short comic "Nits Make Lice," featured in *Slow Death* magazine in 1975. Similar to Nelson's *Soldier Blue,* Jackson provides a harrowing account of the Sand Creek Massacre and encourages the reader to draw parallels between the 1864 massacre and the present-day horrors taking place in Vietnam.

The comic is composed of nine pages. After a short prologue that details how the men that formed the volunteer cavalry regiment were driven by racism, bloodlust, and greed for the Indigenous people's land, Jackson graphically depicts their violent attack on hundreds of Cheyenne and Arapaho people. The comic does not eschew any of the blood-splattered, gory details of the Colorado militia's butchery. The panels coalesce to show a grisly succession of dismemberment, rape, and murder; the most distressing images are centered on the violent acts committed against women and children. One panel depicts a young Cheyenne woman being raped; in the following panel her head is crushed with a rifle butt. Another panel depicts a pregnant woman whose stomach has been cut open, her guts spilling out over the ground. This is positioned next to a panel that shows a young child held atop soldiers' bayonets.

Unlike the scenes of atrocity found in the film *Soldier Blue,* Jackson does not grant his readers a moment of comfortable breathing space. Despite Nelson extending the visualization of unfolding slaughter through cinematic devices like intercutting and slow motion,

FIGURE 7.12. Jack Jackson, "Nits Make Lice," *Slow Death #7*, Last Gasp, 1975.

FIGURE 7.13. Jack Jackson, "Nits Make Lice," *Slow Death #7*, Last Gasp, 1975.

Soldier Blue pales in comparison next to Jackson's representation of the same violent moment from history. Indeed, the unspooling of the film reel—where one image is supplanted by another through a mechanical apparatus—allows respite, as does cinematic editing, where cuts move the action along. However, the static nature of comics requires the reader to decide the pace at which they encounter each image.[52] As one lurid atrocity follows another in a string of continuous barbarity, the comics form itself affords a powerful poignancy to Jackson's illustrated detailing of the immense brutality of the soldiers toward the unsuspecting and peaceful encampment.

Jared Gardner suggests that by nature comics are artifacts that do not let the reader forget their material form. Unlike film or literature, which allow their consumers to immerse themselves in their story-worlds and forget about the production context, comics remind readers of their materiality with each drawn line.[53] Indeed, in documenting the 1864 massacre, Jackson balances the solemnity of portraying this ghastly moment in history with the exuberant and repulsive style of underground comix. Take, for example, his use of comics language: the gruesome "POP" as the scalp comes away from the skull in one image, is both self-referential to the comics material form while appealing to the readers senses in conveying the horrific acts of atrocity (fig. 7.12).

But Jackson blurs the boundaries between comix aesthetic and his type of harrowing historical documentary in other ways. For example, the artist toys with the polarized comics modes of drawing. Joseph Witek details quite standardized rules governing the "naturalistic mode" (relying on the recreation of physical appearance in a realistic art style), and the "cartoon mode" (growing from caricature, with its basic principles of simplification and exaggeration and associations with verbal humor and slapstick comedy).[54] However, as detailed in fig. 7.13, Jackson juxtaposes these competing modes while simultaneously subverting their purpose. The caricatured, gap-toothed, salivating mouth of the soldier does not signal a comedic interpretation of Western history but rather an unbridled bloodlust. Distorted features are common in the underground comix cartoon style of drawing, but here they are starkly contrasted with the depictions of the hopeless Cheyenne and Arapaho people, rendered in a more naturalistic mode. Fusing these differing characterizations creates a jarring visualization of the massacre, at once humanizing the victims while emphasizing the monstrous nature of their attackers.

Witek suggests that underground comix resonate with readers because they "attack authority by means of ruthless exaggerations and repulsive images," while Les Daniels argues that the form sought to "induc[e] drastic changes in America's state of mind" by exposing the reader to the violent and racist undercurrents in contemporary American society.[55] Taken together, these viewpoints would suggest that Jackson's gruesome display of violence in "Nits Make Lice" had a visceral impact that captures the pressing concerns of its readers. Published in the twilight years of the Vietnam War, it is hard not to draw links between Jackson's confrontation of the haunting legacy of settler colonialism and the grim atrocities that were occurring abroad. Witek observes that Jackson's artwork "places the viewer literally within the circle of leering soldiers awaiting their turn at the victim," arguing that this makes "readers become complicit in the action within the panels."[56] This placement has a discomforting effect that not only draws the reader into the barbarism of the past that is played out across the comics page but encourages a relitigation of American imperialism and violence in the present.

Native American studies and settler colonial studies explore the various dominant images and stereotypes of Native peoples that exist in the white American imagination and examines how these troubled representations (whether the romanticized exotic figure or the demonized bloodthirsty "savage") are typically deployed in popular culture as a means by which to articulate myths about race, identity, and national order.[57] Jackson's unflinching hand-drawn representation of violence committed against Native Americans therefore implicates "Nits Make Lice" as functioning within the colonial mechanism at which he takes aim. Although Jackson's graphic depiction of atrocities from the historical West serves to draw attention to the appalling treatment of Indigenous people during the settlement of the American frontier, his retelling of Native American trauma as an allegorical indictment of the Vietnam War situates his comic within a framework of white fictions that co-opt and use images of Native Americans for their own designs. Perhaps showing some awareness of this contention, in later works Jackson would tone down the grotesquely lurid depictions of sexual violence and murder in his retelling of moments from Native American history—a self-censorship that he has attributed to wanting to have his history comics reach a wider audience.[58]

Nevertheless, "Nits Makes Lice" can be read as a specific product of its time and stands out for how it interweaves Jackson's educational impulse as a historian with the burlesque horror that underground comix were known for. The comic intersects with a wide variety of revisionist Westerns that came forth through the late 1960s and 1970s and serves as one of the most sensational and deplorable iterations of the anti-Western's modus operandi: to invert the reverent symbols of the Western myth and attack the mainstream American values and traditions that undergirded the genre. The artist's comic did not have the kind of exposure and distribution networks as similar mainstream Western comics and films. However, the positioning of underground comix outside of the mainstream and beneath the critical radar allowed for an unrestrained and perverse vision of American history.

From Jonah Hex to *The Wild Bunch* to "Nits Make Lice" to *Bury My Heart at Wounded Knee*, the stark articulation of the more barbarous aspects of the Western's historical source material in a variety of popular texts collectively unmasked the hollow façade of American mythmaking, timing perfectly with the sense that American omnipotence had ebbed away by the 1970s. Nevertheless, if the fractious discord of the 1960s and 1970s had given the genre a renewed sense of purpose, the Western's enduring centrality had fragmented under these terms by the later 1970s, and all that remained were the crumbled ruins of the mythic West. On the February 24, 1974, Pauline Kael famously heralded the genre's end in the *New Yorker*: "A few more Westerns may still straggle in, but the Western is dead."[59]

The Western has always projected contemporaneous attitudes onto a historical past, but the negativism and cynicism of its presentation in the 1960s and 1970s marked a dramatic break from the triumphalism and aspirational idealism that had imbued the mythic West of previous decades. While it would be easy to fall into Kael's (and others) observation that the genre was on the cusp of its own violent demise, there was certainly more to this revision. Moving past what Richard A. Maynard observed at the time—that the Western was being "deliberately designed to destroy the previous myths of heroic cowboy literature and films"—the new violent direction of the genre kept pace with the surrounding milieu.[60] Counter to what I described earlier as a failing of mainstream popular culture to effectively engage with the turmoil of the era, and much more an attempt to commodify contemporary themes of social revolt and dissident politics, the importance of the Western lay in its ability to dramatize these concerns under the cover of historical genre fiction. In addition, the infusion of youthful radical criticism demonstrates the appeal of Western themes to new diverse audiences, including the socially conscious comics readers of the late 1960s and 1970s. Yet perhaps this also indicates more than simple revisionism: the genre could continue to be rethought and refashioned in its appeal to contemporaneous audiences and shifting social and political climates.

Walking on the Bones of the Dead

Comics and the Western's "Afterlife"

IN 1974 THE FILM CRITIC Pauline Kael famously declared in the pages of the *New Yorker* that "the western is dead."[1] For much of the nineteenth and twentieth centuries the genre had remained a dominant fixture in American popular culture. At first serving to naturalize the policies of westward expansion, the Western's continued retellings of white American triumph on the contested frontier simultaneously promoted American exceptionalism and reinforced old certainties about race, identity, and national order. However, amid the impacts of the Vietnam War, the civil rights movement, and the women's liberation movement across the 1960s and 1970s, the ideological myths associated with the Western were deeply problematized and came under increasing scrutiny. Due to the dissenting representations of the Old West that prevailed in this era, the genre became unpalatable for many, suffering from a marked downswing in production and circulation. While such an account helps to rationalize Kael's declaration of the genre's "death" by the mid-1970s, such assertions cannot be fully reconciled with the Western's continued, albeit much more moderate, presence in popular culture.

This concluding chapter examines the continued vitality of the Western within late-twentieth- and early twenty-first-century comics storytelling, highlighting traces of the genre that can be found within different forms and settings. Its enquiry is twofold. One strand considers those comics that meld the classic themes and conventions of the Western with the contemporary West, urban locales, or frontiers beyond, revealing the different ways in which comics confront the apparent "death" of the genre while signaling to its continued relevance as a political form. Titles include *Preacher* (1995–2000), a quest narrative set in the modern American Southwest; *Scalped* (2007–2012), a crime drama set on a contemporary Indian reservation; and the relocation of the Western to moribund postapocalyptic wastelands found in *Scout* (1985–1987), *The Walking Dead* (2003–2019), and so on.

Another strand explores the antimythography amplified through New Western History, as new voices and perspectives that had previously been omitted or silenced now come to the fore. These voices are diverse in terms of race, gender, and nationality and help expand the Western beyond the one-dimensional tableau idyll of a white frontier past, adding texture and heterogeneity to the genre. Titles include the expanding body of Indigenous comics (*Trickster* [2010], *Moonshot* [2015], *Sovereign Traces* [2018]) and feminist perspectives (*Pretty Deadly* [from 2013], and *Coyote Doggirl* [2018]), alongside new histories (*Best Shot in the West* [2012], *Indeh* [2016], *Calamity Jane* [2017]), and global interpretations. By way of reflecting on the inherited tropes of the Western and questioning its persistence in popular culture, the chapter reveals how comics continue to challenge and subvert the mythic West and draws attention to the unique and varied transformations of the genre in contemporary graphic narratives.

The Western after the 1970s

In the opening to *The Western Reader* (1998), Jim Kitses observes that "someone is always trying to bury the Western." He further suggests that if all the claims to the genre's death had headstones they would "overflow even Tombstone's cemetery."[2] Indeed, one film critic as early as 1911 would dismiss the Western as "a gold mine that had been worked to the limit."[3] However, such observations about the Western's demise have continually haunted the genre over the years.[4] Like Kael, scholars and critics tend to point to this moment as a turning point in the genre's history, as Westerns began to emphasize the horrors of the nation's history-myth of frontier violence, which doubled as an allegory for the United States' misguided intervention in Vietnam. Other factors besides historical revisionism of the genre also played into the Western's decline by the 1970s. For example, John White observes the shifts in cinema-going demographics: "Westerns had appealed to earlier generations at a time when cinema was the dominant medium for visual entertainment, but that audience was now into middle age and spending their time at home with television for entertainment. For young people, classic Westerns were in effect historical dramas increasingly unrelated to their everyday lives in terms of norms, values, and outlooks."[5] In the aftermath of such shifts, the Western faded from prominence in American cinema, although not without continued resurfacings: *Pale Rider* (1985), *Dances with Wolves* (1990), *Unforgiven* (1992), *Open Range* (2003), *True Grit* (2010), and *The Magnificent Seven* (2016), to name a handful. Given that 1,300 Westerns (mainly B-films) were made in the 1920s, and roughly a thousand were released in each of the next three decades, the sharp decline in the number of Western films being produced into the latter half of the twentieth century certainly helps to inform the exaggerated declarations of the genre's death.[6]

The fluctuation in the number of Western films being produced is of course purely from the perspective of Hollywood, but those numbers can be extended to incorporate mainstream American Western comics, too. For the core comics publishers, Marvel and DC, their flagship Western hero titles (Marvel's *Rawhide Kid*, *Two-Gun Kid*, *Kid Colt, Outlaw*; and DC's Jonah Hex) had all ceased publication by the 1980s. Moreover, bar a series of long-running Jonah Hex reboots (commencing in 2005 and 2011) and a revival of *The Lone Ranger* by Dynamite Entertainment in 2006, the majority of popular Western heroes from comic books made only sparse appearances in limited miniseries into the twenty-first century. Although short-lived, some of these limited series could still offer interesting subversions of the Western genre and the traditional cowboy hero. For instance, Marvel Comics reimagined the Rawhide Kid as a gay character in one 2003 series, while the Native American hero Red Wolf became sheriff of a town called Timely in another from 2015.[7]

Similar to the marked decline of the genre in comic books, most of the Western adventure comic strips from national newspapers had folded by the 1980s, usefully captured in an elegiac cartoon by *Rick O'Shay* cartoonist Stan Lynde, in which a cowboy looks mournfully over the gravestones of various popular Western strips such as *The Lone Ranger*, *Red Ryder*, and *Lance* (fig. 8.1). Printed in 1981, the cartoon's use of gravestones to chart the publication history of a number of noteworthy series is certainly evocative when thinking about the Western as a dead or dying genre in this period.

This account reduces the Western after the 1970s to a conflicting binary, which at once acknowledges the seeming demise of one of America's most traditional genres but also accounts for the Western's continued (albeit modest) presence within the popular-culture landscape. Of course, the latter part of this binary negates the former

FIGURE 8.1. An untitled Stan Lynde cartoon taken from *CARTOONIST PROfiles*, no. 50, June 1981, 79.

and shows how the genre refuses to stay dead and remains a fixture in American culture. However, such an account is also limited, and fails to recognize the genre's reinvention in different forms and settings after the 1970s.

One stark example is the Western's abstraction from the historical context of westward expansion and finding new life repackaged as an element of other popular genres. In cinema, Slotkin observes how visual and thematic elements from the Western were repurposed and redeployed in science fiction, urban crime dramas, and horror films in the 1970s and onwards.[8] Likewise, a similar effect was achieved in comic books. Through the 1980s and 1990s mainstream American comic books were transformed by the rise of the graphic novel publication model, and the medium experienced sophistication through the work of new artists and writers. Christopher Dony uses DC's adult-oriented imprint Vertigo as his exemplar to describe how comics and graphic novels began to explore mature themes and content, participating in "meta- and intertextual meditation[s] on the medium, its status and history," and employing postmodernist strategies of "rewriting" popular genres to "deliberately play with [the] concept of reader familiarity."[9] The Western was part of this shift, and comics creators found imaginative ways to reinterpret the rich symbols and themes of the genre in bleak apocalyptic and dystopian visions. This reinterpretation can be illustrated by a series of remarkable comics from the 1980s.

For example, the closing chapter of Frank Miller's graphic novel *Batman: The Dark Knight Returns* (1986) is indicative of this trend. This superhero story is set against the backdrop of Russia leading an arms race against the United States. As their new "Coldbringer" nuclear warhead plunges Gotham City into darkness, fires break out and chaos ensues on the city's streets. A criminal gang capitalizes on the disorder, hoping to take over Gotham. However, they are quickly interrupted by the sound of oncoming hoofbeats, "like in a Western," and the arrival of Batman on horseback, ready to save Gotham City once more.[10] Equipped only with a lasso, and accompanied by an impromptu posse, the superhero-cum-Western lawman restores order to this crime-ridden town (fig. 8.2).[11]

Similarly, Timothy Truman's *Scout* (1985–1987) melds Western symbols and motifs within a postapocalyptic wasteland, taking its setting in a United States ravaged by nuclear warfare, political corruption, and the degradation of the natural environment. The nation now sits at the bottom of the world order. Within this bleak setting, the comic follows Emmanuel Santana, an Apache who is on a spiritual mission to defeat a series of mythical monsters from Native American folklore that now plague the land. Disguised as humans, they have infiltrated the upper echelons of the nation's power structures.

Amid dwindling sales of its *Jonah Hex* series, DC Comics transported its protagonist from the nineteenth-century Wild West to a twenty-first-century postnuclear setting. Under Michael Fleisher, *Hex* (1985–1987) repurposes the familiar components that comprised the original *Jonah Hex* series—the wandering gunslinger in a pessimistic and bleak frontier setting—but now Hex must try to acclimatize to a barren American landscape that has been devastated by war and famine and contend with a host of robots, mutants, futuristic gangs, and corrupt authoritarian powers alike (which of course replace the stock cast of dastardly villains from the Western).

FIGURE 8.2. Frank Miller, *Batman: The Dark Knight Returns*, New York: DC Comics, 1986.

The texts discussed above can collectively be read with a post-modern steer. As Theo D'haen observes, "The action of the Western takes place against a backdrop of majestic landscapes that illustrate the magnitude of the principles involved and pitted against one another in the plot and via characters: good versus evil, law and justice versus lawlessness, order versus anarchy." As he explains: "These principles, of course, are projections of the cultural codes or metanarratives ruling contemporary society. The typical strategy of the postmodern Western is to reveal the constructed character of these principles by first invoking and then negating the conventions that embody them."[12] The familiar image from the Western of a lone individual wandering amid inhospitable and savage wilderness still remains in these comics, but that symbolism is bereft of the aspirational idealism that once undergirded it. Instead, the use of the Western in these comics has become a metaphor for the contemporaneous United States. The 1980s were characterized by the intensive conservatism and cowboy politics of Ronald Reagan's presidency, in which government expenditure decreased, big business was deregulated, and the military expanded. To uphold his foreign policy of "peace through strength," Reagan reignited previous Cold War tensions, overseeing a buildup of arms to confront the Soviet Union, while at home there were strong fears of domestic unrest and economic downturn.[13] The texts discussed above, from *Batman* to *Hex*, can be read as an encapsulation of nuclear tensions and the erosion of American society in this era, but the bleak postnuclear wasteland settings in some of these comics also provide a grave allegorical premonition of the impact of Reagan's aggressive Cold War posturing. Amid the savage landscapes, the lone American hero-cum-Western lawman once more arrives to master these hostile territories and violently quell disorder to regenerate American civil society. In this regard, such examples illustrate how the Western continued to provide narrative solutions to pressing social and political concerns and persisted as a powerful mode of expression to explore the contemporary American condition after the 1970s.

The Western has gained renewed vitality in American comics through this type of cross-genre blending, which reclaims the themes and motifs of the American West and melds them with other popular genres. Robert Kirkman's *The Walking Dead* (2003–2019) certainly echoes earlier reappropriations of the Western from 1980s comics—the modern-day zombie apocalypse story evokes the genre's familiar themes and motifs through its cast of human survivors who roam the

FIGURE 8.3. Robert Kirkman and Tony Moore, *The Walking Dead* #1, October 2003, Image Comics.

zombie-ravaged urban landscape. This is especially true of early issues from the series: the iconic visual elements of a cowboy on horseback riding through a vast and empty desert landscape with sandstone buttes jutting upwards on the horizon are replaced with a lone survivor in an eerily quiet city with decrepit tower-block buildings rising up in the distance (fig. 8.3).[14] However, Kirkman's title hints at a wider trend shaping playful cross-genre hybrid works that have come to the fore: from horror-supernatural Western comics such as Beau Smith's *Wynonna Earp* (from 1996), Min-Woo Hyung's *Priest* (1998–2007), Cullen Bunn and Brian Hurtt's *The Sixth Gun* (2010–2016), and Chris Dingess and Matthew Roberts's *Manifest Destiny* (from 2013); to science-fiction Westerns like *East of West* (2013–2019), by Jonathan Hickman and Nick Dragotta, and the graphic novel *Cowboys & Aliens* (2006).

Such rearticulations of the Western reveal how the bold action and visual spectacle that the genre has always been known to provide still have currency in contemporary comics storytelling, but they also offer a more general reflection on the hand-drawn medium, which allows for popular genres to be paired and blended with the stroke of the comics artist's pen. The cultural impact of this reimagining of the

Western in comics may best be exemplified in the later film and television adaptations of some of the titles listed above: from hugely popular television series such as AMC's *The Walking Dead* (from 2010) and Syfy's *Wynonna Earp* (from 2016), to the Hollywood films *Cowboys & Aliens* (2011) and *Priest* (2011). Nevertheless, some comics were less concerned with the vibrancy of frontier adventure and instead reflect a stronger interest in the death of the Western—and indeed what remains of the genre in its "afterlife."

Post-Westerns and the Genre's Afterlife

Another direction that creators took the Western was developed most prominently after the 1970s, or rather at the point in which the genre ostensibly "died" (if we take Kael at her word). Consider these films, for example: Peckinpah's *Bring Me the Head of Alfredo Garcia* (1974), John Sayles's *Lone Star* (1996) and *Silver City* (2004), the Coen brothers' *No Country for Old Men* (2007), and David Mackenzie's *Hell or High Water* (2016). In scholarship about the Western, this type of film has been described variously as neo-, postmodern, or post-Western: they are stories that take the classic symbols and themes of the genre and displace them in the contemporary West or in modern-day urban settings.[15] Acknowledging the receding dominance of the Western when writing in 1973, Philip French was in fact looking toward the potential futures of the waning genre when he analyzed a series of modern-day, or rather, "post-Western," films (e.g., *Coogan's Bluff* [1968]).[16]

Observing the decreased production and circulation of the classic Western after the 1960s, Neil Campbell posits that post-Westerns are a reaction to the death of the genre and function as "an archaeological probing into foundations forgotten, repressed, or built over." He suggests that in these modern-day Western stories, "something surges back and into the world again—the dead return (like the genre itself)—and the apparently smooth surface of myth, memory, and history is ruptured." There is, however, more to the post-Western's use of the genre, and Campbell explains how such texts do not merely "perform the histories and identities" of the American West, but "reflect upon these inherited tropes, interrogate their afterlife, and delve into their persistence," while "commenting critically upon the social weight and ideological assumptions embedded within."[17]

This trend can be found at play within various post-Western comics—such as the graphic novels *Holliday* (2012) by Nate Bowden and Doug Dabbs; *The Big Country* (2019) by Quinton Peeples; *Pulp* (2020) by Ed Brubaker and Sean Phillips; and the ongoing series *That Texas Blood* (from 2020) by Chris Condon and Jacob Phillips—which relocate the Western's themes and iconographies into murky (sub)urban crime stories. Earlier examples include Kyle Baker's *The Cowboy Wally Show* (1988), a dark comedy about an aging cowboy actor; and Scott Morse's *Spaghetti Western* (2004), a present-day bank heist story that toys with visual aesthetics from Italian Western films. Another stand-out example is Garth Ennis and Steve Dillon's *Preacher* (1995–2000), which follows the flawed Texan preacher Jesse Custer and his quest across the modern-day United States in a search for God. The series is remarkable for its intertextual reworking of popular genres (from horror to the road movie), its referencing of 1990s popular culture, and its traversal of other iconographic bits of Americana. Unsurprisingly, the creators add the Western to this mix, from the inclusion of iconic backdrops like Monument Valley and the Alamo to invoking ghosts from the Old West, as figures from the past literally haunt the present-day American story.[18] For example, *Preacher*'s cast of characters include the cowboy actor John Wayne, who is an embodiment of Jesse's conscience and advises the protagonist throughout the series. Likewise, the Saint of Killers, a grizzled Western gunfighter drawn straight out of the Wild West, is called upon by angels in Heaven to hunt down and kill Jesse after learning about his mission to find God (fig. 8.4).

Added to the visual conjurations of the Western are the reworking of familiar plot structures from the genre. For example, in one narrative interlude—*Preacher: Salvation* (1999)—Jesse, having lost focus on his quest to find God, takes on the role of sheriff in a small Texan town called Salvation. The story reinterprets the familiar law-and-order formula, in which a lone lawman must use violence to fend off threats to a frontier community, grafting it onto a modern-day setting. In this case, Salvation is in the grip of racial intolerance, the Ku Klux Klan, and the local meat-factory owner, Quincannon, who, with his gang of thugs, rules the town through intimidation. The repurposing of the classic Western narrative provides pleasing resolutions for the reader, and just like in the movies, Sheriff Jesse Custer singlehandedly beats up the bad guys and restores order, ridding this small backwater town of the damaging representations of American racism and corruption. Afterward, Jesse surrenders his sheriff's badge and returns to his search for God.

FIGURE 8.4. Glenn Fabry (cover art). Garth Ennis and Steve Dillon, *Preacher* #2, May 1995, DC Comics.

Campbell asserts that the reinterpretation of Western symbols and themes in these types of present-day stories has a deeper significance and "requires the audience to reconsider the iconic familiarity of western tropes," which are "undone by the garishly unfamiliar modern West [or] urban cityscape" settings that they are situated in. He explains that the deliberate jarring of expectations in post-Westerns encourages "the reader into a space of reflection, [and] a critical dialogue with the form, its assumptions and histories."[19] Ennis and Dillon emphatically capture this space of reflection in one arresting scene from the series, in which we find two of the leading protagonists, Jesse Custer and his friend Cassidy, sitting on the hood of a car deep in the heart of the desert amid the commanding sandstone buttes of Monument Valley. As their discussion turns toward the United States and its promise as a land of opportunity, Jesse marvels at their surroundings, which have been made famous by the Hollywood Western: "This is America to me, Cass," he says, "right outta the movies." In counter to Jesse's reverence for the landscape, Cassidy points out how the United States was "born outta blood an' killin'. We walk on the bones of the dead every fuckin' day."[20]

Cassidy's remark is obviously made in relation to the history of the American West and its legacy of conquest. However, his observation is made more profound by the characters' surroundings. For a long span of the twentieth century, the Western repeatedly retold the national narrative of westward expansion. Particularly in the films of John Ford, the barren terrain of Monument Valley played host to many scenes of Native American slaughter in the name of progress. Campbell explains that where the classic Western is primarily concerned with the violence and drama of settlement on the contested frontier, post-Westerns instead "return to the mythic 'scene' [and are] concerned with . . . what remains from the action the western represented, its dark inheritance and ghostly consequences."[21] It can be argued that in their use of Monument Valley (like the deployment of other tropes from the Western), Ennis and Dillon not only remind the reader of how popular culture has depicted the American West but also reveal how the Western enriches the politics of their series. Primarily, *Preacher* comments on American violence, racism, and inward-looking imperialism—aspects that are readily bound up in symbols from the Western. Cassidy's criticism of the violent history of the West while he sits amid the otherworldly rock formations of Monument Valley creates a spectral encounter with the Old West that carries the reader beyond both the past and the present, reminding them of the omnipresent traces of the frontier that not only haunt the series but also of the enduring burden it places on the American present.

It is this concept of returning to the "scene" in the aftermath of the Western's demise, or rather walking on the bones of the dead (to take Cassidy's phrasing), that I want to explore further. For example, *Preacher* flouts the genre it most overtly recalls. Its spectral status as a Western draws attention to the past's hold over the present, thus reminding the reader that historical transgressions cannot be easily forgotten. Indeed, the series shows the inescapable burden of the American legacy of conquest, as traces of those most repugnant aspects of history remain visible in *Preacher*'s contemporary storyworld. This effect is continually at play in post-Western comics.

Take, for example, Jason Aaron and R. M. Guéra's *Scalped* (2007–2012), a sixty-issue crime drama set on a contemporary Oglala Sioux Indian reservation. The series follows Dashiell Bad Horse, an army veteran who returns to the Prairie Rose Reservation (where he grew up) as an FBI informant. He is under the employ of Agent Nitz—a character who is devoted to convicting Red Crow for the murder of two FBI agents on the reservation in the mid-1970s. In aid of this investigation, Dashiell gains work from Red Crow, the corrupt tribe leader who is opening a new casino on the Prairie Rose Reservation at the start of the series. The comic provides a stark image of reservation life, a place ravaged by alcoholism, drug addiction, and poverty. As Red Crow himself describes, the Prairie Rose Reservation is "a Third World nation in the heart of America."[22]

The Prairie Rose Reservation is a fictional representation of the Pine Ridge Reservation in South Dakota. The geographical location in which Pine Ridge sits is significant for several reasons. It was the site of one of the most tragic chapters from the history of the contested frontier—the Wounded Knee massacre in 1890, in which hundreds of Lakota men, women, and children were murdered by the US Cavalry. Nearly a century later, Pine Ridge was a hotbed for American Indian Movement political activism, including the murder of two FBI agents in 1975. The ensuing controversial trial and conviction of Leonard Peltier for these murders came to symbolize the wider mistreatment of Native Americans and underscored some of the harsh conditions of reservation life. Indeed, the Pine Ridge Reservation boasts massive unemployment rates, and according to Joseph Stromberg, its population has one of the lowest life-expectancy rates in the entire Western Hemisphere.[23] Through the fictional Prairie Rose Reservation Aaron and Guéra conjure the potent symbolism of what Pine Ridge represents. *Scalped* highlights the humiliating living conditions on Indian reservations and also reinterprets moments from history like the murders Peltier was convicted of, which is reworked into a fictional storyline about the murder of two FBI agents that took place at Prairie Rose in the 1970s. As Kate Polak explains: "*Scalped* uses Wounded Knee, the Peltier/FBI shooting case, and other confrontations between whites-Indians as a historical intertext by which present-day life on reservations can be exposed and questioned."[24]

This can be seen through the opening sequence of #25 of the series, in which the creators document key events from the historical West: Custer's defeat at the banks of the Little Bighorn River in 1876 is detailed on one page, and then a harrowing visualization of the aftermath of the Wounded Knee massacre in 1890 on the next page. The reader is then transported to 1900 and a scene of what remains of the Prairie Rose Reservation after these tragic events from the region's history. Hundreds of its people have been murdered, and the territory has been stripped of all its most desirable and profitable land. The next page turn reveals that this series of events is being read about in a history book, *The History of the Prairie Rose Rez*, by a character traveling to Prairie Rose by coach. Taking heed of this grave history he has just read, the character turns to a fellow passenger on the coach—a Native American man living in Prairie Rose—and asks: "The white man put you here to suppress you. . . . So why stick around after all these years? Why not move to a place where there are jobs and the ground isn't littered with the bones of your massacred ancestors?" The man replies, "You're right, the white folks put us here to die. But we fought back by living. We fight back every day, just by surviving."[25]

The resurfacing of the metaphor about walking on the bones of the dead is not lost here and reveals how looking backward to the dark legacies of conquest from the history of the American West allows us to infer messages of hope for the future (such as the persistence of Native American culture after mass genocide), but it also reiterates how the Indian reservation is a symbol of resistance and survivance against the odds. By bringing forth the historic locations and memories of murder that the Western articulates, the creators show how the historical past shapes the lived present of Indigenous people and life on contemporary Indian reservations, restoring what is often a repressed part of American life.

In short, *Scalped* is a murky crime drama squarely set in the present day. However, its infrequent shifts to the past provide the reader with an interesting twist on the Western story of white-Indian conflict. Rather than the common framing of bold action and adventure set on the contested frontier, Aaron and Guéra instead weave the tragic and violent history of the West with the marginalization and deprivation of contemporary Native American life. As Polak argues, "Aaron and Guéra use both textual and imagistic historical artifacts as inspiration for this tale of contemporary reservation life, in order to explore how historical trauma results in intergenerational cycles of poverty and violence."[26]

Bringing together the cultural work of *Preacher* and *Scalped*, we can see how post-Western comics use the Western genre and the regional histories of violence and racism to reconsider the American present through the act of looking backward. However, the narrative setting on a contemporary Indian reservation in *Scalped* alerts us to some of the different types of stories and voices that can be heard through post-Western comics. Indeed, post-Westerns are attached to wider rethinking of the regional West and address a growing need to represent a more complex portrait of its history and myths, shifting the narrative beyond traditional formulas about heroic white individuals who tame "savage" landscapes.

This manner of thinking differently about the Western echoes an idea developed in Patricia Nelson Limerick's *The Legacy of Conquest* (1987), a title that represents a turning point in the study of the American West. Limerick's study highlights the limitations of scholarship surrounding Western history, which had for a long time been preoccupied with the frontier and its supposed end in 1890. Limerick argues it is the role of New Western History to push past these boundaries and see "the continued vitality of issues widely believed to be dead"—or rather, to explore those histories and voices that had previously been omitted.[27] This trail of thought was later expanded by Frieda Knobloch, who outlines a need for a "postwestern history" that is "indigenist, anti-imperialist, and antistatist."[28] Post-Westerns arguably contribute to this important work, providing a platform that can mobilize alternative voices and histories of the West.

This kind of reworking is suggested as much in *Scalped*, which provides a grim look at Indian reservation life and the impact of historical frontier conquest on a contemporary Indigenous population. However, similar patterns have been observed in the wider scholarship on post-Westerns. For example, John Cawelti claims the post-Western examines the "limits and inaccuracies of Western generic formulas." In particular, he suggests that those films "made in other countries [and that] redefined and expanded the meaning of the west itself as mythic terrain or territory" added to the fabric of the post-Western.[29] In 2004 Stephen Tatum recognized the "ongoing reorientation of . . . the literary West," describing it as going through a "postfrontier" phase, wherein old ideas and mythologies about the frontier were being challenged and which encouraged the West to be viewed as "an intercultural contact zone."[30] Finally, Susan Kollin writes that the post-Western "acknowledges Hollywood's legacy . . . but . . . resists this hegemony in an effort to seek another form of storytelling," whether it is a "more self-conscious examination of the genre's conventions and icons" or, given her analysis of how films such as *Dead Man* (1996) and *Smoke Signals* (1998) restore the "indigenous consciousness" in the Western, a space in which to question and disrupt previous modes of representation in the genre.[31]

Taken together, this scholarship not only suggests how post-Westerns present different ways to think critically about the American Western but also offers new points of view, from international interpretations of the genre to providing a vehicle for formerly marginalized voices. While not explicitly mentioned in the above scholarship, comics also enter into this cultural rethinking.

Some recent comics histories about the American West provide an illustrative entry point. For example, Patricia and Fredrick McKissack and Randy DuBurke's *Best Shot in the West* (2012) retells the life of the Black cowboy Nat Love. Ethan Hawke and Greg Ruth's *Indeh* (2016) evokes the earlier work of underground comix creator Jack Jackson, who retold the horrors of the United States history of settler colonialism from the point of view of Indigenous people. Hawke and Ruth tread a similar path, offering a graphic retelling of the Apache Wars told from the perspectives of key players in the conflict, such as Cochise and Geronimo, and in detail represents their desperate fight to protect their land and culture. Likewise, the French comic *Calamity Jane: The Calamitous Life of Martha Jane Cannary* (2017) sees writer Christian Perrissin and artist Matthieu Blanchin play with the distinctions between fact and fiction in their retelling of the life of Martha Cannary, situating the raucous frontierswoman within a similar pantheon of legendary figures from the Old West such as Buffalo Bill Cody and Wild Bill Hickok. These graphic histories add to the rich fabric of the literatures of the American West. Even as they challenge former perceptions about the centrality of white men in the region's history and myth, they provide exciting stories about historic figures from the Old West that are diverse in terms of race and gender and, with the example of *Calamity Jane*, show how different nationalities can author the American West. Drawing on these different points of view, the final portion of this chapter will explore three focuses in recent comics storytelling: the expanding body of Indigenous comics, women and the Western, and international interpretations of the genre.

Indigenous Comics

Writing in 2009, Richard King observed how "comic books increasingly provide American Indian artists and tribes a powerful vehicle through which to reclaim heritage, identity, and language."[32] This postulation is supported by only a few notable comics in his analysis, such as the educational comic *Peace Party* (1999) by Rob Schmidt, and Jon Proudstar and Ryan Huna Smith's *Tribal Force* (2002), which brings together four Native American heroes who battle the federal government and protect tribal land. King describes the latter series as being reminiscent of Marvel's superhero teams like the X-Men or the Avengers, but the group is "charged with a more meaningful mission, one that resists the very acts of appropriation so central to the rendering of indigenous peoples in this genre and the history of native nations in the United States."[33] Nevertheless, in the years since King's essay was printed, Indigenous comics have grown into a burgeoning field. For example, a variety of comics anthologies featuring Indigenous creators from across Canada and the United States have come to the fore, such as *Trickster* (2010), Hope Nicholson's *Moonshot* (2015), Gordon Henry and Elizabeth LaPensée's *Sovereign Traces* (2018), and *Marvel Voices: Heritage* (2022), which covers a diverse mix of popular genres and stories in its pages—science fiction, horror, folklore, superheroes, and forgotten histories, among other subjects. Each comic either implicitly or explicitly serves to promote and preserve the language and culture associated with each artist's and writer's specific tribe or nation, and each of the stories (especially in *Moonshot* and *Sovereign Traces*) has its own foreword to introduce the creator and help contextualize their unique point of view. Added to this, November 2016 marked the first annual Indigenous Comic Con, and the following year saw the opening of the first Indigenous comic book shop, Red Planet Books & Comics, both in Albuquerque, New Mexico. The development of platforms like specialist comics shops and conventions for Indigenous graphic narratives helps to illustrate the wider canon of Indigenous comics that are available—a category that unfortunately cannot be captured fully in any great depth here through this brief snapshot.

So where does the post-Western fit into this? Consider the following examples. In *The 500 Years of Resistance Comic Book* (2010), Gord Hill weaves key events from the history of the American West, such as the Apache Wars and the Battle of the Little Bighorn, into a wider account of the tragic history of Indigenous struggle against European colonization of the Americas, drawing attention to the harmful effects of years of genocide, oppression, and assimilation on the present-day lives of Indigenous people. In Katherena Vermette's 2017 graphic novel *Pemmican Wars* (part one of her *A Girl Called Echo* series), past and present collide as Echo Desjardins, a thirteen-year-old Métis girl who struggles with life in a new adopted family and a new school, discovers her ability to be transported back into the nineteenth century and experience and learn about Métis identity and culture at that moment in history when her people fought against white encroachment of their land. Finally, Cole Pauls's graphic novel *Dakwäkãda Warriors* (2019) is a fun space saga following the protagonists Ts'urk'i (Crow) and Ägay (Wolf), who must defend Nän (the Earth) from the villains Cyber Nàa'i (Bushman) and Space Kwädãy Dän (Long Ago People) (fig. 8.5). The comic is drawn in a striking red-and-black color palette. Pauls pairs a familiar science fiction setting with distinctive Indigenous designs and motifs and organically integrates Southern Tutchone language into his writing. The creator offers a space-age reimagining of the white frontiersmen of old through his wild and wooly antagonists Bushman and Long Ago People; and Crow and Wolf's resistance to the villains' dastardly plan to colonize their homeland reinforces clear messages around sovereignty, resistance, indigeneity, and survivance, which is at the heart of Indigenous comics.

It is important to reaffirm that Indigenous comics are so much more than a narrative form preoccupied with unpicking the harmful representations of the fabled West. However, those Indigenous comics that do engage with the Western's symbols, histories, and myths make an important contribution within the cultural work of the post-Western. The above examples may not be categorized as traditional Westerns, per se; however, each of the above comics in its own way delivers a valuable element of the post-Western, either through the subversion of themes and iconographies of the genre (in the case of *Dakwäkãda Warriors*) or through the reappropriation of historical

FIGURE 8.5. Cole Pauls, *Dakwäkãda Warriors*, Wolfville, NS: Conundrum Press, 2019.

content on which the Western genre is based to illustrate how the legacy of conquest shapes the present and alludes to the scars that remain from North American settler colonialism (as in the case of *The 500 Years of Resistance Comic Book* and *A Girl Called Echo*).

What is significant about these examinations of familiar Western tropes is how they circumvent the Anglo-American hegemonic mastery over the narrative, placing an Indigenous point of view at the fore. In the introduction to *Moonshot: The Indigenous Comics Collection* (2015), Michael Sheyahshe observes this powerful agency. He explains that, given the troubling stereotypes (largely developed through the Western genre) that permeate Native American representation in popular culture, the comics medium "provides a wonderful venue for Indigenous storytellers to shrug off these misrepresentations and amplify our collective voice: here *we* are."[34]

Over the course of this cultural history of the Western genre in American comics storytelling, I have revealed how the medium is a prime example of the American imperial imaginary. Native Americans have been present in the history of comics and cartooning dating back to the nineteenth century, but their representation has been confined to troubled stereotypes, dehumanizing images, and ideologies that diminish their power and humanity. Alongside a few circumscribed roles within the Western, from the wily aggressor to the noble and friendly "savage" who holds an intimate connection with the natural landscape, Indigenous people have largely been subject to their status within the mythology of the West—menacing "savages" that oppose the will of white Americans' Manifest Destiny.[35] The objective of Indigenous comics then, according to King, is "to use popular art media to reclaim Indianness from culture industries and imperial idioms content with, if not intent on, circulating false, hurtful, and dehumanizing representations of American Indians. They affirm indigenous identities and tribal traditions as they put into circulation new representations and alter/native heroes."[36]

Given the medium's status as a hand-drawn form, unlike other popular media comics have provided an accessible and effective mode of expression for Indigenous writers and artists to produce their own narratives. Within these comics, Indigenous storytellers can cast off the colonial baggage of the past and the misrepresentation from within the Western, constructing Indigenous characters devoid of stereotypes and providing a vibrant and textured mode of storytelling to capture the imagination of Native American readers and creators alike.[37]

Women and the Western

The status of women presents another troubling mode of representation in the Western that has been challenged by contemporary comics storytelling. Westerns have often been criticized for carrying misogynistic representations of its female characters and of providing them with circumscribed roles and limited aspirations. For example, Pam Cook and John Cawelti both have catalogued the impoverished range of roles for women in Westerns, which include the mother, the schoolmarm, the saloon girl, and the sex worker.[38] Likewise, Jane Tompkins argues that Westerns corral female ambition and that women characters are often found "cowering in the background," as their main function is to "legitimize the violence men practice in order to protect them."[39]

Over the course of this study, I have singled out examples of strong and empowered women. For example, chapter 6 highlights a spate of independent and often aggressive gunslinging female characters that emerged out of the Cold War milieu in Western comic books. However, because they were created by men, these characters were often highly sexualized. Nevertheless, contemporary comics storytelling has produced a number of female-led, female-produced Western comics that transcend any former troubled representations.

One example is Emma Ríos and Kelly Sue DeConnick's *Pretty Deadly* (from 2013), which blends Western tropes with folklore and mysticism and is rendered in stylized artwork inspired by Japanese samurai films, manga, and surrealism, which gives the storyworld a distinctive aesthetic. The plot largely focuses on Ginny, the Reaper of Vengeance and the daughter of Death, and Sissy, a young girl who takes on the role of Death after Ginny's father is killed. The first arc of the series, across issues #1–5, takes place in the Old West and follows Sissy's discovery of her history and traces her ascendancy in becoming the next iteration of Death. The series is remarkable for its violent shootouts and gory sword-fighting sequences in which Ginny slices at and maims her foes across the comics page. Ayanni Cooper argues that these action scenes are a response to misogyny and violence committed against women and that the excessive violence dealt out by *Pretty Deadly*'s female characters gives them agency. For Cooper, the very accentuation of bloodshed and graphic violence serves to "challenge the ideas of 'acceptable femininity' . . . such as softness and gentleness," and encourages the reader to identify with the more monstrous representations of characters like Ginny in the comic.[40] Furthermore, we can contend that by casting women in the typical gunslinging leading roles in this Western, Ríos and DeConnick disrupt and challenge the conventions of the genre and toy with former perceptions about the circumscribed role of women.

Another example of this break from the codes and conventions of the Western can be found in Lisa Hanawalt's *Coyote Doggirl* (2018), which follows the adventures of the anthropomorphized (part dog–part coyote) Coyote Doggirl and her trusty horse, Red. Hanawalt adds light-hearted elements to her narrative through the one-sided conversations the protagonist has with her horse in a storyworld rendered in bub-blegum pinks and vibrant yellows. However, there is a darkness that imbues the story, and *Coyote Doggirl* reinterprets the familiar West-ern revenge plot, showing the central character's survival of sexual trauma. The story concludes with Coyote Doggirl killing her abuser after being pursued by him throughout the course of the comic.

Hanawalt toys with readerly assumptions about the Western from the outset. On the opening page the artist puts forth the common per-ception about the Western and the American West as a male-dominated space, as we see Coyote Doggirl having to flee after noticing that "guys" are following her on the Western range (fig. 8.6). However, this coding is quickly challenged by Hanawalt, as we see throughout the story that Coyote Doggirl is an adept hunter and a skilled rider, and she boasts a strong survival instinct. She is able to outwit her male pursuers, and her story culminates in the cathartic moment when she finally kills her sexual abuser—shouting, "Don't fuck with meeeeee," as she tri-umphantly rides away.[41]

More recent scholarship has rethought the role of women in the history of Western fiction and film, highlighting the significant con-tributions women have made in authoring the popular West, alongside observing some of the more empowered roles women have previously been cast in.[42] However, earlier scholarship by Cook, Cawelti, and Tompkins certainly highlights a significant gender gap that did pre-vail in the history of the Western. Examples like *Pretty Deadly* and *Coyote Doggirl* reveal how comics can comment critically upon the limited space formerly offered to women in the history of Westerns. Rather than cowering away from the violence in the background of the story (like Tompkins has described), in both examples the creators push back against these passive constructions, showing strong female characters who command much more primacy over the narrative than their male peers.

FIGURE 8.6. Lisa Hanawalt, *Coyote Doggirl*, Montreal: Drawn and Quarterly, 2018.

Likewise, the aforementioned biography *Calamity Jane: The Ca-lamitous Life of Martha Jane Cannary* (2017) shows how the limits of gender in the Western, not least in fiction but as historical subject matter, too, is still being rethought in comics. Nevertheless, produced by two French creators, the graphic biography highlights the different national voices that have added to the rich fabric of the popular West.

Global Perspectives: "Foreign" Western Comics

Writing in 1987, Richard Cracroft observed how "only when confronted by the shock of seeing Westerns in translation do some Americans experience an intellectual epiphany, a realization that Europeans (along with Asians, South Americans, Australians, and nearly everyone else) have distinctive, indigenous, deep-seated literary and cultural traditions regarding life in the American West."[43] In retrospect, the impact of Cracroft's statement proves less revelatory since the "postfrontier" (to borrow Tatum's wording) rethinking of the Western as a global genre in recent decades. Indeed, scholarship has documented the widespread production, circulation, and reception of the Western in a variety of international contexts, placing a particular emphasis on how the distinctly American mythology has been picked up and reshaped in global cinema.[44] The most striking point of reference is probably the Spaghetti Western, the term coined to describe a series of Italian films that were mass-produced across the 1960s and 1970s as the production of American Westerns began to wane. Italian Westerns were heavily inspired by the themes and iconographies of the Hollywood Western, but their anti-imperialist disposition placed them at odds with the myth of the American West. As Christopher Frayling points out: "After the 'rules' of the Italian Western genre had been established . . . a group of writers . . . managed to *use* the genre for overtly political purposes, manipulating audience expectations while putting over their ideas about American interventionism, particularly the role of the CIA in Latin America."[45] When viewed in this light, the Western can be understood as a cultural space that has expanded beyond the confines of American mythology and has readily been co-opted and reimagined by storytellers from outside the borders of the United States.

Sticking with the distinctly European example of the Spaghetti Westerns, the powerful appeal of Western adventure has its roots in the early 1800s, when reprintings of James Fenimore Cooper's *Leatherstocking Tales* were circulated around the continent. However, translations of American-produced fiction soon gave way to a vast array of locally produced frontier adventure stories, authored by popular writers like Germany's Karl May and France's Gustave Aimard, among many others.[46] Notwithstanding earlier instances such as George Catlin's exhibition of his Native American paintings, which toured London and Paris in the late 1830s, Buffalo Bill's Wild West show traveled through vast reaches of Europe in the late 1800s and offered eager audiences their first visual encounter with the mythic West. Kasson describes that the success of the Wild West lay in how it "displayed American military and cultural adventurism in a way that seemed familiar to Europeans at the high tide of imperialism."[47]

The turn of the century brought newfound opportunities in the transnational circulation of the American Western. Indeed, the arrival of mass-entertainment media like comics and film prompted attempts by US producers to export these commodities to untapped markets across Europe throughout the first half of the twentieth century—with varied success. This brief history provides a basis to show how the American Western gradually seeped into the European imagination and how its stories of cowboys and Indians, law and order, conquest and justice, set against lush prairies and commanding desert vistas, held a tremendous appeal to a variety of national audiences.[48] Likewise, it gives better context for the subsequent locally produced interpretations of the genre that came to the fore, such as the spate of Italian Western films, but also the local versions of the Western that have flourished in various national comics traditions, of which little has been written.

The arresting cover image from *Sun* #226 (1953) is a useful start point. It depicts Billy the Kid paired with a Union Jack flag and the caption "Long Live the Queen!" (fig. 8.7). Printed days after Queen Elizabeth II's coronation, the cover captures a jubilant moment in British history. Interestingly, David Huxley's close reading of the "Billy the Kid" series, which appeared in the British comics anthology *Sun* between 1952 and 1959, makes clear how the makeup of the adventure strip took influence from Hollywood Westerns and the popular masked hero the Lone Ranger.[49] However, the odd pairing of the American gunslinger waving a British flag in Queen Elizabeth's honor indicates a more nationalistic reorientation of the legendary Western outlaw. Indeed, the Western was entrenched in the fabric of British boys' comics from the midcentury, with Far West adventure stories about lone gunfighters who must battle for order on the contested frontier making a regular feature in popular anthology titles such as *Sun* (1947–1959), *The Comet* (1946–1959), and *Eagle* (1950–1969), among others.

James Chapman and Nicholas Cull contend that the appeal of Western adventure in British culture related to how closely the genre chimed with films celebrating British Empire: "The two genres share common ground—the narrative of expansion, the taming of the frontier, the clash between civilization and savagery."[50] In fact, the Western was interchangeable with other exciting genres at the time, and

FIGURE 8.7. "Long Live the Queen!," SUN #226, June 6, 1953, Amalgamated Press.

comics anthology titles often paired stories about frontier action with colonial adventures and science fiction. The tone of these stories is typically imperialist (featuring white heroes who conquer exotic landscapes), and they collectively attempt to assimilate ideas about Britain's place on the world stage in the twilight years of empire. Nevertheless, Chris Murray's history of British comics points out that the huge influx of American comics and film (especially after World War II) had an enduring influence on British comics, an observation that suggests that the absorption and internalization of iconographic and thematic elements from the American Western was much more varied and widespread.[51] For example, *The Dandy* (from 1937), features the comedic character Desperate Dan, a hulking cowboy whose storyworld pairs iconography from an imagined Wild West with contemporary Britain. Likewise, British science fiction comic *2000AD* (from 1977)—and particularly the adventures of Judge Dredd, a law enforcement officer in the dystopian futuristic city Mega City One—did little to hide its influence from Hollywood's American West. Brian Ireland observes here a hybridization of the familiar Western genre: Dredd's characterization draws on the figure of the hardened frontier lawman; and the irradiated postnuclear deserts of the Cursed Earth and its bands of hostile mutants reimagine the savage frontier setting of the classic Western—a pleasing genre mashup that is still sold on newsstands today.[52]

The expanding popularity of the Western outside the borders of the United States intensified in the postwar milieu, as American Cold War politics aimed to prop up European allies with financial aid to restore devastated economies, alongside flooding these foreign markets with vast assortments of American products, including popular fiction and films.

The impact was particularly evident upon Franco-Belgian comics. Despite some early forays, as creators confronted their title heroes with characters and settings from the American West (the Fenouillard family in 1889, Bécassine in 1921, and Tintin in 1932), the flurry of frontier adventure comics that emerged after 1945 was indicative of the deluge of American popular culture that blanketed Europe.[53] Comics creators openly embraced and imitated exotic American genres like the Hollywood Western, and stories about cowboys and Indians featured prominently amid a range of different adventure genres in Franco-Belgian boys' comics like *Coq Hardi*, *Le Journal de Tintin*, *Spirou*, and *Vaillant*.[54] Similar to the recoding of the myth of the American West in midcentury British comics, the boom in Franco-Belgian Western comics coincided with two decolonial wars that France fought in Vietnam

(1946–1954) and Algeria (1954–1962).[55] The contested American frontier was reinscribed as a space in which to test imperial ambition, promoting the safeguarding of empire through rugged cowboy heroes who tame savage and inhospitable landscapes.[56]

However, some comics dissented, turning this familiar story on its head. For example, Jijé's *Jerry Spring* (1954–1977) follows an antiracist gunslinger who fights for justice for the oppressed and features a variety of stories concerning Spring mediating peace among Native Americans tribes and Mexican revolutionaries south of the border. Spring's mission to uplift the downtrodden and bring calm between warring parties can be read as much as an antiwar statement amid fraught midcentury geopolitics as a critical comment about the United States. Other postwar series achieved a similar effect but through a more lighthearted approach. Morris's *Lucky Luke* (from 1946) provides a raucous take on the Wild West, following the adventures of a wandering cowboy and his talking horse. Each story takes inspiration from the history and folklore of the West, and the humor often derives from its overt parodying of the American Western. The affectionate ribbing of the Western genre paired with clever allusions to a more critical disposition about its country of origin continues to strike a pleasing chord with readers: a recent album, *Un cow-boy dans le Coton* (2020) by Achdé & Jul, makes comment about race in the United States through a storyline that pits Lucky Luke against the Ku Klux Klan.

The ability of Franco-Belgian Western comics to shift with changing times and speak to the contemporaneous concerns of their readers is evident in a wide array of series. For example, *Blueberry* (1963–2005), by Jean Giraud and Jean-Michel Charlier, follows the adventures of the undisciplined army lieutenant Mike "Blueberry" Donovan across several epochs from post–Civil War history, from the coming of the railroads to the Indian Wars. Unlike the imperialist tone carried in European Western comics from the previous decade, *Blueberry* was instead receptive to the developing radical politics from which it emerged in 1960s France and stood out for its rebellious antihero, experimental artwork, and stark violence that took influence from the bleak frontier setting of Spaghetti Western films.[57] It is possible to chart the robust influence that *Blueberry* has had on the Franco-Belgian Western through the successive titles that followed, which carried a similar style and tone: Hermann's *Comanche* (1972–1983); Michel Blanc-Dumont and Laurence Harlé's *Jonathan Cartland* (1974–1989); Yves Swolfs's *Durango* (from 1980); and Alejandro Jodorowsky and François Boucq's *Bouncer* (from

2002), among others. For creators like Hermann, the American West offered a platform from which to explore themes of violence, pessimism,
Puritanism, and domination.[58] Even more compelling is the fact that
decades later, these creators are still exploring their unique vision of
the American West in the form of comic books (e.g., Hermann's *Duke*
[from 2017] and Swolfs's *Lonesome* [from 2018]). Their ongoing output is
part of a wide range of artistically detailed, well-researched, and gritty
Franco-Belgian Western series that remain popular with readers today.

In a similar manner to earlier titles like *Jerry Spring*, other comics continued to display a sensitivity to race, such as the Swiss comic
Buddy Longway (1972–1987; 2002–2006), which centers on the white
trapper Longway, his Sioux family, and their adventures in the heart
of the American wilderness. Later examples include Swolfs and
Marc-Rénier's harrowing *Black Hills 1890* (from 1999) and TaDuc and
Serge Le Tendre's *Chinaman* (from 1997). Elsewhere, comics have added
elements of humor and parody in a similar vein to series like *Lucky
Luke*: Raoul Cauvin's *Les Tuniques Bleues* (from 1970); Christophe
Blain's *Gus* (2007–2017), which follows a group of bank robbers whose
elaborately planned heists always fall into the backdrop of a story
about their complex love lives; and Kickliy's *Perdy* (from 2018), which
toys with the circumscribed role of women through bawdy humor, following the adventure of the middle-aged, big-bosomed outlaw.

Other European countries boast an equally vibrant heritage of
Western comics. For instance, the Italian industry was punctuated by
a variety of significant Westerns like the horror-infused *Zagor* (from
1961), the historical epic *Storia del West* (1967–1980), and the socially
charged *Ken Parker* (1977–2014). Much like other European comics
traditions, the growth in Italian-produced Westerns was largely fueled
by the postwar infiltration of American products into the region. For
example, the popular cowboy comic *Tex Willer* appeared in 1948 and
was emphatically attuned to the codes and conventions of the American Western formula. However, its setting took influence not from the
dramatic landscapes of the American West but from the mountains,
valleys, and gorges of the Dolomites, Trentino, and Sardinia. As Austin Fisher describes: "On one hand Tex Willer displays a fascination
with the Western myth in postwar Italy, [but] it also betrays a sense,
however subconsciously, of disorientation and a desire to situate this
imaginary 'America' in a familiar locale."[59]

The complex tangling of Italian-inspired vistas and sensational
Wild West action not only offered a form of escapism for a readership

still reeling from the devastation of war after 1945, but interestingly *Tex Willer* had a significant transnational influence abroad. For example, *Sergeant Kirk* (1953–1961) appeared in the pages of the Argentinian comic book *Misterix*. Kirk was known for his unusual egalitarian sensibilities, and he often fights to defend the typically oppressed people from the Western milieu. Designed by an international creative team—written by the Argentinian journalist Héctor Germán Oesterheld and drawn by the Italian emigrant Hugo Pratt—the comic paired exciting American adventure with Italian cultural influences that Pratt had brought with him—*Tex Willer* being one of them.[60]

Comics scholarship has unmasked a wider trajectory for the transnational flow of Western comics around the globe. Sticking with the appropriation of the mythic West in Latin American comics like *Sergeant Kirk*, Christopher Conway's study of Mexican-produced Western comic books identifies how the highly sexed and violent titles from the latter decades of the twentieth century, such as *El libro vaquero* (from 1978) and *Aguila Solitaria* (from 1976), evoked conversations about Mexican national identity, immigration, and race.[61] Elsewhere, in a study of postwar Australian Western comic books, Kevin Patrick observes how the nation was not immune from entering the American cultural sphere of influence after 1945, and the successive importation of American Western films and comic books led to "the fantasy world of the Wild West form[ing] an integral part of daily life for many Australian children." Furthermore, Patrick describes the Australian cultural affinity with the American West stemming from shared experiences of frontier expansion.[62] Paired with a variety of American imports, key Australian-produced Western comic books included the Lone Ranger–inspired cowboy comic *The Lone Avenger* (1946–1957), *El Lobo* (1956–1957), and *Davy Crockett* (1955–1957). Likewise, in earlier research into the South Korean comic *Priest*, I describe how the familiar iconographies of the Western are easily picked up and redeployed through a series that blends the classic Western with gothic horror, influence from computer games, and stylistic elements of the Spaghetti Western, all rendered in an art style redolent of Southeast Asian comics storytelling (fig. 8.8).[63]

The wide-reaching production of the Western in comics from around the globe is in large part owed to the materiality of comics form itself. For global audiences the adventurous American frontier was a distant and exotic landscape that was out of reach. Especially in the twentieth century, for many worldwide consumers the only way to peek into this mythic world was through cinema screens that played

FIGURE 8.8. Min-Woo Hyung, *Priest: A Pale Rider's Chorus*, Los Angeles: Tokyopop, 2003.

Hollywood Western films. Therefore, the pen and paper became powerful tools. John Berger, in his writings on the art of drawing, observes how drawing has a quality of becoming rather than being.[64] This act of drawing—marking out lines on the page—allows the comics artist to easily conjure imaginative storyworlds, and, in relation to the Western, explicitly frame those most intense and exciting aspects from the genre's visual narrative in sequential panels, capturing the imaginations of their local readerships by taking this most American of genres and reinterpreting it in their own designs. In short, comics democratized the American Western for global audiences. When asked about the popularity of the genre outside of the United States, French comics artist Jean Giraud (best known for his Western comic *Blueberry*) explained how "the Western is perceived as something extremely exotic" and that its "story takes place in a society with few rules, and in a framework where there is always more open, unexplored space ahead. This is something very powerful and appealing to a European."[65] The lack of rules and the promise of adventure just on the horizon are only some of the reasons why the genre continues to resonate in international contexts. Such explanations help inform the wide-ranging reappropriations and reimaginings of the genre in global comics storytelling: whether they are recrafting the exciting world of the fabled West for new readerships (e.g., *Tex Willer*), reinterpreting Manifest Destiny mythologies of the American West as a vehicle for critique (e.g., *Jerry Spring*), or reshaping the genre's familiar themes and iconographies in hybrid works (e.g., *2000AD*), to mention only a few possibilities.

Maurice Horn asserts that "the production of the Western comics from foreign lands is immense and far outstrips . . . the American contribution to the field."[66] Perhaps recognizing the impossible task of documenting the phenomenon in its entirety, Horn only devotes one chapter to "foreign" Westerns in his own history of comics and the American West. Likewise, my own brief historical account here serves as an introductory overview of the subject rather than a comprehensive documentation. Indeed, it omits a wide array of critical titles and national traditions of Far West adventure comics, and it merely touches on the transnational travel and influence of Western comics: from how certain titles have been translated and circulated around the globe (e.g., *Lucky Luke*) to how certain series have inspired and influenced other "foreign" Western comics (e.g., *Blueberry*). Instead, this overview of the Western in global comics intersects with this closing chapter's concern with the postmodern rethinking of the genre, which includes a turn toward the transnationalism of the American West. Campbell roundly asserts that the Western was "already always transnational."[67] However, given the fact that Western studies and comics studies have done little to unpack the massive global canon of Western comics and their continued production and circulation in various transcultural and transnational contexts, it would suggest that this is one area of study that warrants further exploration.[68]

End of the Road . . .

The chapter opened with Pauline Kael's declaration of the death of the Western genre—a call that probably felt very plausible within the surrounding milieu of 1970s America. However, with hindsight this observation proves wholly inaccurate; instead, the conceptualization of the Western as a dead genre provides a useful launchpad from which to consider the genre in different contexts: from postmodern stories that build on the dilapidated ruins of the Old West (e.g., *Preacher*) to new voices that recast the genre (e.g., the wide array of Indigenous comics) to a shift in focus toward the global expansion of the American Western.

The volume, diversity, and vibrancy of the stories discussed in this concluding chapter demonstrate the power and continuing appeal of the Western in contemporary comics storytelling and indeed popular culture more broadly. Part of the great thing about this moment in comics history is seeing how the medium continues to innovate and challenge the Western, but also marking how the genre continues to persist in contemporary culture. The longevity of the Western relates to how the genre has epitomized the American Dream, speaking to audiences about the merits of hard work, determination, and true grit to attain success. Given the fictive West's roots in the very development of the United States, its stories of an ascendent civilization's quest for progress and order in an untamed and boundless wilderness way out West have helped Americans not only through periods of great hardship and anxiety but also in times of peace and prosperity. While some of the Western's elements have been rethought and have changed over time, the genre's penchant for adventure and colorful characters and its grandiose landscapes have continued to offer a unique platform from which to explore American myth and identity and promote traditional ideals and values, but also to mobilize counternarratives that critique and subvert the contemporaneous political milieu.

From its beginnings in folklore to its transformation into a narrative genre and mythical vehicle for reflecting contemporaneous concerns and values, the Western has remained a powerful force in popular culture precisely for its ability to entertain and inspire its audience. Western comics ostensibly told simple morality tales about the march of progress and of good triumphing over evil, but beneath this lay complex and nuanced psychological narratives that embodied mythic expressions of their given publication context. Through the continued biweekly and monthly printing of Western comics, the medium could offer much more dynamic interactions with shifts in national mood and posture than other versions of the Western from popular culture. Likewise, comics' ability to go below the critical radar has allowed creators to steadily provide subversive content and dissenting representations of the Western that reach an alternative (and primarily younger) reader. Moreover, given the hand-drawn nature of the form, time and again the comics medium has managed to transform and reimagine the genre in some striking and unusual ways.

On the one hand, the image of the Western has remained unchanged in over a century. But on the other hand, the genre has regularly experienced transformations that permit it to maintain its compelling hold on audiences. The history of the Western in American comics is a brilliant exemplar of this evolution as it experienced continual shifts since the late 1800s. The important relationship of history and myth at work within the genre has allowed its narratives to reflect not only a given era but also the different attitudes that exist within such time frames. The first part of this book outlined the development of the Western genre first in the fledgling illustrated press and later in the developing newspaper comic strip medium. It clarified the various influences (from popular fiction to films) that coalesced to inform comics' typical brand of exciting Western adventure fiction by the late 1930s. Equally, it traced the shifts in the representation of the Western in the very early stages of the genre's formation. In its initial form in magazine cartoons from the nineteenth century, the word-and-image medium played a vital role in reinforcing the American mission of Manifest Destiny through reportage of the ongoing Indian Wars, normalizing US acts of conquest and genocide. However, this changed with the closing of the frontier at the turn of the century. Comic strips at once captured the sense of loss for a way of life that had vanished (like other forms of popular culture such as fiction, film, and painting), but did so in their own unique style through stories about present-day tourist encounters with the mythic West.

The second part of the book revealed a much more politically engaged take on the Western genre. Comic books, like other forms of popular culture, took up the Western as an expression of Cold War culture, utilizing the righteous and imperialist stories of frontier conquest to help promote new ideological rationales of exceptionalism, hegemony, and consensus after 1945. The Western genre's association with such politics became its own undoing, as US Cold War foreign policy soured during the Vietnam War in the 1960s and 1970s. The Western myth of conquest ruptured under a backlash against the genre in popular culture, and a host of acerbic retellings of the Western emerged. Rather than perish, new life has sprouted from the remains of this ostensibly dead genre, and contemporary comics storytelling provides a platform for a whole host of new voices to narrate the American West and reimagine the Western genre once more.

At the outset, this book was driven by a contention laid out in scholarly writing that called for a broadening of focus in comics studies and Western studies to look at those texts that fall outside the margins of scholarship. Western comics are one such area—the medium's omission formed a large chasm in the wider corpus. This book serves as just one addition in helping to fill this gap, and hopefully its focus on comics contributes to shifting the way in which scholars consider the Western and its significance to American society, providing a novel interpretation of a familiar chronology (that is, the history of the Western in and around the twentieth century). However, there is more work to be done. This book was never intended to be all-encompassing, and this cultural history of the Western genre in American comics should be read as a useful starting point into a rich area of study that has been largely overlooked. Indeed, some areas for further research have been outlined in this concluding chapter, from the vast culture of Western comics that exists in a multitude of global comics traditions to the development of new genres of storytelling, such as the rich canon of Indigenous comics that reclaims the representation of Native American people and cultures from the Western genre. Throughout this study I have indicated the crucial contributions that Western comics have made to the discussions about the genre, whether by extending current ways of thinking about the Western or by developing new ones. In mythical terms, the Western narrative from its origins served to address the transition from wilderness to modern civilization in America. However, this study has revealed how the history of Western popular culture in comics is much more transformative than its initial subject matter; how it was stretched in some unusual directions and was even taken beyond the borders of its country of origin. In short, the Western in its purest form is a story of odyssey. *Redrawing the Western* demonstrates how this odyssey is not only found in the pages of Western comics and their thrilling stories of conflict and adventure but is also expressed through the expansive and ever-evolving history of the genre itself.

ACKNOWLEDGMENTS

I began research for this book over ten years ago, and in the years since I have benefitted from the advice and guidance of a wide array of people. Foremost I must thank David Huxley and Joan Ormrod, who inspired and nurtured my interest in comics studies and the American West way back when I was a directionless film studies undergrad at Manchester Metropolitan University. Over the years they have been a tremendous support in all my academic endeavors. In equal measure, I owe a huge debt of gratitude to my former PhD supervisor, Chis Murray, who has been a brilliant source of inspiration and guidance during the course of writing my doctoral thesis. This book is a revision of parts of my doctoral thesis undertaken at the University of Dundee, and I think the finished manuscript and my ideas within would be much worse for wear without him. The Department of Humanities at the University of Dundee provided me with funding to both study and attend conferences, without which I would not have been able to complete the research presented here. I must also thank staff from the University of Dundee's English faculty for their enthusiasm for my research and for offering different perspectives on my work: in particular, Daniel Cook, Nicole Devarenne, Brian Hoyle, Phillip Vaughan, and Keith Williams. In addition, thanks to the comics studies community at the University of Dundee: Hailey Austin, Madeline Gangnes, Andrew Godfrey, Damon Herd, Ollie Hicks, Kelly Kanayama, Stephen O'Donnell, Megan Sinclair, and Jules Valera, among others.

Over the years I have been fortunate to have met many different people who have taken the time to brainstorm ideas, read drafts, offer critical feedback, share words of encouragement, offer intel, or otherwise stand as inspiring role models and mentors. Thanks to, among many others: Casey Brienza, Rikke Platz Cortsen, Eliza Bourque

Dandridge, Harriet Earle, Charlotte Johanne Fabricius, Mel Gibson, Ian Gordon, Paul Gravett, Maggie Gray, Ian Hague, Ian Horton, Hattie Kennedy, Pascal Lefèvre, Anna Madill, John McShane, Nina Mickwitz, John Miers, Mihaela Precup, Julia Round, Roger Sabin, Joe Sutliff Sanders, Nicola Streeten, Lise Tannahill, Laurike in 't Veld, and Paul Williams. I am also grateful for the work, guidance, and support of the team at the University of Texas Press who have made the publication process an enjoyable one (Danni Bens, Jim Burr, Lynne Ferguson, Mia Uribe Kozlovsky, Leslie Tingle, and others), as well for the helpful feedback I received from the reviewers of my book manuscript: Christopher Conway and two other anonymous readers. Their opinions and suggestions on how to improve the manuscript were extremely beneficial.

The life of a scholar can at times be a quite lonely and insular one, especially when you're sat at your desk writing for days on end. So a special thanks to all my friends for keeping me grounded in the real world over the years: Holly Brown, Sophie Carnegie, Selina Cole, Ella Condron, Hayley Cunningham, Adam Grant, Berro Griffiths, Sophie Helps, Martin Jackson, Katie Knight, Ashley Long, Emma Morrow, Sarah Oldfield, Chris Twigg, and Meg Wilson. Also a big shout-out to my family pub quiz team—Thursday nights at the Oak were really important to me when I was writing up my PhD: Daniel Barlow, Sue Barlow, Sue Beesley, Jean Davies, Jamie Viggers, Julie Viggers, and our team's matriarch, big bad Maureen (may she rest in peace).

To Suz and Ian, I'm so lucky to have such amazing parents, I truly can't thank you enough for everything.

And finally, thanks to Peter, my steadfast companion who stuck by me as I navigated the dusty trails of academia. I look forward to our future adventures together.

NOTES

Introduction. Rethinking the Western Genre through Comics

1. Jim Kitses, *Horizons West: Directing the Western from John Ford to Clint Eastwood*, new ed. (London: BFI Publishing, 2004), 8.
2. Earl Pomeroy, "Rediscovering the West," *American Quarterly* 12 (1960): 30.
3. Richard Slotkin, *Regeneration through Violence: The Mythology of the American Frontier, 1600–1860* (Middletown, CT: Wesleyan University Press, 1973), 18.
4. Robert J. Higgs and Ralph L. Turner, *The Cowboy Way: The Western Leader in Film, 1945–1995* (Santa Barbara, CA: Praeger, 1999), xix.
5. For an overview of popular Western fiction, see Christine Bold, *Selling the Wild West: Popular Western Fiction, 1860 to 1960* (Bloomington: Indiana University Press, 1987). Regarding the painted West, and particularly the important contributions made by Frederic Remington and Charles Russell from this specific era (post-1865), see Brian W. Dippie, *Remington and Russell: The Sid Richardson Collection* (Austin: University of Texas Press, 1994). For a detailed history of Buffalo Bill's frontier performances, see Joy S. Kasson, *Buffalo Bill's Wild West: Celebrity, Memory, and Popular History* (New York: Hill and Wang, 2000).
6. Frederick Jackson Turner, "The Significance of the Frontier in American History" (1893), reprinted in Frederick Jackson Turner, *The Frontier in American History* (New York: Holt, 1920), 4.
7. John Belton, *American Cinema/American Culture*, 4th ed. (New York: McGraw Hill, 2013), 260.
8. Stephen McVeigh, *The American Western* (Edinburgh: Edinburgh University Press, 2007), 155. Regarding film, the migration of the Western into other genres after 1970 is discussed in Geoff King, *Spectacular Narratives: Hollywood in the Age of the Blockbuster* (London: I. B. Tauris, 2000), 1–69; Patrick McGee, *From "Shane" to "Kill Bill": Rethinking the Western* (Oxford: Blackwell, 2007), 235–244. In relation to the Western in comics, see William Grady, "Western Comics," in *The Routledge Companion to Comics*, ed. Frank Bramlett, Roy T. Cook, and Aaron Meskin (London: Routledge, 2016), 164–173.
9. Henry Nash Smith, *Virgin Land: The American West as Symbol and Myth* (Cambridge, MA: Harvard University Press, [1950] 1978), 91.

10. Richard Slotkin, *Gunfighter Nation: The Myth of the Frontier in Twentieth-Century America* (Norman: University of Oklahoma Press, [1992] 1998), 5.

11. Edwin Fussell, *Frontier: American Literature and the American West* (Princeton, NJ: Princeton University Press, 1965); J. Golden Taylor and Thomas J. Lyon, eds., *A Literary History of the American West*, sponsored by the Western Literature Association (Fort Worth: Texas Christian University Press, 1987); Thomas J. Lyon et al., eds., *Updating the Literary West*, sponsored by the Western Literature Association (Fort Worth: Texas Christian University Press, 1999); Nicolas S. Witschi, ed., *A Companion to the Literature and Culture of the American West* (Chichester, UK: Wiley-Blackwell, 2011); Susan Kollin, ed., *A History of Western American Literature* (Cambridge: Cambridge University Press, 2015).

12. While scholarship on Western films is vast, some notable cultural histories include John H. Lenihan, *Showdown: Confronting Modern America in the Western Film* (Urbana: University of Illinois Press, 1985); Slotkin, *Gunfighter Nation*; Michael Coyne, *The Crowded Prairie: American National Identity in the Hollywood Western* (London: I. B. Tauris, 1998). Equally, more recent cultural histories illustrate a continued interest in the interconnections between the genre and American history: see, for example, McVeigh, *American Western*; McGee, *From "Shane" to "Kill Bill"*; Mary Lea Bandy and Kevin Stoehr, *Ride, Boldly Ride: The Evolution of the American Western* (Berkeley: University of California Press, 2012); Richard Aquila, *The Sagebrush Trail: Western Movies and Twentieth-Century America* (Tucson: University of Arizona Press, 2015).

13. J. Fred MacDonald, *Who Shot the Sheriff? The Rise and Fall of the Television Western* (New York: Praeger, 1987). More contemporary considerations can be found in Andrew Patrick Nelson, ed., *Contemporary Westerns: Film and Television since 1990* (Lanham, MD: Scarecrow Press, 2013).

14. William H. Goetzmann and William N. Goetzmann, *The West of the Imagination*, 2nd ed. (Norman: University of Oklahoma Press, 2009).

15. Paul Reddin, *Wild West Shows* (Urbana: University of Illinois Press, 1999); Roger A. Hall, *Performing the American Frontier, 1870–1906* (Cambridge: Cambridge University Press, 2006).

16. Beth E. Levy, *Frontier Figures: American Music and the Mythology of the American West* (Berkeley: University of California Press, 2012).

17. Notwithstanding Maurice Horn's popular illustrated history: *Comics of the American West* (South Hackensack, NJ: Stoeger Publishing, 1978). While Horn provides a useful overview of Western genre comics, the work lacks a theoretical framework for understanding the social processes that inform and work within Western comics. Equally, it does not offer a clear interpretation or understanding of why certain Western comics emerged and resonated within specific time frames. In addition, some work has been done on the presentation of the cowboy hero in postwar comics from the United States, Britain, and France (David Huxley's short monograph *Lone Heroes and the Myth of the American West in Comic Books, 1945–1962* [Cham: Palgrave Macmillan, 2018]). Largely, the limited scholarship that does consider the Western in comics does so in relation to other genres. For works discussing the blending of Westerns and superheroes, see Lorrie Palmer, "'Le Western Noir': *The Punisher* as Revisionist Superhero Western," in Terrence R. Wandtke, ed., *The Amazing Transforming Superhero!* (Jefferson, NC: McFarland,

2007), 192–208; Theo Finigan, "'To the Stables, Robin!': Regenerating the Frontier in Frank Miller's *Batman: The Dark Knight Returns,*" *ImageTexT* 5, no. 1 (2010): n.p.; and Chad A. Barbour, *From Daniel Boone to Captain America: Playing Indian in American Popular Culture* (Jackson: University Press of Mississippi, 2016). For the blending of Westerns with science fiction and horror themes in comics, see the various essays in Cynthia Miller and A. Bowdoin Van Riper, eds., *Undead in the West II: They Just Keep Coming* (Lanham, MD: Scarecrow Press, 2013).

18. Smith, *Virgin Land*, 91; Christine Bold, "Malaeska's Revenge; or, The Dime Novel Tradition in Popular Fiction," in *Wanted Dead or Alive: The American West in Popular Culture*, ed. Richard Aquila (Urbana: University of Illinois Press, 1996), 21–42.

19. Horn, *Comics of the American West*, 215.

20. Jack Jackson, "The Good, the Bad, the Foreign," *Comics Journal*, no. 144 (1991): 52.

21. Bold, "Malaeska's Revenge," 35.

22. Richard Slotkin, *The Fatal Environment: The Myth of the Frontier in the Age of Industrialization, 1800–1890* (New York: Atheneum, 1985), 23–24.

23. Slotkin, *Fatal Environment*, 28–29.

24. John G. Cawelti, *Adventure, Mystery, and Romance* (Chicago: University of Chicago Press, 1976), 6.

25. See, for instance, William W. Savage, *Comic Books and America, 1945–1954* (Norman: University of Oklahoma Press, 1990); Bradford W. Wright, *Comic Book Nation: The Transformation of Youth Culture in America* (Baltimore: Johns Hopkins University Press, 2001); James Chapman, *British Comics: A Cultural History* (London: Reaktion Books, 2011).

26. Wright, *Comic Book Nation*, xv, xiv.

27. Roland Barthes, *Mythologies*, trans. Annette Lavers (London: Cape, 1972), 11.

28. One of the clearest applications of this approach can be found in Christopher Murray, "The Pleasures of Persuasion: Comics and Propaganda," in *Critical Approaches to Comics and Graphic Novels*, ed. Matthew Smith and Randy Duncan (New York: Routledge, 2011), 129–141.

29. Scott McCloud, *Understanding Comics: The Invisible Art* (New York: Harper Perennial, 1994); Thierry Groensteen, *The System of Comics* (Jackson: University Press of Mississippi, [1999] 2007).

30. Corey Creekmur, "The American Western in Film," in *A Companion to the Literature and Culture of the American West*, ed. Nicolas S. Witschi (Chichester, UK: Wiley-Blackwell, 2011), 407.

31. Jon Tuska, *The Filming of the West* (New York: Doubleday, 1976), xviii.

32. Douglas Pye, "Introduction: Criticism and the Western," in *The Movie Book of the Western*, ed. Ian Cameron and Douglas Pye (London: Studio Vista, 1996), 10–11.

33. Horn, *Comics of the American West*, 137.

34. Neil Campbell, *The Rhizomatic West: Representing the American West in a Transnational, Global, Media Age* (Lincoln: University of Nebraska Press, 2008), 41.

35. Andrew Patrick Nelson, *Still in the Saddle: The Hollywood Western, 1969–1980* (Norman: University of Oklahoma Press, 2015), 7.

36. Bart Beaty and Benjamin Woo, *The Greatest Comic Book of All Time: Symbolic Capital and the Field of American Comic Books* (Basingstoke, UK: Palgrave Macmillan, 2016), 95; Marc Singer, *Breaking the Frames: Populism and Prestige in Comics Studies* (Austin: University of Texas Press, 2019).

Chapter 1. "Print the Legend"

1. Deborah A. Carmichael, *The Landscape of Hollywood Westerns: Ecocriticism in an American Film Genre* (Salt Lake City: University of Utah Press, 2006), 2–3.
2. Bold, "Malaeska's Revenge," 22.
3. For more details about dime novel production, plot formulas, and popular Western fiction's significance to nineteenth-century American society, see Smith, *Virgin Land*, 90–111; Michael Denning, *Mechanic Accents: Dime Novels and Working-Class Culture in America* (London: Verso, 1987); Bold, "Malaeska's Revenge," 21–42; Slotkin, *Gunfighter Nation*, 125–155.
4. For a history of popular Western fiction, see Bold, *Selling the Wild West*.
5. Kasson, *Buffalo Bill's Wild West*, 255–263; Bandy and Stoehr, *Ride, Boldly Ride*, 5, 10.
6. For a history of nineteenth-century pictorial reportage, see Joshua Brown, *Beyond the Lines: Pictorial Reporting, Everyday Life, and the Crisis of Gilded-Age America* (Berkeley: University of California Press, 2002).
7. M. L. Carlebach, *The Origins of Photojournalism in America* (Washington, DC: Smithsonian Institution Press, 1992); Patricia Mainardi, *Another World: Nineteenth-Century Illustrated Print Culture* (New Haven, CT: Yale University Press, 2017), 114–115.
8. A range of magazine cartoons and illustrations that detail life in the nineteenth-century American West, particularly a large collection from *Harper's Weekly*, can be found in John Grafton, *The American West in the Nineteenth Century* (New York: Dover, 1993).
9. Elisabeth El Refaie, "Metaphor in Political Cartoons: Exploring Audience Responses," in *Multimodal Metaphor*, ed. C. Forceville and E. Urios-Aparisi (Berlin: De Gruyter, 2009), 175–176.
10. R. L. Craig, "Fact, Public Opinion, and Persuasion: The Rise of the Visual in Journalism and Advertising," in *Picturing the Past: Media, History, and Photography*, ed. B. Brennan and H. Hardt (Urbana: University of Illinois Press, 1999), 47.
11. Jodi Byrd, *The Transit of Empire: Indigenous Critiques of Colonialism* (Minneapolis: University of Minnesota Press, 2011), xx.
12. John M. Coward, "Making Sense of Savagery: Native American Cartoons in *The Daily Graphic*," *Visual Communication Quarterly* 19, no. 4 (2012): 209–210.
13. Russell notes that the *Daily Graphic*'s speedy publication of the Custer image beat major competitors like *Harper's Weekly* by ten days. Don Russell, *Custer's Last* (Fort Worth, TX: Amon Carter Museum of Western Art, 1968).
14. William de la Montagne Cary, "The Battle on the Little Big Horn River—The Death Struggle of General Custer," *Daily Graphic*, July 19, 1876, 122.
15. Using Cary's magazine cartoon as a starting point, Dippie has provided a much more detailed discussion of the various attempts to capture Custer's Last Stand in paintings. See Brian W. Dippie, *Custer's Last Stand: The Anatomy of an American Myth* (Lincoln: University of Nebraska Press, [1976] 1994), 32–61.
16. Gerald Vizenor, *Manifest Manners: Postindian Warriors of Survivance* (Hanover, NH: Wesleyan University Press, 1994), 5–6.

17. Aileen Moreton-Robinson, *Sovereign Subjects: Indigenous Sovereignty Matters* (Crows Nest, NSW: Allen & Unwin, 2007), 89, 95.

18. Byrd, *Transit of Empire*, xviii.

19. Livingston Hopkins, "The True Solution of the Indian Problem," *Daily Graphic*, July 8, 1876.

20. Patricia Nelson Limerick, *The Legacy of Conquest: The Unbroken Past of the American West* (New York: Norton, 1988), 197–198.

21. Thomas Nast, "Patience until the Indian Is Civilized—So to Speak," *Harper's Weekly*, December 28, 1878.

22. See discussions in Roger A. Fischer, *Them Damned Pictures: Explorations in American Political Cartoon Art* (North Haven, CT: Archon, 1996), 101–120; John M. Coward, *The Newspaper Indian: Native American Identity in the Press, 1820–90* (Urbana: University of Illinois Press, 1999); Coward, "Making Sense of Savagery," 200–215.

23. Coward, "Making Sense of Savagery," 212.

24. Mainardi, *Another World*, 119.

25. McCloud, *Understanding Comics*, 8.

26. Robert C. Harvey, "How Comics Came to Be: Through the Juncture of Word and Image from Magazine Gag Cartoons to Newspaper Strips, Tools for Critical Appreciation plus Rare Seldom Witnessed Historical Facts," in *A Comics Studies Reader*, ed. Jeet Heer and Kent Worcester (Jackson: University Press of Mississippi, 2009), 25–45.

27. Harvey, "How Comics Came to Be," 29.

28. Harvey, "How Comics Came to Be," 38–39.

29. Charles Hatfield's extensive reading of comics form develops and unites these various processes. Hatfield argues, quite like Harvey, that the tensions between word and image are a fundamental element in comics form. However, this visual-verbal interplay is interdependent with other tensions in the comic that require a reader's participation in creating signification. These include the tension between the singular image and the image-in-series and between narrative sequence and the broader comics page. Charles Hatfield, *Alternative Comics: An Emerging Literature* (Jackson: University Press of Mississippi, 2005), 36–65.

30. For instance, Gordon and Gardner have both closely analyzed the cartoons of Franklin Morris Howarth from magazines of the early 1890s (just before comic strips emerged in American newspapers), who narrowed the relationship of word and image and placed increased emphasis on sequential images, characters, and narratives. See Ian Gordon, *Comic Strips and Consumer Culture, 1890–1945* (Washington, DC: Smithsonian Institution Press, 1998), 20–24; Jared Gardner, *Projections: Comics and the History of Twenty-First-Century Storytelling* (Stanford, CA: Stanford University Press, 2012), 7–10.

31. Roger Sabin, *Adult Comics: An Introduction* (London: Routledge, 1993), 133–143.

32. Fischer, *Them Damned Pictures*, 118.

33. Fischer, *Them Damned Pictures*, 120.

34. Turner, "Significance of the Frontier," 1–38.

35. Gerald D. Nash, *Creating the West: Historical Interpretation 1890–1990* (Albuquerque: University of New Mexico Press, 1993), 4.

Chapter 2. The Spectacle of the Southwest

1. William Bloodworth, "Writers of the Purple Sage: Novelists and the American West," in *Wanted Dead or Alive: The American West in Popular Culture,* ed. Richard Aquila (Urbana: University of Illinois Press, 1996), 45.
2. Pascal Lefèvre, "Newspaper Strips," in *The Routledge Companion to Comics,* ed. Frank Bramlett, Roy T. Cook, and Aaron Meskin (London: Routledge, 2016), 17.
3. Thomas Schatz, *Hollywood Genres* (New York: Random House, 1981), 46.
4. Scott Simmon, *The Invention of the Western Film: A Cultural History of the Genre's First Half-Century* (Cambridge: Cambridge University Press, 2003), 46.
5. Gregory S. Jay, "'White Man's Book No Good': D. W. Griffith and the American Indian," *Cinema Journal* 39, no. 4 (2000): 6.
6. Bold, "Malaeska's Revenge," 34.
7. Richard Schickel, *D. W. Griffith: An American Life* (New York: Simon and Schuster, 1984), 139.
8. Bandy and Stoehr, *Ride, Boldly Ride,* 13.
9. Simmon, *Invention of the Western Film,* 18.
10. Jean-Paul Gabilliet points to varying proto–comic books that marked this century, from a translation of Rodolphe Töpffer's work, *The Adventures of Mr. Obadiah Oldbuck* (1842) to the American-produced comic *Journey to the Gold Diggins by Jeremiah Saddlebags* (1849). In contrast, Sabin suggests that much of the early comics material was reserved for the humorous cartoon-based magazines of the latter decades of the century (like those discussed in the previous chapter). Jean-Paul Gabilliet, *Of Comics and Men: A Cultural History of American Comic Books,* trans. Bart Beaty and Nick Nguyen (Jackson: University Press of Mississippi, 2010), 3–4; Sabin, *Adult Comics,* 133.
11. George Juergens, *Joseph Pulitzer and the New York World* (Princeton, NJ: Princeton University Press, 1966), 94.
12. On the history of the American comic strip, see Gordon, *Comic Strips and Consumer Culture;* Robert C. Harvey, *The Art of the Funnies: An Aesthetic History* (Jackson: University Press of Mississippi, 1994); Judith O'Sullivan, *The Great American Comic Strip: One Hundred Years of Cartoon Art* (Boston: Bullfinch, 1990); M. Thomas Inge, *Comics as Culture* (Jackson: University Press of Mississippi, 1990); Brian Walker, *The Comics before 1945* (New York: Harry N. Abrams, 2004).
13. David Hajdu, *The Ten-Cent Plague: The Great Comic Book Scare and How It Changed America* (New York: Farrar, Straus and Giroux, 2008), 11.
14. Gardner, *Projections,* 9–10.
15. Gordon, *Comic Strips and Consumer Culture,* 6.
16. Sabin and Walker provide overviews of the large set of homelife comic strips that emerged on the back of *Hogan's Alley.* See Roger Sabin, *Comics, Comix and Graphic Novels: A History of Comic Art* (London: Phaidon, 1996), 24; Walker, *Comics before 1945,* 74–75, 83, 116–117, 124–129, 162–163.
17. Nash, *Creating the West,* 198.
18. Horn, *Comics of the American West,* 20.
19. "Hyperreality" is a term developed by Jean Baudrillard that refers to the notion that media simulations and reality coincide to such a degree that the "real" has disappeared. "Reality" has become virtual, or rather the virtual has taken the

place of the real, which can no longer be experienced except through simulations. Christopher Butler, *Postmodernism: A Very Short Introduction* (New
York: Oxford University Press, 2002), 112–114.

20. Horn, *Comics of the American West*, 19.
21. This thesis is more thoroughly explored in Katherine Roeder, *Wide Awake
in Slumberland: Fantasy, Mass Culture, and Modernism in the Art of Winsor
McCay* (Jackson: University Press of Mississippi, 2014).
22. Winsor McCay, *Little Nemo in Slumberland*, February 21, 1909, reprinted in
McCay, *The Complete Little Nemo in Slumberland*, vol. 3, *1908–1910* (London:
Titan, 1990).
23. McCay, *Little Nemo in Slumberland*, August 28, 1910.
24. Patricia Nelson Limerick, "Seeing and Being Seen: Tourism in the American
West," in *Over the Edge: Remapping the American West*, ed. Valerie J. Matsumoto
and Blake Allmendinger (Berkeley: University of California Press, 1999), 19.
25. Limerick, "Seeing and Being Seen," 21.
26. Marguerite S. Shaffer, " 'The West Plays West': Western Tourism and the Landscape of Leisure," in *A Companion to the American West*, ed. William Deverell
(Oxford: Blackwell, 2004), 377.
27. Shaffer, "West Plays West," 378–379.
28. Shaffer, "West Plays West," 380.
29. See Earl Pomeroy, *In Search of the Golden West: The Tourist in Western America* (Lincoln: University of Nebraska Press, 1990); Leah Dilworth, *Imagining
Indians in the Southwest: Persistent Visions of a Primitive Past* (Washington,
DC: Smithsonian Institution Press, 1996), 77–124; Hal K. Rothman, *Devil's Bargains: Tourism in the Twentieth-Century American West* (Lawrence: University
Press of Kansas, 1998); Shaffer, "West Plays West," 375–389.
30. Pomeroy, *In Search of the Golden West*, 225.
31. Shaffer, "West Plays West," 385.
32. Gardner, *Projections*, 15 (emphasis in original).
33. For an overview of Swinnerton's life and artwork, see Gary Fillmore, *Desert
Horizons: Images of James Swinnerton's Southwest* (Cave Creek, AZ: Blue Coyote Gallery, 2009).
34. Michael Tisserand, *Krazy: George Herriman; A Life in Black and White* (New
York: HarperCollins, 2016), 312–313.
35. James Swinnerton, interview with Master Sergeant Percy Brown Jr. for Armed
Forces Radio, 1963, accessed November 4, 2012, https://www.youtube.com/watch
?v=eeNKnxeR_mM.
36. James Swinnerton, "Jimmy—He Smokes the Pipe of Peace," *Seattle Times*, May
18, 1913.
37. James Swinnerton, "Jimmy—He's Among the Navajos!," March 23, 1913.
38. Swinnerton, "Jimmy—He's Among the Navajos!"
39. Between 1914 and 1917, the production of automobiles in the United States soared
from a little over half a million to almost two million. John B. Rae, *The American
Automobile: A Brief History* (Chicago: University of Chicago Press, 1965). Macy
and Bonnemaison look at the popular activity of car camping in the range of
national parks and across the American countryside in the early decades of the
twentieth century, suggesting it "touched a deep chord in the American psyche"

and "corresponded to a pioneer spirit of individualism that evoked the covered wagon and outdoor life." Christine Macy and Sarah Bonnemaison, *Architecture and Nature: Creating the American Landscape* (London: Routledge, 2003), 114.

40. For instance, King made a cross-country trip to Yellowstone National Park in 1922, which would later be replicated in *Gasoline Alley* through his comic strip characters who took the same journey.

41. Jeet Heer, introduction to Frank O. King, *Walt & Skeezix: 1923–1924* (Montreal: Drawn & Quarterly Books, 2006), 9.

42. Carolyn O'Bagy Davis and Harvey Leake, *Kayenta and Monument Valley* (Charleston, SC: Arcadia Publishing, 2010), 64–65; Tisserand, *Krazy*, 284–286.

43. Shaffer, "West Plays West," 377.

44. Frank King, *Gasoline Alley*, June 21 and 30, 1924, reprinted in Frank King, *Walt & Skeezix (1923–1924)* (Montreal: Drawn & Quarterly Books, 2006), n.p.

45. Frank King, *Gasoline Alley*, July 3, 1924, reprinted in King, *Walt & Skeezix: 1923–1924*.

46. Patrick McDonnell, Georgia Riley De Havenon, and Karen O'Connell, *Krazy Kat: The Comic Art of George Herriman* (New York: Abrams, 1986), 71.

47. Tisserand, *Krazy*, 293, 277–278, 297–301.

48. Tisserand, *Krazy*, 289, 295.

49. Herriman quoted in McDonnell et al., *Krazy Kat*, 68–69.

50. Shaffer, "West Plays West," 385.

51. A concise but substantive list of references to Navajo customs and culture in *Krazy Kat* can be found in Daniel Stein, "The Comic Modernism of George Herriman," in *Crossing Boundaries in Graphic Narrative: Essays on Forms, Series and Genres*, ed. Jake Jakaitis and James F. Wurtz (Jefferson, NC: McFarland, 2012), 60–61; Tisserand, *Krazy*, 287–288.

52. This included the painters Emil Bistram, Ernest Blumenschein, John Marin, and B. J. O. Nordfeldt (among others); and the writers Mary Austin, Max Weber, and Carl Sandburg (to name but a few). A fantastic overview of modernist arts cultures' use of, and inspiration from, Native American arts and crafts can be found in Dilworth, *Imagining Indians in the Southwest*, 173–210.

53. Dilworth, *Imagining Indians in the Southwest*, 187, 203.

54. Dilworth, *Imagining Indians in the Southwest*, 199; Marianna Torgovnick, *Gone Primitive: Savage Intellects, Modern Lives* (Chicago: University of Chicago Press, 1990), 151.

55. A brilliant account of how modernism inspired the creation of *Krazy Kat* can be found in Tisserand, *Krazy*, 237–244. See also Stein, "Comic Modernism of George Herriman," 40–70.

56. Tisserand, *Krazy*, 299.

57. Bloodworth, "Riders of the Purple Sage," 45; Gordon, *Comic Strips and Consumer Culture*, 6; and Shaffer, "West Plays West," 377.

58. Renato Rosaldo, "Imperialist Nostalgia," *Representations* 26 (Spring 1989): 107–122.

Chapter 3. Saddling Up in the Slump

1. Goulart provides a concise account of *White Boy*'s tumultuous publication history before being dropped by the *Chicago Tribune* in 1935. See Ron Goulart,

The Adventurous Decade: Comic Strips in the Thirties (New York: Arlington House, 1975), 191–192.

2. Walker, *Comics before 1945*, 116, 185.

3. The etymology of the word "comics" stems from the comical drawings and amusing short essays and droll verse offered in *Life, Puck,* and *Judge*—dubbed "comic weeklies." See Harvey, "How Comics Came to Be," 36.

4. Pascal Lefèvre, "Newspaper Strips," 18.

5. Goulart, *Adventurous Decade.*

6. Les Daniels, *Marvel: Five Fabulous Decades of the World's Greatest Comics* (London: Virgin Books, 1991), 16.

7. Maldwyn A. Jones, *The Limits of Liberty: American History 1607-1992* (Oxford: Oxford University Press, 1995), 453–476; David Reynolds, *America: Empire of Liberty* (London: Penguin Books, 2010), 339–351.

8. Reynolds, *America,* 341.

9. For discussions about 1930s popular culture, see Andrew Bergman, *We're in the Money: Depression America and Its Films* (New York: NYU Press, 1971); Colin Shindler, *Hollywood in Crisis: Cinema and American Society, 1929-1939* (London: Routledge, 1996); Warren I. Susman, *Culture as History: The Transformation of American Society in the Twentieth Century* (New York: Pantheon Books, 2003), 184–210; David W. Stowe, *Swing Changes: Big-Band Jazz in New Deal America* (Cambridge, MA: Harvard University Press, 1994).

10. See discussion in John Shelton Lawrence and Robert Jewett, *The Myth of the American Superhero* (Grand Rapids, MI: William B. Eerdmans, 2002), 36–48.

11. Discussions of 1930s adventure strips and their relationship to cinema can be found in Harvey, *Art of the Funnies;* and Gardner, *Projections,* 29–67.

12. It is worth highlighting Couperie's use of filmmaking terms (Foster's panels are described as "shots," highlighting his use of perspective), which both emphasizes and fuses the critical appreciation of comics with film. Pierre Couperie, *A History of the Comic Strip* (New York: Crown, 1972), 57.

13. Byron B. Jones, "Fred Harman," *Southwest Art* 20 (1990): 135–136, 138.

14. Ian Rakoff, "Red Ryder," in *1001 Comics You Must Read before You Die,* ed. Paul Gravett (London: Cassell Illustrated, 2011), 108.

15. Jones, "Fred Harman," 136.

16. Robert Sklar, *Movie-Made America: A Cultural History of American Movies* (New York: Random House, 1994), 196.

17. Peter Stanfield, "Country Music and the 1939 Western: From Hillbillies to Cowboys," in *The Movie Book of the Western,* ed. Ian Cameron and Douglas Pye (London: Studio Vista, 1996), 22.

18. Stanfield, "Country Music and the 1939 Western," 24.

19. For a discussion of the intersection of classical music and the American frontier, see Levy, *Frontier Figures.*

20. See Peter Stanfield, *Hollywood, Westerns, and the 1930s: The Lost Trail* (Exeter, UK: University of Exeter Press, 2001); Simmon, *Invention of the Western Film,* 160–170.

21. Bold, *Selling the Wild West,* 7.

22. Slotkin, *Gunfighter Nation,* 195.

23. Slotkin, *Gunfighter Nation,* 271, 273.

24. Reynolds, *America*, 347–350, 354; Godfrey Hodgson, *America in Our Time: From World War II to Nixon—What Happened and Why* (Princeton, NJ: Princeton University Press, 2005), 88–89.

25. Franklin D. Roosevelt's speech at the Democratic National Convention, June 27, 1936, UVA, Miller Center, https://millercenter.org/the-presidency/presidential -speeches/june-27-1936-democratic-national-convention.

26. Savage, *Comic Books and America*, 7.

27. See Lawrence and Jewett, *Myth of the American Superhero*, 37–43.

28. Lawrence and Jewett, *Myth of the American Superhero*, 40.

29. Ariel Dorfman, *The Empire's Old Clothes: What the Lone Ranger, Babar, and Other Innocent Heroes Do to Our Minds* (Durham, NC: Duke University Press, [1983] 2010), 105–106.

30. Dorfman, *Empire's Old Clothes*, 102–103.

31. Storyline initiated with Fran Striker, "The Lone Ranger," King Features Syndicate, October 1, 1939.

32. The cattle rustling storyline initiated with Striker, "The Lone Ranger," March 12, 1939; the gold mine storyline is initiated with Striker, "The Lone Ranger," July 23, 1939; and the claim-jumper's storyline initiated with Striker, "The Lone Ranger," November 5, 1939.

33. Bob Leffingwell, *Little Joe*, November 12, 1939, reprinted in *Ed Leffingwell's Little Joe: The Sunday Comics*, by Harold Gray (Palo Alto, CA: Sunday Press, 2019).

34. Bob Leffingwell, *Little Joe*, April 13, 1941, reprinted in *Ed Leffingwell's Little Joe*.

35. Ed Leffingwell, *Little Joe*, Chicago Tribune Syndicate, April 15, 1934.

36. Ed Leffingwell, *Little Joe*, April 22, 1934.

37. Jeet Heer, "Who's [sic] Strip Is This Anyway? The Birth and Rebirth of a Western Comic," in *Ed Leffingwell's Little Joe*, 5–7.

38. Horn, *Comics of the American West*, 25–26.

39. Ed Leffingwell, *Little Joe*, October 28, 1934.

40. Ed Leffingwell, *Little Joe*, November 4, 1934.

41. Bob Leffingwell, *Little Joe*, July 12, 1942.

42. Walter Prescott Webb, *Divided We Stand: The Crisis of a Frontierless Democracy* (New York: Farrer & Rinehart, 1937), 158.

43. A discussion of the potency of superheroes to World War II America can be found in Chris Murray, *Champions of the Oppressed: Superhero Comics, Propaganda and Popular Culture in America during World War Two* (Cresskill, NJ: Hampton Press, 2010).

Chapter 4. Cowboys, Crooks, and Comic Books

1. Irwin Hasen and John Broome, "The Ghost of Billy the Kid," *All-Star Comics* #47, June–July 1949, DC Comics.

2. Slotkin, *Gunfighter Nation*, 347.

3. Shawna Kidman, *Comic Books Incorporated: How the Business of Comics Became the Business of Hollywood* (Oakland: University of California Press, 2019), 1.

4. Henry Luce, "The American Century," *Life*, February 17, 1941, 61–65.

5. Reynolds, *America*, 365; Paul Levine and Harry Papasotiriou, *America since 1945: The American Moment*, 2nd ed. (Basingstoke, UK: Palgrave Macmillan, 2011), 13.

6. Jones, *Limits of Liberty*, 517.

7. Richard Hofstadter, *Anti-Intellectualism in American Life* (New York: Vintage Books, 1966), 415.

8. Edmund Wilson, *Europe without Baedeker: Sketches among the Ruins of Italy, Greece, and England* (New York: Doubleday, 1947), 340.

9. Timothy Donovan, "Annie Get Your Gun: A Last Celebration of Nationalism," *Journal of Popular Culture* 12, no. 3 (1978): 539.

10. Leonard Quart and Albert Auster, *American Film and Society since 1945*, 2nd ed. (New York: Praeger, 1991), 39.

11. Coyne, *Crowded Prairie*, 33.

12. Pye, "Introduction: Criticism and the Western," 10.

13. Sabin, *Comics, Comix and Graphic Novels*, 35; Wright, *Comic Book Nation*, 2–4; Hajdu, *Ten-Cent Plague*, 19–22.

14. An article from November 1945 found that the comic book's reading demographic broke down thus: over 90 percent of boys and girls under eleven years of age; over 80 percent of twelve- to seventeen-year-olds; 41 percent of men and 28 percent of women aged eighteen to thirty; and over 10 percent of men and women over the age of thirty. Sanderson Vanderbilt, "The Comics," *Yank: The Army Weekly*, November 23, 1945 (cited in Wright, *Comic Book Nation*, 57).

15. Savage estimates that 60 million comic books were sold per month in the postwar decade (1945–1954), while Hajdu observes that monthly sales reached highs of between 80 and 100 million throughout 1948. Savage, *Comic Books and America*, xi; Hajdu, *Ten-Cent Plague*, 112.

16. *Superman* comics alone were selling 1.25 million copies per month by 1940. Hajdu, *Ten-Cent Plague*, 31.

17. Wright suggests that the strong federal government and the abundance of America's consumer economy in the postwar years alleviated the social inequalities that the superhero had previously fought against and that the superpowers that these heroes wielded were overshadowed by the might of the nation's atomic weaponry. Wright, *Comic Book Nation*, 30–55, 59, 72.

18. Nolan suggests that this figure climbed to as many as 5,000 different Western comic book titles sometime later. Michelle Nolan, "Collecting the Western Genre!," *Comic Book Marketplace* 61 (July 1998): 23.

19. John Cawelti, *The Six-Gun Mystique* (Bowling Green, OH: Bowling Green University Popular Press, 1971), 14, 38, 40.

20. Robert Warshow, "The Westerner," in *The Western Story: Fact, Fiction and Myth*, ed. Philip Durham and Everett L. Jones (New York: Harcourt Brace Jovanovich, 1975), 345.

21. Max Elkan, "Six-Gun Justice" and "Injun Gun-Bait!," both in *Western Adventures* #1, October 1948, Ace Magazines.

22. Michael Barrier, *Funnybooks: The Improbable Glories of the Best American Comic Books* (Oakland: University of California Press, 2014), 295.

23. Various numbers of *John Wayne Adventure Comics*: "The Cowboy and the Gambler," #1, December 1949; "Link-Up in Korea," #12, December 1951; "How Many Deaths Build a Bridge?," #20, May 1953; "Tall Timber," #13, February 1952.

24. Henry Jenkins, *Convergence Culture: Where Old and New Media Collide* (New York: New York University Press, 2006), 95.

25. Kidman, *Comic Books Incorporated*, 29.
26. Kidman, *Comic Books Incorporated*, 29, 31.
27. Blair Davis, *Movie Comics: Page to Screen/Screen to Page* (New Brunswick, NJ: Rutgers University Press, 2017), 234.
28. Barrier, *Funnybooks*, 293.
29. Davis, *Movie Comics*, 233.
30. *Business Weekly*, January 19, 1952, 151 (cited in Savage, *Comic Books and America*, 133.)
31. Barrier, *Funnybooks*, 292.
32. Huxley provides an overview of midcentury film and television Western comic books in *Lone Heroes and the Myth of the American West*, 51–82.

Chapter 5. Nuclear Showdown

1. Stephen Kirkel, "Swift Deer and the Russian Bear," *Buffalo Bill* #9, December 1951, Youthful Magazines.
2. While the origins of the Cold War are widely debated, with much disagreement as to whether it started before, during, or after World War II, this chapter will focus on the various strands that defined the American-Russian conflict after 1945. The literature surrounding the conflict is vast: John Lewis Gaddis's *The Cold War: A New History* (New York: Penguin, 2005) offers an important overview; Stephen J. Whitfield's *The Culture of the Cold War* (Baltimore: Johns Hopkins University Press, 1996) provides a useful summary of the political and social events that informed the anticommunist crusade in the United States; Lary May's *The Big Tomorrow: Hollywood and the Politics of the American Way* (Chicago: University of Chicago Press, 2000), 175–214, offers a good examination of the impact that the anticommunist crusade had on Hollywood.
3. David Caute, *The Great Fear: The Anti-Communist Purge under Truman and Eisenhower* (New York: Simon and Schuster, 1978), 11.
4. Jones, *Limits of Liberty*, 518–519; Michael Barson and Steven Heller, *Red Scared: The Commie Menace in Propaganda and Popular Culture* (San Francisco: Chronicle Books, 2001), 41.
5. Jones, *Limits of Liberty*, 529–530.
6. See Arthur M. Schlesinger Jr., *The Vital Center: Our Purposes and Perils on the Tightrope of American Liberalism* (Boston: Houghton Mifflin, 1949).
7. See discussion in Elaine Tyler May, *Homeward Bound: American Families in the Cold War Era* (New York: Basic Books, 1988); Jane Sherron de Hart, "Containment at Home: Gender, Sexuality, and National Identity in Cold War America," in *Rethinking Cold War Culture*, ed. Peter J. Kuznick and James Gilbert (Washington, DC: Smithsonian Books, 2001), 124–155; Robert J. Corber, "All about the Subversive Femme: Cold War Homophobia in *All about Eve*," in *American Cold War Culture*, ed. Douglas Field (Edinburgh: Edinburgh University Press, 2005), 34–49.
8. Jones, *Limits of Liberty*, 529–531.
9. For discussion of the anticommunist crusade from the perspective of politics and society, see Whitfield's *Culture of the Cold War*. For details on the anticommunist crusade within Hollywood and its impact on the film industry, see Larry Ceplair and Steven Englund, *The Inquisition in Hollywood: Politics in the Film*

Community, 1930-1960 (Garden City, NY: Doubleday, 1980), 254-360; Victor S. Navasky, *Naming Names* (New York: Penguin Books, 1981).

10. The Korean War erupted as North Korea—supported by China and Soviet Russia—invaded South Korea in June 1950 in an attempt to unify the country, which had been divided after World War II. The United States, hoping to make a stand that would deter any further Communist aggression elsewhere in the world, entered the conflict in support of South Korea. Ultimately the war ended in a stalemate in 1953, with no real victor.

11. "Introduction: U.S. Culture and the Cold War," in Kuznick and Gilbert, *Rethinking Cold War Culture*, 11.

12. Cynthia Hendershot, *Anti-Communism and Popular Culture in Mid-Century America* (Jefferson, NC: McFarland, 2003); Martin Halliwell, *American Culture in the 1950s* (Edinburgh: Edinburgh University Press, 2007), 147-189; Chris York and Rafiel York, eds., *Comic Books and the Cold War, 1946-1962: Essays on Graphic Treatment of Communism, the Code and Social Concerns* (Jefferson, NC: McFarland, 2012).

13. May, *The Big Tomorrow*, 206-207.

14. John H. Lenihan, "Westbound: Feature Films and the American West," in Aquila, *Wanted Dead or Alive*, 123.

15. Al Micale, "The Strange Man Hunt," *Roy Rogers* #66, June 1953, Dell. Rogers was in frequent tangles with Communist spies in the West. For example, in Al Micale, "Poisoned Water" (*Roy Rogers* #57, December 1952), Rogers uncovers Soviet saboteurs who are to blame for the poisoned water supply at a local military base. Likewise, Rogers would clash with wicked Communists in "Christmas at Corbett's Curve" and "Mountain Mystery," from *Roy Rogers* #61, January 1953.

16. Nicholas Firfires, "The Oil Hijackers," *Gene Autry Comics* #86, April 1954, Dell.

17. "Mysterious Mountain," *Buster Crabbe* #1, November 1951, Famous Funnies Publications; Mike Roy, "The Saboteurs," *Buster Crabbe* #12, September 1953.

18. Additional discussion on this topic can be found in Savage, *Comic Books and America*, 66-73.

19. Wright, *Comic Book Nation*, 110.

20. For an overview, see Jeanne Emerson Gardner, "'Dreams May End, But Love Never Does': Marriage and Materialism in American Romance Comics, 1947-1954," in *Comic Books and American Cultural History*, ed. Matthew Pustz (London: Continuum, 2012), 94-109; Peter Lee, "Decrypting Espionage Comic Books in 1950s America," in York and York, *Comic Books and the Cold War*, 30-44; Leonard Rifas, *Korean War Comic Books* (Jefferson, NC: McFarland, 2021).

21. Savage, *Comic Books and America*, 67.

22. Savage, *Comic Books and America*, 68.

23. Roland Barthes explicates this as mythology, or the rendering of complex political values and beliefs into simple meanings. With regard to the Western, this is the approach Slotkin adopts in *Fatal Environment* and continues in *Gunfighter Nation*. See Barthes, *Mythologies*, 109-159; Slotkin, *Fatal Environment*, 11, 13-32.

24. Hatfield, *Alternative Comics*, 27.

25. These include *High Noon* (1952); *Shane* (1953); *Law and Order* (1953); *A Man Alone* (1955); *Bad Day at Black Rock* (1955); *Man without a Star* (1955); *Top Gun* (1955);

Wichita (1955); *Johnny Concho* (1956); *Gunfight at the OK Corral* (1957); *Tall T* (1957); *Proud Rebel* (1958); *The Tin Star* (1957); *Rio Bravo* (1959); and *Warlock* (1959).

26. Matthew Costello, "Rewriting 'High Noon': Transformations in American Popular Political Culture during the Cold War," *Film and History* 33, no. 1 (2003): 30.

27. Robert Kanigher and Alex Toth, various numbers of DC Comics' *All-American Western*: "The City without Guns!," #103, November 1948; "Snow Mountain Ambush," #106, February–March 1949; "The Iron Horse's Last Run!," #124, February–March 1952; "The Secret of Crazy River!," #109, August–September 1949; "Ambush at Scarecrow Hills!," #110, October–November 1949.

28. Kanigher and Toth, "Double Danger!," *All-American Western* #112, February 1950.

29. Robert Kanigher and Carmine Infantino, "Phantoms of the Desert," *All-American Western* #126, June–July 1952.

30. "Hopalong Cassidy and the Mysterious Wolf Pack!" *Hopalong Cassidy* #39, January 1950, Fawcett Publications.

31. Doug Wildey, "Case of the Supernatural," *Six-Gun Heroes* #20, May 1953, Fawcett; "The Mysterious Valley of Violence," *John Wayne* #1, December 1949; Syd Shores, "Trapped in the Baron's Den!," *Two-Gun Kid* #8, June 1949, Atlas Comics; Dick Ayers, "Death's Stagecoach!," *The Ghost Rider* #2, December 1950, Magazine Enterprise.

32. Ayers, "Death's Stagecoach!"

33. Lenihan, *Showdown*, 13.

34. Stanley Corkin, *Cowboys as Cold Warriors: The Western and U.S. History* (Philadelphia: Temple University Press, 2004), 23.

35. Mike Sekowsky, "Aztec Gold Brings Hot-Lead Justice!," *Two-Gun Kid* #4, October 1948, Atlas Comics.

36. Carlos E. Cortés, "To View a Neighbor: The Hollywood Textbook on Mexico," in *Images of Mexico in the United States*, ed. John Coatsworth and Carlos Rico (San Diego: Centre for U.S.-Mexican Studies, University of California, 1989), 95; Camilla Fojas, *Border Bandits: Hollywood on the Southern Frontier* (Austin: University of Texas Press, 2008), 16.

37. George McTurnan Kahin, *Intervention: How America Became Involved in Vietnam* (New York: Anchor Books, 1987), 27–30; John Ranelagh, *The Agency: The Rise and Decline of the CIA* (London: Weidenfeld and Nicolson, 1986), 237–238; Odd Arne Westad, *The Global Cold War: Third World Interventions and the Making of Our Times* (Cambridge: Cambridge University Press, 2005), 111; Levine and Papasotiriou, *America since 1945*, 71.

38. See overview in Westad, *Global Cold War*, 110–157.

39. Corkin, *Cowboys as Cold Warriors*, 20.

40. Slotkin, *Gunfighter Nation*, 404.

41. See Noel Carroll, "The Professional Western: South of the Border," in *Back in the Saddle Again: New Essays on the Western*, ed. Edward Buscombe and Roberta Pearson (London: British Film Institute, 1998), 46–62; Slotkin, *Gunfighter Nation*, 405–440; Corkin, *Cowboys as Cold Warriors*, 164–204.

42. Similar Western stories, which much more forcefully underscored US anxieties regarding the democratic order of contemporary developing nations being threatened and subverted by Soviet influence/local Communist movements, can be found in Ed Moritz, "Injun Jones," *Blazing West* #9, January–February

1950, American Comics Group; "The Cossack of Mexico," *Dead-Eye Western* #12, October–November 1950, Hillman.

43. *Two-Gun Kid* #17, October 1954, Atlas Comics.

44. Alex Blum, "Mission of Murder!," *Cowboy Action* #5, March 1955, Atlas Comics; Christopher Rule, "The Spider Strikes," *Black Rider* #27, March 1955, Atlas Comics; Joe Maneely, "Duel on the Rio Grande," *The Gunhawk* #14, April 1951, Atlas Comics.

45. Leonard Starr, "Cowboy Sahib," *The Hooded Horseman* #27, January–February 1953, American Comics Group.

46. McCloud, *Understanding Comics*, 30.

47. Kanigher and Toth, "Double Danger!"

48. Corkin, *Cowboys as Cold Warriors*, 10.

Chapter 6. "I Know It's Not in the Romantic Western Spirit"

1. Bob Fujitani, "The Yella Lawman!," *Wild Western* #30, October 1953, Atlas Comics. Atlas had previously published similar unusual interpretations of the Western hero. One example, by Gene Colan, features a sheriff who is reduced to tears when he thinks about all the people he has shot and killed: "He Was Branded Yellow," *Two Gun Western* #5, November 1950, Atlas Comics.

2. For a discussion of the postwar psychological Western, see Bandy and Stoehr, *Ride, Boldly Ride*, 156–184.

3. Corkin, *Cowboys as Cold Warriors*, 95.

4. Levine and Papasotiriou, *America since 1945*, 79.

5. Reinhold Niebuhr, *The Irony of American History* (Chicago: University of Chicago Press, [1952] 2010), 7.

6. Tom Engelhardt, *The End of Victory Culture: Cold War America and the Disillusioning of a Generation* (Amherst: University of Massachusetts Press, 2007), 3–10.

7. Warren Tufts, *Lance*, December 11 and 18, 1955, reprinted in Warren Tufts, *Lance* (River Forest, IL: Classic Comics Press, 2018).

8. Reprinted in Stan Lynde, *Rick O'Shay, Hipshot, and Me: A Memoir by Stan Lynde* (Billings, MT: Cottonwood Graphics, 1990), 94–125.

9. Lynde, *Rick O'Shay, Hipshot, and Me*, 25.

10. Reynolds, *America*, 410; Neil Campbell and Alasdair Kean, *American Cultural Studies* (London: Routledge, 1997), 200.

11. Lynde, *Rick O'Shay* (August 1959), 39. Ellipsis in original.

12. Bold, "Malaeska's Revenge," 38.

13. Engelhardt, *End of Victory Culture*, 7–8.

14. Engelhardt, *End of Victory Culture*, 8.

15. Irving Howe, "This Age of Conformity," *Partisan Review* 21 (January–February 1954): 7–33.

16. Hajdu, *Ten-Cent Plague*, 179. For more detailed analyses of crime and horror comic books from the era, see Wright, *Comic Book Nation*, 75–84, 147–152; and Hajdu, *Ten-Cent Plague*, 59–70, 175–181.

17. Reading and circulation figures found in US Senate Committee on the Judiciary to Investigation Juvenile Delinquency in the United States, *Comic Books and*

Juvenile Delinquency—Interim Report, 84th Cong., 1st Session (Washington, DC, 1955), 3; Wright, *Comic Book Nation*, 155. "The Hundred Million Dollar Market for Comics," *Publishers Weekly*, May 1, 1954, 1906.

18. An excellent analysis of how EC's genre comics grappled with pressing social and political concerns can be found in Qiana Whitted, *EC Comics: Race, Shock, and Social Protest* (New Brunswick, NJ: Rutgers University Press, 2019).

19. Matthew J. Pustz, *Comic Book Culture: Fanboys and True Believers* (Jackson: University Press of Mississippi, 1999), 38.

20. For a broader discussion on Entertaining Comics and its output, see Wright, *Comic Book Nation*, 135–153; Hajdu, *Ten-Cent Plague*, 175–200; Whitted, *EC Comics*.

21. Harvey Kurtzman, *From Aargh! to Zap!* (New York: Prentice Hall, 1991), 41.

22. Jack Davis, "Cowboy!," *MAD* #20, February 1955, EC.

23. Karin Kukkonen, *Studying Comics and Graphic Novels* (Chichester, UK: Wiley-Blackwell, 2013), 18. The semiotic potential of the comics page and the complex operations at work within its space are more broadly explored in Groensteen, *System of Comics*.

24. Harvey Kurtzman and Jack Davis, "Vera's Cruz," *MAD* #24, July 1955.

25. Kurtzman and Davis, "Hah! Noon!," *MAD* #9, March 1954. Ellipsis in original.

26. Joseph Witek, "Comics Modes: Caricature and Illustration in the Crumb Family's *Dirty Laundry*," in *Critical Approaches to Comics: Theories and Methods*, ed. Matthew J. Smith and Randy Duncan (New York: Routledge, 2012), 28.

27. McCloud, *Understanding Comics*, 30.

28. Kurtzman and Davis, "Hah! Noon!"

29. Other examples include a spoof of the Lone Ranger in Kurtzman and Davis's "The Lone Stranger," *MAD* #3, January–February 1953; George Stevens's 1953 film *Shane* in Kurtzman and Serverin's "Sane!," *MAD* #10, April 1954; and John Sturges's 1957 film *Gunfight at the OK Corral* in Woodbridge's "O.K.! Gunfight at the Corral!," *MAD* #36, December 1957, among others.

30. Whitted, *EC Comics*, 5.

31. John Severin, "Justice!," *Two-Fisted Tales* #36, January 1954, EC.

32. Harvey Kurtzman and Wally Wood, "Custer's Last Stand," *Two-Fisted Tales* #27, May/June 1952.

33. Harvey Kurtzman and John Severin, "Geronimo!," *Frontline Combat* #10, January 1953, EC.

34. Wright, *Comic Book Nation*, 146.

35. Harvey Kurtzman, "War Is Not Glamorous," *The EC Archives: Two-Fisted Tales* (West Plains, MD: Gemstone, 2005), 1:76.

36. Whitted, *EC Comics*, 8.

37. Gerald Early and Alan Lightman, "Race, Art, and Integration: The Image of the African American Soldier in Popular Culture during the Korean War," *Bulletin of the American Academy of Arts and Sciences* 57, no. 1 (2003): 36.

38. Charles Quinlan, "Hopalong Cassidy in the Land Grabbers!," *Hopalong Cassidy* #42, April 1950; John Buscema, "Massacre at Fort Madison," *Two-Gun Western* #5, November 1950, Atlas Comics (ellipses in original). The story of a white hero who averts a military confrontation with warring Native Americans can be found in further comics, such as Syd Shores, "Duel to the Death!," *Two-Gun Kid* #2, June 1948, Atlas Comics; "Kit Carson's Revenge," *Kit Carson* #2, August

1951, Avon Periodicals; Bruno Premiani, "The Race to Peril Point," *Tomahawk* #11, May–June 1952, DC Comics; Stan Lee and Bob Forgione, "Indian Attack!," *Frontier Western* #3, June 1956, Atlas Comics.

39. Found in comics such as Fred Meagher, "The Buffalo Hide of Peace," *Straight Arrow* #4, August 1950, Magazine Enterprise; Howard Larsen, "The Dakota Renegades," *Fighting Indians of the Wild West!* #1, March 1952, Avon Periodicals.

40. "The Duel of the Devil Knives," *Indians* #15, Fall 1952, Fiction House.

41. Huxley, *Lone Heroes*, 66–70.

42. Grady, "Western Comics," 169.

43. This resembles Joe Simon and Jack Kirby's comic book *Boy Commandos*, DC Comics, 1942–1949, which combined a kid gang comic with a war story, following a cast of young boys fighting Nazis during World War II.

44. Jack Kirby and Joe Simon, "Lead Will Fly at Sunset!," *Boys' Ranch* #2, December 1950, Harvey Comics.

45. Kirby and Simon, "The Man Who Hated Boys" and "Mother Delilah," both in *Boys' Ranch* #1, October 1950, and #3, February 1951, respectively.

46. Savage, *Comic Books and America*, 67.

47. Jack Kamen, "John Ringo and Curly Bill: The Unholy Two," *Western True Crime* #15, August 1948, Fox Features Syndicate.

48. "Cattle Kate: The Queen of the Rustlers," *Women Outlaws* #1, July 1948, Fox Features Syndicate.

49. Elaine Tyler May, "Explosive Issues: Sex, Women, and the Bomb," in *Recasting America: Culture and Politics in the Age of the Cold War*, ed. Lary May (Chicago: University of Chicago Press, 1989), 157.

50. Betty Friedan, *The Feminine Mystique* (London: Gollancz, 1963), 432.

51. Christopher Rule, "Big City Blues!," *Annie Oakley* #4, November 1948, Atlas Comics.

52. Fredric Wertham, *Seduction of the Innocent* (New York: Rinehart & Co., 1954).

53. Wertham, *Seduction of the Innocent*, 10.

54. Denning, *Mechanic Accents*, 50–52.

55. Daniel Worden, *Masculine Style: The American West and Literary Modernism* (Basingstoke, UK: Palgrave Macmillan, 2011), 19.

56. Sterling North, "A National Disgrace and a Challenge to American Parents," reprinted in *Childhood Education* 17, no. 2 (1940): 56.

57. Discussed in Amy Kiste Nyberg, *Seal of Approval: The History of the Comics Code* (Jackson: University Press of Mississippi, 1998), 2–3; Hajdu, *Ten-Cent Plague*, 11–13.

58. James Gilbert, *Cycle of Outrage: America's Reaction to the Juvenile Delinquent in the 1950s* (Oxford: Oxford University Press, 1986), 77.

59. Gilbert, *Cycle of Outrage*, 12–14.

60. Discussed in Wright, *Comic Book Nation*, 86–108.

61. Research by Carol Tilley highlights how Wertham "manipulated, overstated, compromised, and fabricated evidence," particularly in his misreading of comic book content and his misrepresentation of conversations he had held with subjects, to draw his conclusions about the harmful effects of comic books. See Carol L. Tilley, "Seducing the Innocent: Fredric Wertham and the Falsifications that Helped Condemn Comics," *Information and Culture* 47, no. 4 (2012): 383–413.

62. US Senate, *Juvenile Delinquency (Comic Books): Hearing before the Subcommittee to Investigate Juvenile Delinquency*, 83rd Congress, 2nd Session (Washington, DC, 1954), 29.

63. The 1954 Comics Code is reprinted in Nyberg, *Seal of Approval*, 166–169.

64. Wright, *Comic Book Nation*, 179. Hadju provides an overview of the aftermath of the "comics scare" in *Ten-Cent Plague*, 305–330.

65. Sabin, *Comics, Comix and Graphic Novels*, 69; Nyberg, *Seal of Approval*, 136–137; Wright, *Comic Book Nation*, 201–223.

66. Quart and Auster, *American Film and Society*, 93.

Chapter 7. Blood on the Borders

1. John Albano and Tony De Zuñiga, "Welcome to Paradise," *All-Star Western* #10, March 1972, DC Comics. (Ellipses in original.)

2. An important account of this time frame is provided in Mark Hamilton Lytle's *America's Uncivil Wars: The Sixties Era from Elvis to the Fall of Richard Nixon* (Oxford: Oxford University Press, 2006).

3. Hodgson, *America in Our Time*, 471.

4. Leo Braudy, "Realists, Naturalists, and Novelists of Manners," in *Harvard Guide to Contemporary American Writing*, ed. Daniel Hoffman (Cambridge, MA: Harvard University Press, 1979), 116.

5. John F. Kennedy, Democratic National Convention nomination acceptance address, "The New Frontier," July 15, 1960, Los Angeles, Shapell Manuscript Collection, https://www.shapell.org/manuscript/jfk-1960-new-frontier-speech/.

6. Paul Goodman, *Growing Up Absurd* (New York: Random House, 1960); Arthur Marwick, *The Sixties: Cultural Revolution in Britain, France, Italy, and the United States, c. 1958–c. 1974* (Oxford: Oxford University Press, 1998), 31–36; Levine and Papasotiriou, *America since 1945*, 120–127.

7. Wright, *Comic Book Nation*, 201.

8. Sabin, *Comics, Comix and Graphic Novels*, 69, 74; Wright, *Comic Book Nation*, 180–225; Paul Douglas Lopes, *Demanding Respect: The Evolution of the American Comic Book* (Philadelphia: Temple University Press, 2009), 61–68.

9. Stan Lee, Jack Kirby, and Dick Ayers, "Beware! The Rawhide Kid," *Rawhide Kid* #17, August 1960, Marvel Comics.

10. Edward Gallafent, "Not with a Bang: The End of the West in *Lonely Are the Brave*, *The Misfits*, and *Hud*," in *The Movie Book of the Western*, ed. Ian Cameron and Douglas Pye (London: Studio Vista, 1996), 254.

11. See, for example, Marvel Comics' Stan Lee and Jack Keller, "Behind the Iron Mask!," *Kid Colt, Outlaw* #110, May 1963; Stan Lee and Dick Ayers, "The Rattler Strikes!," *Rawhide Kid* #37, December 1963; Lee and Ayers, "Revenge of the Red Raven!," *Rawhide Kid* #38, February 1964; Al Hartley and Dick Ayers, "The Panther Will Get You If You Don't Watch Out!," *Two-Gun Kid* #77, September 1965.

12. T. K. Ryan, *Presenting the Best of "Tumbleweeds"* (Boca Raton, FL: Cool Hand Communications, 1993), 59. Ellipsis in original.

13. Ryan quoted in Horn, *Comics of the American West*, 61.

14. The satirical reimagining of the Western found in *MAD* magazine's comic strips

(discussed in the previous chapter) continued in the 1960s. In film, the decade saw a range of comedic Westerns, such as *McLintock!* (1963), *The Hallelujah Trail* (1965), *Support Your Local Sheriff* (1969), and, later, *Blazing Saddles* (1974).

15. Coyne, *Crowded Prairie*, 124.

16. Sergio Aragonés, Dennis O'Neil, and Nick Cardy, *Bat Lash* #3, March 1969, DC Comics.

17. This type of content certainly resonated with readers. One submission to the letters page praised Bat Lash's rebellious nature ("a true picaresque rogue hero"), while signaling their distaste for Marvel's version of the Western, suggesting that *Bat Lash* "vastly [stands] above the three or four publications that hit the stands regularly, usually concerning 'Kid This' or 'Kid That.'" Aragonés, O'Neil, and Cardy, *Bat Lash* #4, May 1969.

18. Michael K. Johnson provides a brilliant overview of the efforts of film and television industries in the 1960s to represent the African American West on screen and to incorporate the Black cowboy into the Western mise-en-scène. See Michael K. Johnson, *Hoo-Doo Cowboys and Bronze Buckaroos: Conceptions of the African American West* (Jackson: University Press of Mississippi, 2014), 154–185.

19. Controversy surrounds the title; some argue that the comic book was cancelled due to poor sales, while another account suggests distributors were overly cautious about promoting a comic book with a Black hero on the cover, so boxes of *Lobo* were set aside and went unopened. Blair Davis, "All-Negro Comics and the Birth of Lion Man, the First African American Superhero," *Inks: The Journal of the Comics Studies Society* 3, no. 3 (2019): 278.

20. Wright and Davis discuss some of the small efforts made by mainstream comic book publishers to address the highly publicized situation of Black Americans brought to light by the civil rights movement. For example, several Back characters (most notably Marvel's Black Panther) appeared by the late 1960s, but only in supporting roles. Wright, *Comic Book Nation*, 218; Davis, "All-Negro Comics," 278.

21. Don Arneson and Tony Tallarico, *Lobo* #1, December 1965, Dell. Ellipsis in original.

22. Morris Dickstein, *Leopards in the Temple: The Transformation of American Fiction, 1945–1970* (Cambridge, MA: Harvard University Press, 2002), 1.

23. James T. Patterson, *Grand Expectations: The United States, 1945–1974* (Oxford: Oxford University Press, 1996), 593–636; Hodgson, *America in Our Time*, 225–260, 384–398; Levine and Papasotiriou, *America since 1945*, 106–107, 111–116.

24. Richard Polenberg, *One Nation Divisible: Class, Race, and Ethnicity in the United States since 1938* (New York: Viking, 1980), 164–207; Hodgson, *America in Our Time*, 179–224; Levine and Papasotiriou, *America since 1945*, 116–117.

25. Levine and Papasotiriou, *America since 1945*, 145.

26. Levine and Papasotiriou, *America since 1945*, 146.

27. Larry Lieber, "Day of the Outcast," *Rawhide Kid* #94, December 1971, Marvel Comics. Ellipsis in original.

28. John Romita, "Crisis on Campus!," *The Amazing Spider-Man* #68, January 1969, Marvel Comics; Stan Lee and Gene Colan, "The Sting of the Scorpion," *Captain America* #122, February 1970, Marvel Comics; Dennis O'Neil and Neal Adams, "No Evil Shall Escape My Sight," *Green Lantern* #76, April 1970, DC Comics.

29. Saul Braun, "Shazam! Here Comes Captain Relevant," *New York Times*, May 2, 1971; Richard J. Howe, "Updating Superman: Comic Book Heroes Are Being

Modernized," *Wall Street Journal*, April 15, 1970; "Comic Realities," *Newsweek*, November 23, 1970.

30. Gabilliet, *Of Comics and Men*, 76.
31. Belton, *American Cinema/America Culture*, 357.
32. Belton, *American Cinema/America Culture*, 357.
33. "The Gun under Fire," *Time*, June 21, 1968, 13.
34. Jones, *Limits of Liberty*, 565.
35. Engelhardt, *End of Victory Culture*, 236.
36. Coyne, *Crowded Prairie*, 164.
37. John Albano and Tony De Zuñiga, "Grasshopper Courage," *Weird Western Tales* #16, March 1973, DC Comics. Ellipsis in original.
38. Albano and De Zuñiga, "Promise to a Princess," and De Zuñiga, "Killers Die Alone," *Weird Western Tales* #12, July 1972, and #14, November 1972, respectively.
39. Albano and De Zuñiga, "The Hangin' Woman," *Weird Western Tales* #17, May 1973.
40. Albano and De Zuñiga, "Promise to a Princess!"
41. The metaleptic possibilities afforded by comics form is much more broadly explored in Karin Kukkonen, "Metalepsis in Comics and Graphic Novels," in *Metalepsis in Popular Culture*, ed. Karin Kukkonen and Sonja Klimek (Berlin: De Gruyter, 2011), 213–231; Tommi Kakko and Mervi Miettinen, "'The Image Rules the World': Focalization, Hallucinations and Metalepsis in *The Invisibles*," *ImageTexT* 8, no. 2 (2015): n.p.
42. Vizenor, *Manifest Manners*, 6–7.
43. Gary Friedrich and Dick Ayers, "Massacre at Medicine Creek!," *The Gunhawks* #3, February 1973, Marvel Comics. Ellipses in original.
44. Hampton Sides, foreword to *Bury My Heart at Wounded Knee: An Indian History of the American West*, by Dee Brown (New York: Henry Holt, 2007), xvi.
45. The differences between the original novel and the film adaptation are discussed in John W. Turner, "*Little Big Man*, the Novel and the Film," *Literature/Film Quarterly* 5 (Spring 1977): 154–163.
46. Coyne, *Crowded Prairie*, 162.
47. Quote from a review of *Soldier Blue* in *New York Times*, September 20, 1970 (cited in Coyne, *Crowded Prairie*, 162–163).
48. See Sabin, *Comics, Comix and Graphic Novels*, 92–107; Patrick Rosenkranz, *Rebel Visions: The Underground Comix Revolution, 1963–1975* (Seattle: Fantagraphics, 2006); Gabilliet, *Of Comics and Men*, 61–67; Dan Mazur and Alexander Danner, *Comics: A Global History, 1968 to the Present* (London: Thames & Hudson, 2014), 22–40.
49. Joshua Abraham Kopin, "'With Apologies to the Old Masters': Jack Jackson's Citational Practice and the History of Comic Book History," *Inks: The Journal of the Comics Studies Society* 3, no. 1 (2019): 28.
50. The relationship between Jackson's comics and the artwork of "serious" artists Charles Russell, Frederic Remington, and others is discussed in Martha Sandweiss, "Redrawing the West: Jack Jackson's *Comanche Moon*," in *The Graphic Novel*, ed. Jan Baetens (Leuven, Belgium: Leuven University Press, 2001), 123–124.
51. Kopin, "With Apologies to the Old Masters," 28–29.

52. Bart Beaty echoes this difference in storytelling between comics and film in the article "In Focus: Comics Studies—Fifty Years after Film Studies," *Cinema Journal* 50, no. 3 (2011): 108.

53. Jared Gardner, "Storylines," *SubStance* 40, no. 1 (2011): 64–65.

54. Witek, "Comics Modes," 28.

55. Joseph Witek, *Comic Books as History: The Narrative Art of Jack Jackson, Art Spiegelman, and Harvey Pekar* (Jackson: University Press of Mississippi, 1989), 55; Les Daniels, *Comix: A History of Comic Books in America* (London: Wildwood House, 1973), 166.

56. Witek, *Comic Books as History*, 71–72.

57. Robert Berkhofer, *The White Man's Indian: Images of the American Indian from Columbus to the Present* (New York: Knopf, 1978); Devon A. Mihesuah, *American Indians: Stereotypes and Realities* (Atlanta: Clarity Press, 1996); Philip J. Deloria, *Playing Indian* (New Haven, CT: Yale University Press, 1998).

58. Bruce Sweeney, "Bruce Sweeney Talks with Jaxon," *Cascade Comix Monthly*, May 1980, 7.

59. Pauline Kael, "The Street Western," reprinted in Kael, *Reeling* (London: Marion Boyars, 1977), 283.

60. Richard A. Maynard, *The American Western Film: Myth and Reality* (Rochelle Park, NJ: Hayden Book Co., 1974), 93.

Coda. Walking on the Bones of the Dead

1. Kael, "The Street Western," 283.

2. Jim Kitses and Gregg Rickman, eds., *The Western Reader* (New York: Limelight Editions, 1998), 15.

3. Quoted in Edward Buscombe, *The BFI Companion to the Western* (London: André Deutsch, 1990), 24.

4. Anthony Lejeune, "The Disappearing Cowboy: The Rise and Fall of the Western," *National Review*, December 31, 1989, 23–26; J. Hoberman, "How the West Was Lost—Tracking the Decline of an American Genre: From Appomattox to Vietnam to Disney World," *Voice*, August 27, 1991, 49–54; Alex Cox, "A Bullet in the Back," *Guardian*, May 5, 2006; Michael Agresta, "How the Western Was Lost (and Why It Matters)," *Atlantic*, July 24, 2013.

5. John White, *Westerns* (London: Routledge, 2011), 33.

6. Film production figures found in Belton, *American Cinema/American Culture*, 266.

7. Ron Zimmerman and John Severin, *Rawhide Kid: Slap Leather* (New York: Marvel Comics, 2003); Nathan Edmondson, *Red Wolf: Man Out of Time* (New York: Marvel Comics, 2016).

8. Slotkin, *Gunfighter Nation*, 634.

9. Christophe Dony, "The Rewriting Ethos of the Vertigo Imprint: Critical Perspectives on Memory-Making and Canon Formation in the American Comics Field," *Comicalités: Études de culture graphique* (2014), https://doi.org/10.4000/comicalites.1918.

10. Frank Miller, *Batman: The Dark Knight Returns* (New York: DC Comics, 1986), n.p.

11. Theo Finigan provides a useful study of the relationship of Miller's *Batman* and the Western in "'To the Stables, Robin!'"

12. Theo D'haen, "The Western," in *International Postmodernism: Theory and Literary Practice*, ed. Hans Bertens (Amsterdam: John Benjamins, 1997), 186.

13. Robert M. Collins, *Transforming America: Politics and Culture during the Reagan Years* (New York: Columbia University Press, 2007); John Ehrman, *The Eighties: America in the Age of Reagan* (New Haven, CT: Yale University Press, 2005).

14. Dan Hassler-Forest provides a useful reading of *The Walking Dead*'s reinterpretation of the Western in "Cowboys and Zombies: Destabilizing Patriarchal Discourse in *The Walking Dead*." *Studies in Comics* 2, no. 2 (2012): 339–355.

15. See, for example, Gilles Deleuze, *Cinema II: The Time-Image* (London: Bloomsbury, 2013), 222–230; Bandy and Stoehr, *Ride, Boldly Ride*, 269–280; Neil Campbell, *Post-Westerns: Cinema, Region, West* (Lincoln: University of Nebraska Press, 2013).

16. Philip French, *Westerns* (London: Carcanet, [1973] 2005), 82–101.

17. Neil Campbell, "Post-Western Cinema," in *A Companion to the Literature and Culture of the American West*, ed. Nicolas S. Witschi (Chichester, UK: Wiley-Blackwell, 2011), 411–412.

18. Discussions about *Preacher* as a Western can be found in William Grady, "Transcending the Frontier Myth: Dime Novel Narration and (Jesse) Custer's Last Stand in *Preacher*," in *Comic Books and American Cultural History*, ed. Matthew J. Pustz (London: Continuum, 2012), 40–58; William Grady, "Garth Ennis Interview," *Studies in Comics* 3, no. 1 (2012): 17–24.

19. Campbell, "Post-Western Cinema," 413, 414.

20. Garth Ennis and Steve Dillon, *Preacher: War in the Sun* (London: Titan Books, 1999), 102–103.

21. Campbell, "Post-Western Cinema," 412.

22. Jason Aaron and R. M. Guéra, *Scalped* #1 (2007), reprinted in Aaron and Guéra, *Scalped*, Book One (Burbank, CA: DC Comics, 2017), n.p.

23. Joseph Stromberg, *Lands of the Lakota: Policy, Culture, and Land Use on the Pine Ridge Reservation* (Saarbrucken, Germany: LAP LAMBERT Academic Publishing, 2013), 4.

24. Kate Polak, *Ethics in the Gutter: Empathy and Historical Fiction in Comics* (Columbus: Ohio State University Press, 2017), 119.

25. Aaron and Guéra, *Scalped* #25 (2009), reprinted in Aaron and Guéra, *Scalped*, Book Three (Burbank, CA: DC Comics, 2018), n.p.

26. Polak, *Ethics in the Gutter*, 119.

27. Limerick, *Legacy of Conquest*, 18.

28. Frieda Knobloch, *The Culture of Wilderness* (Chapel Hill: University of North Carolina Press, 1996), ix.

29. John G. Cawelti, *The Six-Gun Mystique Sequel* (Bowling Green, OH: Popular Press, 1999), 101, 103.

30. Stephen Tatum, "Postfrontier Horizons," *Modern Fiction Studies* 50 (2004): 462.

31. Susan Kollin, "Dead Man, Dead West," *Arizona Quarterly* 56, no. 3 (2000): 129, 142, 150.

32. C. Richard King, "Alter/native Heroes: Native Americans, Comic Books, and the Struggle for Self-Definition," *Cultural Studies/Critical Methodologies* 9, no. 2 (2009): 222.

33. King, "Alter/native Heroes," 220.

34. Michael A. Sheyahshe, introduction to *Moonshot: The Indigenous Comics Collection*, ed. Hope Nicholson (Toronto: Inhabit Education Books, 2015), n.p.

35. Much more detailed interrogations of the representations of Native Americans in popular culture can be found in L. G. Moses, *Wild West Shows and the Images of American Indians, 1883–1933* (Albuquerque: University of New Mexico Press, 1996); Jacquelyn Kilpatrick, *Celluloid Indians: Native Americans and Film* (Lincoln: University of Nebraska Press, 1999); Carol Spindel, *Dancing at Halftime: Sports and the Controversy over American Indian Mascots* (New York: New York University Press, 2000); Michael A. Sheyahshe, *Native Americans in Comic Books* (Jefferson, NC: McFarland, 2008); John M. Coward, *Indians Illustrated: The Image of Native Americans in the Pictorial Press* (Champaign: University of Illinois Press, 2016).

36. King, "Alter/native Heroes," 221–222.

37. For a deeper analysis of Indigenous comics, see Susan Bernardin, "Future Pasts: Comics, Graphic Novels, and Digital Media," in *The Routledge Companion to Native American Literature*, ed. Deborah L. Madsen (London: Routledge, 2015), 480–493; Sylvain Rheault, "A Surge of Indigenous Graphic Novels," *Journal of Graphic Novels and Comics* 11, no. 5–6 (2020): 501–521; Frederick Luis Aldama, ed., *Graphic Indigeneity: Comics in the Americas and Australasia* (Jackson: University Press of Mississippi, 2020).

38. Pam Cook, "Women," in *The BFI Companion to the Western*, ed. Edward Buscombe (London: André Deutsch, 1990), 240; Cawelti, *Six-Gun Mystique Sequel*, 31.

39. Jane Tompkins, *West of Everything: The Inner Life of Westerns* (Oxford: Oxford University Press, 1992), 41.

40. Ayanni C. H. Cooper, "'There Is More to Me Than Just Hunger': Female Monsters and Liminal Spaces in *Monstress* and *Pretty Deadly*," in *Monstrous Women in Comics*, ed. Samantha Langsdale and Elizabeth Rae Coody (Jackson: University Press of Mississippi, 2020), 55.

41. Lisa Hanawalt, *Coyote Doggirl* (Montreal: Drawn and Quarterly, 2018), n.p.

42. Victoria Lamont, *Westerns: A Women's History* (Lincoln: University of Nebraska Press, 2016); Mark E. Wildermuth, *Feminism and the Western in Film and Television* (London: Palgrave Macmillan, 2018).

43. Richard Cracroft, "World Westerns: The European Writer and the American West," in *A Literary History of the American West*, ed. J. Golden Taylor and Thomas J. Lyon (Fort Worth: Texas Christian University Press, 1987), 159.

44. See, for example, Cynthia J. Miller and A. Bowdoin Van Riper, eds., *International Westerns: Re-Locating the Frontier* (Lanham, MD: Scarecrow Press, 2013); MaryEllen Higgins, Rita Keresztesi, and Dayna Oscherwitz, eds., *The Western in the Global South* (London: Routledge, 2015); Stephen Teo, *Eastern Westerns: Film and Genre Outside and Inside Hollywood* (London: Routledge, 2016); Lee Broughton, *The Euro-Western: Reframing Gender, Race and the "Other" in Film* (London: I. B. Tauris, 2016).

45. Christopher Frayling, *Spaghetti Westerns: Cowboys and Europeans from Karl May to Sergio Leone* (London: I. B. Tauris, 1981), 62.

46. Ray Allen Billington, *Land of Savagery, Land of Promise: The European Image of the American Frontier in the Nineteenth Century* (New York: Norton, 1981), 29–57.

47. Kasson, *Buffalo Bill's Wild West*, 65–66.
48. Film studies provide some useful examples of how Hollywood Westerns were received and reinterpreted by audiences in unlikely regions, such as Soviet-occupied East Germany and colonial French North Africa. See Rosemary Stott, *Crossing the Wall: The Western Feature Film Import in East Germany* (Oxford: Peter Lang, 2012); Peter J. Bloom, "Beyond the Western Frontier: Reappropriations of the 'Good Badman' in France, the French Colonies, and Contemporary Algeria," in *Westerns: Films through History*, ed. Janet Walker (New York: Routledge, 2001), 197–216.
49. Huxley, *Lone Heroes*, 44–45.
50. James Chapman and Nicholas J. Cull, *Projecting Empire: Imperialism and Popular Cinema* (London: I. B. Tauris, 2009), 7.
51. Christopher Murray, "British Comics," in *The Routledge Companion to Comics*, ed. Frank Bramlett, Roy T. Cook, and Aaron Meskin (London: Routledge, 2016), 44–52.
52. Brian Ireland, "Errand into the Wilderness: *The Cursed Earth* as Apocalyptic Road Narrative," *Journal of American Studies* 43, no. 3 (2009): 497–534.
53. Reprinted in Christophe, *La Famille Fenouillard* (Paris: A. Colin, 1893); Caumery and Pinchon, *Bécassine Voyage* (Gautier et Languereau, 1921); and Hergé, *Tintin en Amérique* (Brussels: Les Éditions du Petit Vingtième, 1932).
54. For an overview of postwar Franco-Belgian comics, see Laurence Grove, *Comics in French: The European Bande Dessinée in Context* (New York: Berghahn Books, 2010), 137–141.
55. McKinney's study highlights how French genre comics interacted with these surrounding geopolitics, although he misses the opportunity to incorporate the allegorically engaged Westerns of the midcentury into his discussion. See Mark McKinney, *Redrawing French Empire in Comics* (Columbus: Ohio State University Press, 2013).
56. This is a thesis explored more fully by Eliza Borque Dandridge in her unpublished doctoral dissertation, "Cowboys and Indians in Africa: The Far West, French Algeria, and the Comics Western in France" (Duke University, 2017).
57. Described in William Grady, "For a Few Comic Strips More: Reinterpreting the Spaghetti Western through the Comic Book," in *Spaghetti Westerns at the Crossroads: Studies in Relocation, Transition and Appropriation*, ed. Austin Fisher (Edinburgh: Edinburgh University Press, 2016), 213–238.
58. This talk is partially transcribed in Paul Gravett, "Hermann: A Man of Characters," *Comic Heroes*, January 2017, 96–101.
59. Austin Fisher, *Radical Frontiers in the Spaghetti Western: Politics, Violence and Popular Italian Cinema* (London: I. B. Tauris, 2014), 25.
60. Domingos Isabelinho, "Sgt. Kirk," in Gravett, *1001 Comics You Must Read before You Die*, 175.
61. Christopher Conway, *Heroes of the Borderlands: The Western in Mexican Film, Comics, and Music* (Albuquerque: University of New Mexico Press, 2019), 155–186.
62. Kevin Patrick, "The Contested Frontier: Western Comics and Australian Identity, 1945–1960," *International Journal of Comic Art* 13, no. 2 (2011): 224, 226.
63. William Grady, "A Baptism of Blood: *Priest* and the Regeneration of Violence on Min-Woo Hyung's Frontier," in *Undead in the West II: They Just Keep*

Coming, ed. Cynthia Miller and A. Bowdoin Van Riper (Lanham, MD: Scarecrow Press, 2013), 177–194.

64. John Berger, *Berger on Drawing* (Aghabullogue, Ireland: Occasional Press, 2005), 124.

65. The interview appears on the dust jacket of Jean-Michel Charlier and Jean Giraud, *Moebius 9: Blueberry* (Anaheim, CA: Graphitti Designs, 1991).

66. Horn, *Comics of the American West,* 137.

67. Campbell, *The Rhizomatic West,* 4.

68. Some existing scholarship includes an overview of Western comics from South America, Europe, and Asia in Horn, *Comics of the American West,* 137–174; and a focused examination of Western comics from Europe (particularly France, Germany, and Italy) in Randall W. Scott, "European Western Comics: A Kind of Round-Up," *International Journal of Comic Art* 9, no. 2 (2007): 413–424. As I was finishing up this project, an edited collection on global Western comics was released, indicating the possibility of growing interest in this area: see Christopher Conway and Antoinette Sol, eds., *The Comic Book Western: New Perspectives on a Global Genre* (Lincoln: University of Nebraska Press, 2022).

BIBLIOGRAPHY

Cartoons and Comic Strips

"Are You Satisfied?" In George Ward Nichols, "Wild Bill." *Harper's New Monthly Magazine*, February 1867.

Cary, William de la Montagne. "The Battle on the Little Big Horn River—The Death Struggle of General Custer." *Daily Graphic*, July 19, 1876.

Crichton, A. T. *Little Growling Bird in Windego Land*. Darke County, OH: Coachwhip Publications. Ebook.

Farny, H. F. "The Last Scene of the Last Act of the Sioux War." *Harper's Weekly*, February 14, 1891.

Gillam, Bernhard. "Ever Our Indian Policy." *Judge*, January 3, 1891.

Grey, Zane, and Jack Abbott. *Riders of the Purple Sage*. Register and Tribune Syndicate, 1932.

Harman, Fred. *Red Ryder*. Newspaper Enterprise Association, December 18, 1938.

Herriman, George. *Krazy Kat*. King Features Syndicate, September 4, 1927.

Hopkins, Livingston. "The True Solution of the Indian Problem." *Daily Graphic*, July 8, 1876.

King, Frank O. *Walt & Skeezix: 1923-1924*. [*Gasoline Alley*.] Montreal: Drawn & Quarterly, 2006.

Leffingwell, Bob. *Little Joe*. Chicago Tribune Syndicate, July 12, 1942.

Leffingwell, Ed. *Little Joe*. Chicago Tribune Syndicate, April 15 and 22, October 28, November 4, 1934.

Leffingwell, Ed, and Harold Gray (with Bob Effingwell). *Ed Leffingwell's Little Joe: The Sunday Comics*. Edited by Peter Maresca and Sammy Harkham. Palo Alto, CA: Sunday Press, 2019.

Lynde, Stan. *Rick O'Shay, Hipshot, and Me: A Memoir by Stan Lynde*. Billings, MT: Cottonwood Graphics, 1990.

Lynde, Stan. Untitled cartoon. *CARTOONIST PROfiles*, no. 50, June 1981, 79.

McCay, Winsor. *The Complete Little Nemo in Slumberland*. Vol. 3, *1908-1910*. London: Titan, 1990.

Nast, Thomas. "Patience until the Indian Is Civilized—So to Speak." *Harper's Weekly*, December 28, 1878.

O'Neill, Harry F. "Broncho Bill—Hell Doesn't Approve." United Features, September 30, 1938.

O'Neill, Harry F. "Broncho Bill—The Smash Up." United Features, October 5, 1938.

O'Neill, Harry F. "Broncho Bill—Back Home Again." United Features, November 3, 1938.

Opper, Frederick Burr. "Woes of the Western Agriculturalist." *Puck*, July 20, 1881.

Penfield, Edward. "The Modern Dick Turpin." *Harper's Weekly*. January 16, 1892.

Poland, H. "The Right Way to Dispose of Sitting Bull and His Braves." *Daily Graphic*, August 11, 1876.

Price, Garrett. *White Boy in Skull Valley*. Palo Alto, CA: Sunday Press, 2015.

Ryan, T. K. *Presenting the Best of "Tumbleweeds."* Boca Raton, FL: Cool Hand Communications, 1993.

Striker, Fran, and Charles Flanders. *The Lone Ranger*. King Features Syndicate, March 12, July 23, October 1, November 5, December 31, 1939.

Swinnerton, James. "Jimmy—He's Among the Navajos!," March 23, 1913.

Swinnerton, James. "Jimmy—He Sees the Grand Canyon." *Los Angeles Examiner*, April 27, 1913.

Swinnerton, James. "Jimmy—He Smokes the Pipe of Peace." *Seattle Times*, May 18, 1913.

Tufts, Warren. *Lance*. River Forest, IL: Classic Comics Press, 2018.

Williams, J. R. *Out Our Way*. Newspaper Enterprise Association, March 25, 1922.

Comic Books and Graphic Novels

Aaron, Jason, and R. M. Guéra. *Scalped*. Book One. Burbank, CA: DC Comics, 2017.

Aaron, Jason, and R. M. Guéra. *Scalped*. Book Three. Burbank, CA: DC Comics, 2018.

Achdé and Jul. *Un cow-boy dans le coton*. Paris: Les Arènes, 2020.

Albano, John, and Tony De Zuñiga. "Welcome to Paradise." *All-Star Western* #10, March 1972. DC Comics.

Albano, John, and Tony De Zuñiga. "Promise to a Princess!" *Weird Western Tales* #12, July 1972. DC Comics.

Albano, John, and Tony De Zuñiga. "Killers Die Alone." *Weird Western Tales* #14, November 1972. DC Comics.

Albano, John, and Tony De Zuñiga. "Grasshopper Courage." *Weird Western Tales* #16, March 1973. DC Comics.

Albano, John, and Tony De Zuñiga. "The Hangin' Woman." *Weird Western Tales* #17, May 1973. DC Comics.

Allison, W. M. Cover art. *Star Ranger* #1, February 1937. Chesler Publications.

Aragonés, Sergio, Dennis O'Neil, and Nick Cardy. *Bat Lash* #3, March 1969. DC Comics.

Aragonés, Sergio, Dennis O'Neil, and Nick Cardy. *Bat Lash* #4, May 1969, DC Comics.

Arneson, Don, and Tony Tallarico. *Lobo* #1, December 1965. Dell.

Ayers, Dick. "Death's Stagecoach!" *The Ghost Rider* #2, December 1950. Magazine Enterprise.

Ayers Dick. Cover art. *Rawhide Kid* #91, September 1971. Marvel Comics.

Baker, Kyle. *The Cowboy Wally Show*. New York: Vertigo/DC Comics, 1988.

Blum, Alex. "Mission of Murder!" *Cowboy Action* #5, March 1955. Atlas Comics.

Bowden, Nate, and Doug Dabbs. *Holliday*. Portland: Oni Press, 2012.

Brubaker, Ed, and Sean Phillips. *Pulp*. Portland: Image Comics, 2020.

Buscema, John. "Massacre at Fort Madison." *Two-Gun Western* #5, November 1950. Atlas Comics.

"Cattle Kate: The Queen of the Rustlers." *Women Outlaws* #1, July 1948. Fox Features Syndicate.

Caumery, M.-L., and J. Pinchon. *Bécassine voyage*. Paris: Gautier et Languereau, 1921.

Charlier, Jean-Michel, and Jean Giraud. *Moebius 9: Blueberry*. Anaheim, CA: Graphitti Designs, 1991.

Christophe. *La Famille Fenouillard*. Paris: A. Colin, 1893.

Colan, Gene. "He Was Branded Yellow." *Two-Gun Western* #5, November 1950. Atlas Comics.

"The Cossack of Mexico." *Dead-Eye Western* #12, October-November 1950. Hillman.

"The Cowboy and the Gambler." *John Wayne Adventure Comics* #1, December 1949. Toby Press.

Cowgirl Romances #1, January 1950. Fiction House.

Davis, Jack. "Cowboy!" *MAD* #20, February 1955. EC.

"The Duel of the Devil Knives." *Indians* #15, Fall 1952. Fiction House.

Edmondson, Nathan. *Red Wolf: Man Out of Time*. New York: Marvel Comics, 2016.

Elkan, Max. "Injun Gun-Bait!" *Western Adventures* #1, October 1948. Ace Magazines.

Elkan, Max. "Six-Gun Justice." *Western Adventures* #1, October 1948. Ace Magazines.

Ennis, Garth, and Steve Dillon. *Preacher* #2, May 1995. DC Comics.

Ennis, Garth, and Steve Dillon. *Preacher: Salvation*. London: Titan Books, 1999.

Ennis, Garth, and Steve Dillon. *Preacher: War in the Sun*. London: Titan Books, 1999.

Fawcette, Gene. Cover art. *Custer's Last Fight*. Avon Periodicals, 1950.

Firfires, Nicholas. "The Oil Hijackers." *Gene Autry Comics* #86, April 1954. Dell.

Fleisher, Michael, and Dick Ayers. "Feather for a Savage!" *Weird Western Tales* #43, December 1977. DC Comics.

Friedrich, Gary, and Dick Ayers, "Massacre at Medicine Creek!" *The Gunhawks* #3, February 1973. Marvel Comics.

Fujitani, Bob. "The Yella Lawman!" *Wild Western* #30, October 1953. Atlas Comics.

Hanawalt, Lisa. *Coyote Doggirl*. Montreal: Drawn and Quarterly, 2018.

Hartley, Al, and Dick Ayers. "The Panther Will Get You If You Don't Watch Out!" *Two-Gun Kid* #77, September 1965. Marvel Comics.

Hasen, Irwin, and John Broome. "The Ghost of Billy the Kid." *All-Star Comics* #47, June-July 1949. DC Comics.

Hawke, Ethan, and Greg Ruth. *Indeh: A Story of the Apache Wars*. New York: Grand Central, 2016.

Heck, Don. "Trouble in Mexico." *Death Valley* #6, August 1954. Comic Media.

Henry, Gordon, Jr., and Elizabeth LaPensée, eds. *Sovereign Traces*. Vol. 1, *Not (Just) (An)other*. East Lansing: Michigan State University Press, 2018.

Hergé, *Tintin en Amérique*. Brussels: Les Éditions du Petit Vingtième, 1932.

Hill, Gord. *The 500 Years of Resistance Comic Book*. Vancouver: Arsenal Pulp Press, 2010.

"Hopalong Cassidy and the Mysterious Wolf Pack!" *Hopalong Cassidy* #39, January 1950. Fawcett Publications.

"How Many Deaths Build a Bridge?" *John Wayne Adventure Comics* #20, May 1953. Toby Press.

Hyung, Min-Woo. *Priest: A Pale Rider's Chorus*. Los Angeles: Tokyopop, 2003.

Jackson, Jack. *Comanche Moon*. San Francisco: Rip Off Press, 1979.

Jackson, Jack. *Los Tejanos*. Seattle: Fantagraphics, 1982.

Jackson, Jack. "Nits Make Lice." *Slow Death* #7. Last Gasp, 1975.

Kamen, Jack. "John Ringo and Curly Bill: The Unholy Two." *Western True Crime* #15, August 1948. Fox Features Syndicate.

Kanigher, Robert, and Alex Toth. "The City without Guns!" *All-American Western* #103, November 1948. DC Comics.

Kanigher, Robert, and Alex Toth. "Snow Mountain Ambush." *All-American Western* #106, February-March 1949. DC Comics.

Kanigher, Robert, and Alex Toth. "The Secret of Crazy River!" *All-American Western* #109, August-September 1949. DC Comics.

Kanigher, Robert, and Alex Toth. "Ambush at Scarecrow Hills!" *All-American Western* #110. October-November 1949. DC Comics.

Kanigher, Robert, and Alex Toth. "Double Danger!" *All-American Western* #112, February 1950. DC Comics.

Kanigher, Robert, and Alex Toth. "The Iron Horse's Last Run!" *All-American Western* #124, February-March 1952. DC Comics.

Kanigher, Robert, and Carmine Infantino. "Phantoms of the Desert." *All-American Western* #126, June-July 1952. DC Comics.

Kinstler, Everett Raymond. *Chief Victorio's Apache Massacre*. 1951. Avon Periodicals.

Kinstler, Everett Raymond. *Fighting Indians of the Wild West* #2, November 1952. Avon Periodicals.

Kinstler, Everett Raymond. "Western Marshal." *Four Color* #534, February 1954. Dell.

Kinstler, Everett Raymond. Cover art. *Kit Carson* #1, October 1950. Avon Periodicals.

Kirby, Jack, and Joe Simon. "The Man Who Hated Boys." *Boys' Ranch* #1, October 1950. Harvey Comics.

Kirby, Jack, and Joe Simon. "Lead Will Fly at Sunset!" *Boys' Ranch* #2, December 1950. Harvey Comics.

Kirby, Jack, and Joe Simon. "Mother Delilah." *Boys' Ranch* #3, February 1951. Harvey Comics.

Kirkel, Stephen. "Swift Deer and the Russian Bear." *Buffalo Bill* #9, December 1951. Youthful Magazines.

Kirkman, Robert, and Tony Moore. *The Walking Dead* #1, October 2003. Image Comics.

"Kit Carson on the Santa Fe Trail." *Kit Carson* #1, October 1950. Avon Periodicals.

"Kit Carson's Revenge." *Kit Carson* #2, August 1951. Avon Periodicals.

Kurtzman, Harvey, and John Severin. "Geronimo!" *Frontline Combat* #10, January 1953. EC.

Kurtzman, Harvey, and Jack Davis. "The Lone Stranger." *MAD* #3, January-February 1953. EC.

Kurtzman, Harvey, and Jack Davis. "Hah! Noon!" *MAD* #9, March 1954. EC.

Kurtzman, Harvey, and Jack Davis. "Vera's Cruz." *MAD* #24, July 1955. EC.

Kurtzman, Harvey, and John Severin. "Sane!" *MAD* #10, April 1954. EC.

Kurtzman, Harvey, and Wally Wood. "Custer's Last Stand." *Two-Fisted Tales* #27, May-June 1952. EC.

Larsen, Howard. "The Dakota Renegades." *Fighting Indians of the Wild West!* #1, March 1952. Avon Periodicals.

Lee, Stan, and Gene Colan. "The Sting of the Scorpion." *Captain America* #122, February 1970. Marvel Comics.

Lee, Stan, and Bob Forgione. "Indian Attack!" *Frontier Western* #3, June 1956. Atlas Comics.

Lee, Stan, and Jack Keller. "Behind the Iron Mask!" *Kid Colt, Outlaw* #110, May 1963. Marvel Comics.

Lee, Stan, and Jack Keller. "The Return of Iron Mask." *Kid Colt, Outlaw* #114, January 1964. Marvel Comics.

Lee, Stan, Jack Kirby, and Dick Ayers. "Beware! The Rawhide Kid." *Rawhide Kid* #17, August 1960. Marvel Comics.

Lee, Stan, and Dick Ayers. "The Rattler Strikes!" *Rawhide Kid* #37, December 1963. Marvel Comics.

Lee, Stan, and Dick Ayers. "Revenge of the Red Raven!" *Rawhide Kid* #38, February 1964. Marvel Comics.

Lieber, Larry. "Day of the Outcast." *Rawhide Kid* #94, December 1971. Marvel Comics.

"Link-Up in Korea." *John Wayne Adventure Comics* #12, December 1951. Toby Press.

"Long Live the Queen!" *SUN* #226, June 6, 1953. Amalgamated Press.

Maneely, Joe. "Duel on the Rio Grande." *The Gunhawk* #14, April 1951. Atlas Comics.

Marvel Voices: Heritage. New York: Marvel Comics, 2022.

McKissack, Patricia, Fredrick McKissack, and Randy DuBurke. *Best Shot in the West: The Adventures of Nat Love.* San Francisco: Chronicle Books, 2012.

Meagher, Fred. "The Buffalo Hide of Peace." *Straight Arrow* #4, August 1950. Magazine Enterprise.

Micale, Al. "Poisoned Water." *Roy Rogers* #57, December 1952. Dell.

Micale, Al. "Christmas at Corbett's Curve." *Roy Rogers* #61, January 1953. Dell.

Micale, Al. "Mountain Mystery." *Roy Rogers* #61, January 1953. Dell.

Micale, Al. "The Strange Man Hunt." *Roy Rogers* #66, June 1953. Dell.

Miller, Chuck. *Two-Gun Kid* #17, October 1954. Atlas Comics.

Miller, Frank. *Batman: The Dark Knight Returns.* New York: DC Comics, 1986.

Moritz, Ed. "Injun Jones." *Blazing West* #9, January-February 1950. American Comics Group.

Morse, Scott. *Spaghetti Western.* Portland: Oni Press, 2004.

"Mysterious Mountain." *Buster Crabbe* #1, November 1951. Famous Funnies Publications.

"The Mysterious Valley of Violence." *John Wayne Adventure Comics* #1, 1949. Toby Press.

Nicholson, Hope, ed. *Moonshot: The Indigenous Comics Collection.* Toronto: Inhabit Education Books, 2015.

O'Neil, Dennis, and Neal Adams. "No Evil Shall Escape My Sight." *Green Lantern* #76, April 1970. DC Comics.

Pauls, Cole. *Dakwäkãda Warriors.* Wolfville, NS: Conundrum, 2019.

Peeples, Quinton, Dennis Calero, and Darick Robertson. *The Big Country.* Los Angeles: Humanoids, 2019.

Perrissin, Christian, and Matthieu Blanchin. *Calamity Jane: The Calamitous Life of Martha Jane Cannary.* San Diego: IDW, 2017.

Premiani, Bruno. "The Race to Peril Point." *Tomahawk* #11, May-June 1952. DC Comics.

Quinlan, Charles. "Hopalong Cassidy in the Land Grabbers!" *Hopalong Cassidy* #42, April 1950. Fawcett.

Romita, John. "Crisis on Campus!" *The Amazing Spider-Man* #68, January 1969. Marvel Comics.

Rosenberg, Scott Mitchell, Fred Van Lente, Andrew Foley, Dennis Calero, and Luciano Lima. *Cowboys & Aliens*. Los Angeles: Platinum Studios, 2006.

Roy, Mike. "The Saboteurs." *Buster Crabbe* #12, September 1953. Famous Funnies Publications.

Rule, Christopher. "Big City Blues!" *Annie Oakley* #4, November 1948. Atlas Comics.

Rule, Christopher. "The Spider Strikes." *Black Rider* #27, March 1955. Atlas Comics.

Sekowsky, Mike. "Aztec Gold Brings Hot-Lead Justice!" *Two-Gun Kid* #4, October 1948. Atlas Comics.

Severin, John. Cover art. *Rawhide Kid* #9, July 1956. Atlas Comics.

Severin, John. "Justice!" *Two-Fisted Tales* #36, January 1954. EC.

Shores, Syd. Cover art. *The Gunhawks* #3, February 1973. Marvel Comics.

Shores, Syd. Cover art. *Red Wolf* #3, September 1972. Marvel Comics.

Shores, Syd. "Duel to the Death!" *Two-Gun Kid* #2, June 1948. Atlas Comics.

Shores, Syd. "Trapped in the Baron's Den!" *Two-Gun Kid* #8, June 1949. Atlas Comics.

Starr, Leonard. "Cowboy Sahib." *The Hooded Horseman* #27, January-February 1953. American Comics Group.

"Tall Timber." *John Wayne Adventure Comics* #13, February 1952. Toby Press.

Trickster: Native American Tales; A Graphic Collection. Golden, CO: Fulcrum Publishing, 2010.

Vermette, Katherena. *A Girl Called Echo*. Vol. 1, *Pemmican Wars*. Winnipeg: Highwater Press, 2017.

Wildey, Doug. "Case of the Supernatural." *Six-Gun Heroes* #20, May 1953. Fawcett Publications.

Woodbridge, George. "O.K.! Gunfight at the Corral!" *MAD* #36, December 1957. EC.

Zimmerman, Ron, and John Severin. *Rawhide Kid: Slap Leather*. New York: Marvel Comics, 2003.

Films

Annie Oakley, dir. William Kennedy Dickson. Edison Manufacturing Co., 1894.

Bad Day at Black Rock, dir. John Sturges. Metro-Goldwyn-Mayer, 1955.

Barbarella, dir. Roger Vadim. Paramount Pictures, 1968.

The Big Trail, dir. Raoul Walsh. Fox Film Corporation, 1930.

Blazing Saddles, dir. Mel Brooks. Warner Bros., 1974.

Bring Me the Head of Alfredo Garcia, dir. Sam Peckinpah. United Artists, 1974.

Broken Arrow, dir. Delmer Daves. 20th Century Fox, 1950.

Bronco Billy's Redemption, dir. Gilbert M. Anderson. Essanay Film Manufacturing Co., 1910.

Brush between Cowboys and Indians, dir. Edwin S. Porter. Edison Manufacturing Co., 1904.

Bucking Broncho, dir. William Kennedy Dickson and William Heise. Edison Manufacturing Co., 1894.

Butch Cassidy and the Sundance Kid, dir. George Roy Hill. 20th Century Fox, 1969.

Cat Ballou, dir. Elliot Silverstein. Columbia Pictures, 1965.

Colt .45, dir. Edwin L. Marin. Warner Bros., 1950.

Coogan's Bluff, dir. Don Siegel. Universal Pictures, 1968.

Cowboys & Aliens, dir. Jon Favreau. Paramount Pictures, 2011.

Dances with Wolves, dir. Kevin Costner. Orion Pictures, 1990.

Dead Man, dir. Jim Jarmusch. Miramax Films, 1996.

Devil's Doorway, dir. Anthony Mann. Metro-Goldwyn-Mayer, 1950.

A Fistful of Dollars, dir. Sergio Leone. United Artists, 1964.

For a Few Dollars More, dir. Sergio Leone. United Artists, 1965.

The Good, the Bad, and the Ugly, dir. Sergio Leone. United Artists, 1966.

The Graduate, dir. Mike Nichols. United Artists, 1967.

The Great Train Robbery, dir. Edwin S. Porter. Edison Manufacturing Co., 1903.

Guess Who's Coming to Dinner, dir. Stanley Kramer. Columbia Pictures, 1967.

Gunfight at the O.K. Corral, dir. John Sturges. Paramount Pictures, 1957.

The Gunfighter, dir. Henry King. 20th Century Fox, 1950.

The Hallelujah Trail, dir. John Sturges. United Artists, 1965.

Hell or High Water, dir. David Mackenzie. Lionsgate, 2016.

High Noon, dir. Fred Zinnemann. United Artists, 1952.

Hud, dir. Martin Ritt. Paramount Pictures, 1963.

The Indian Massacre, dir. Thomas Ince. New York Motion Picture, 1912.

Johnny Concho, dir. Don McGuire. United Artists, 1956.

The Last of the Fast Guns, dir. George Sherman. Universal Pictures, 1958.

Law and Order, dir. Nathan Juran. Universal Pictures, 1953.

The Life and Times of Judge Roy Bean, dir. John Huston. National General Pictures, 1972.

Little Big Man, dir. Arthur Penn. Paramount, 1970.

Little Train Robbery, dir. Siegmund Lubin. S. Lubin, 1904.

Lonely Are the Brave, dir. David Miller. Universal Pictures, 1962.

Lone Star, dir. John Sayles. Sony Pictures, 1996.

The Magnificent Seven, dir. John Sturges. United Artists, 1960.

The Magnificent Seven, dir. Antoine Fuqua. Sony Pictures, 2016.

A Man Alone, dir. Ray Milland. Republic Pictures, 1955.

The Man Who Shot Liberty Valance, dir. John Ford. Paramount Pictures, 1962.

Man without a Star, dir. King Vidor. Universal Pictures, 1955.

The Massacre, dir. D. W. Griffith. General Film Co., 1912.

McCabe & Mrs. Miller, dir. Robert Altman. Warner Bros., 1971.

McLintock!, dir. Andrew V. McLaglen. United Artists, 1963.

The Mended Lute, dir. D. W. Griffith. Biograph Co., 1909.

The Misfits, dir. John Huston. United Artists, 1961.

No Country for Old Men, dir. Joel and Ethan Coen. Miramax Films, 2007.

On the War Path, dir. Kenean Buel. Kalem Co., 1911.

Open Range, dir. Kevin Costner. Buena Vista Pictures, 2003.

Pale Rider, dir. Clint Eastwood. Warner Bros., 1985.

Pat Garrett and Billy the Kid, dir. Sam Peckinpah. Metro-Goldwyn-Mayer, 1973.

Priest, dir. Scott Stewart. Screen Gems, 2011.

Proud Rebel, dir. Michael Curtiz. Metro-Goldwyn-Mayer, 1958.

The Redman's View, dir. D. W. Griffith. Biograph Co., 1909.

Red River, dir. Howard Hawks. United Artists, 1948.

Ride the High Country, dir. Sam Peckinpah. Metro-Goldwyn-Mayer, 1962.

Rio Bravo, dir. Howard Hawks. Warner Bros., 1959.

Ruggles of Red Gap, dir. Leo McCarey. Paramount Pictures, 1935.

Shane, dir. George Stevens. Paramount Pictures, 1953.

The Shootist, dir. Don Siegel. Paramount Pictures, 1976.

Silver City, dir. John Sayles. Newmarket Films, 2004.

Sioux Ghost Dance, dir. William Kennedy Dickson and William Heise. Edison Manufacturing Co., 1894.

Smoke Signals, dir. Chris Eyre. Miramax Films, 1998.

Soldier Blue, dir. Ralph Nelson. Avco Embassy Pictures, 1970.

Stagecoach, dir. John Ford. United Artists, 1939.

The Strawberry Statement, dir. Stuart Hagmann. Metro-Goldwyn-Mayer, 1970.

Support Your Local Sheriff, dir. Burt Kennedy. United Artists, 1969.

The Tall T, dir. Budd Boetticher. Columbia Pictures, 1957.

The Tin Star, dir. Anthony Mann. Paramount Pictures, 1957.

Top Gun, dir. Ray Nazarro. United Artists, 1955.

The Treasure of Pancho Villa, dir. George Sherman. RKO Radio Pictures, 1955.

True Grit, dir. Joel and Ethan Coen. Paramount Pictures, 2010.

Ulzana's Raid, dir. Robert Aldrich. Universal Pictures, 1972.

Unforgiven, dir. Clint Eastwood. Warner Bros, 1992.

Vera Cruz, dir. Robert Aldrich. United Artists, 1954.

Warlock, dir. Edward Dmytryk. 20th Century Fox, 1959.

Western Stage Coach Hold Up, dir. Edwin S. Porter. Edison Manufacturing Co., 1904.

Wichita, dir. Jacques Tourneur. Allied Artists Pictures, 1955.

The Wild Bunch, dir. Sam Peckinpah. Warner Bros, 1969.

The Wonderful Country, dir. Robert Parrish. United Artists, 1959.

Paintings

Adams, Cassilly. *Custer's Last Fight*. Lithograph from original painting, ca. 1884. (Original destroyed by fire in 1946). National Museum of American History.

Mulvaney, John. *Custer's Last Rally*. Chromolithograph, 1883. Amon Carter Museum of American Art, Fort Worth.

Paxson, Edgar Samuel. *Custer's Last Stand*, 1899. Oil on canvas. Whitney Gallery of Western Art Collection, Buffalo Bill Center of the West, Cody, WY.

Remington, Frederic. *The Last of His Race*, 1908. Oil on composition board. Yale University Art Gallery, New Haven, CT.

Scholarly Works and Other Sources

Agresta, Michael. "How the Western Was Lost (and Why It Matters)." *Atlantic*, July 24, 2013.

Aldama, Frederick Luis, ed. *Graphic Indigeneity: Comics in the Americas and Australasia*. Jackson: University Press of Mississippi, 2020.

Aquila, Richard. *The Sagebrush Trail: Western Movies and Twentieth-Century America*. Tucson: University of Arizona Press, 2015.

Bandy, Mary Lea, and Kevin Stoehr. *Ride, Boldly Ride: The Evolution of the American Western*. Berkeley: University of California Press, 2012.

Barbour, Chad A. *From Daniel Boone to Captain America: Playing Indian in American Popular Culture*. Jackson: University Press of Mississippi, 2016.

Barrier, Michael. *Funnybooks: The Improbable Glories of the Best American Comic Books*. Berkeley: University of California Press, 2014.

Barson, Michael, and Steven Heller. *Red Scared: The Commie Menace in Propaganda and Popular Culture*. San Francisco: Chronicle Books, 2001.

Barthes, Roland. *Mythologies*. Translated by Annette Lavers. London: Cape, 1972.

Beaty, Bart. "In Focus: Comics Studies: Fifty Years after Film Studies." *Cinema Journal* 50, no. 3 (2011): 106–110.

Beaty, Bart, and Benjamin Woo. *The Greatest Comic Book of All Time: Symbolic Capital and the Field of American Comic Books*. Basingstoke, UK: Palgrave Macmillan, 2016.

Belton, John. *American Cinema/American Culture*. 4th ed. New York: McGraw Hill, 2013.

Berger, John. *Berger on Drawing*. Aghabullogue, Ireland: Occasional Press, 2005.

Berger, Thomas. *Little Big Man*. New York: Dial Press, 1964.

Bergman, Andrew. *We're in the Money: Depression America and Its Films*. New York: NYU Press, 1971.

Berkhofer, Robert. *The White Man's Indian: Images of the American Indian from Columbus to the Present*. New York: Knopf, 1978.

Bernardin, Susan. "Future Pasts: Comics, Graphic Novels, and Digital Media." In *The Routledge Companion to Native American Literature*, edited by Deborah L. Madsen, 480–493. London: Routledge, 2015.

Billington, Ray Allen. *Land of Savagery, Land of Promise: The European Image of the American Frontier in the Nineteenth Century*. New York: Norton, 1981.

Bloodworth, William. "Writers of the Purple Sage: Novelists and the American West." In *Wanted Dead or Alive: The American West in Popular Culture*, edited by Richard Aquila, 43–68. Urbana: University of Illinois Press, 1996.

Bloom, Peter J. "Beyond the Western Frontier: Reappropriations of the 'Good Badman' in France, the French Colonies, and Contemporary Algeria." In *Westerns: Films through History*, edited by Janet Walker, 197–216. New York: Routledge, 2001.

Bold, Christine. "Malaeska's Revenge; or, The Dime Novel Tradition in Popular Fiction." In *Wanted Dead or Alive: The American West in Popular Culture*, edited by Richard Aquila, 21–42. Urbana: University of Illinois Press, 1996.

Bold, Christine. *Selling the Wild West: Popular Western Fiction 1860 to 1960*. Bloomington: Indiana University Press, 1987.

Braudy, Leo. "Realists, Naturalists, and Novelists of Manners." In *Harvard Guide to Contemporary American Writing*, edited by Daniel Hoffman, 84–152. Cambridge, MA: Harvard University Press, 1979.

Braun, Saul. "Shazam! Here Comes Captain Relevant." *New York Times*, May 2, 1971.

Broughton, Lee. *The Euro-Western: Reframing Gender, Race and the "Other" in Film*. London: I. B. Tauris, 2016.

Brown, Dee. *Bury My Heart at Wounded Knee*. New York: Holt, Rinehart & Winston, 1970.

Brown, Joshua. *Beyond the Lines: Pictorial Reporting, Everyday Life, and the Crisis of Gilded-Age America*. Berkeley: University of California Press, 2002.

"Buffalo Bill rode into their midst." Illustration. In Colonel Prentiss Ingraham, "Buffalo Bill's Death-Deal." *The New York Dime Library* #1004. New York: Beadle and Adams, 1898.

Buscombe, Edward. *The BFI Companion to the Western*. London: André Deutsch, 1990.

Butler, Christopher. *Postmodernism: A Very Short Introduction*. New York: Oxford University Press, 2002.

Byrd, Jodi. *The Transit of Empire: Indigenous Critiques of Colonialism*. Minneapolis: University of Minnesota Press, 2011.

Campbell, Neil. "Post-Western Cinema." In *A Companion to the Literature and Culture of the American West*, edited by Nicolas S. Witschi, 409–424. Chichester, UK: Wiley-Blackwell, 2011.

Campbell, Neil. *Post-Westerns: Cinema, Region, West*. Lincoln: University of Nebraska Press, 2013.

Campbell, Neil. *The Rhizomatic West: Representing the American West in a Transnational, Global, Media Age*. Lincoln: University of Nebraska Press, 2008.

Campbell, Neil, and Alasdair Kean. *American Cultural Studies*. London: Routledge, 1997.

Carlebach, M. L. *The Origins of Photojournalism in America*. Washington DC: Smithsonian Institution Press, 1992.

Carmichael, Deborah A. *The Landscape of Hollywood Westerns: Ecocriticism in an American Film Genre*. Salt Lake City: University of Utah Press, 2006.

Carroll, Noel. "The Professional Western: South of the Border." In *Back in the Saddle Again: New Essays on the Western*, edited by Edward Buscombe and Roberta Pearson, 46–62. London: British Film Institute, 1998.

Caute, David. *The Great Fear: The Anti-Communist Purge under Truman and Eisenhower*. New York: Simon and Schuster, 1978.

Cawelti, John G. *Adventure, Mystery, and Romance*. Chicago: University of Chicago Press, 1976.

Cawelti, John G. *The Six-Gun Mystique*. Bowling Green, OH: Bowling Green University Popular Press, 1971.

Cawelti, John G. *The Six-Gun Mystique Sequel*. Bowling Green, OH: Bowling Green University Popular Press, 1999.

Ceplair, Larry, and Steven Englund. *The Inquisition in Hollywood: Politics in the Film Community, 1930-1960*. Garden City, NY: Doubleday, 1980.

Chapman, James. *British Comics: A Cultural History*. London: Reaktion Books, 2011.

Chapman, James, and Nicholas J. Cull. *Projecting Empire: Imperialism and Popular Cinema*. London: I. B. Tauris, 2009.

Collins, Robert M. *Transforming America: Politics and Culture during the Reagan Years*. New York: Columbia University Press, 2007.

"Comic Realities." *Newsweek*, November 23, 1970.

Conway, Christopher. *Heroes of the Borderlands: The Western in Mexican Film, Comics, and Music*. Albuquerque: University of New Mexico Press, 2019.

Conway, Christopher, and Antoinette Sol, eds. *The Comic Book Western: New Perspectives on a Global Genre*. Lincoln: University of Nebraska Press, 2022.

Cook, Pam. "Women." In *The BFI Companion to the Western*, edited by Edward Buscombe, 240–243. London: André Deutsch, 1990.

Cooper, Ayanni C. H. "'There Is More to Me Than Just Hunger': Female Monsters and Liminal Spaces in *Monstress* and *Pretty Deadly*." In *Monstrous Women in Comics*, edited by Samantha Langsdale and Elizabeth Rae Coody, 51–68. Jackson: University Press of Mississippi, 2020.

Corber, Robert J. "All about the Subversive Femme: Cold War Homophobia in *All about Eve*." In *American Cold War Culture*, edited by Douglas Field, 34–49. Edinburgh: Edinburgh University Press, 2005.

Corkin, Stanley. *Cowboys as Cold Warriors: The Western and US History*. Philadelphia: Temple University Press, 2004.

Cortés, Carlos E. "To View a Neighbor: The Hollywood Textbook on Mexico." In *Images of Mexico in the United States*, edited by John Coatsworth and Carlos Rico, 91–118. San Diego: Centre for US-Mexican Studies, University of California, 1989.

Costello, Matthew. "Rewriting 'High Noon': Transformations in American Popular Political Culture during the Cold War." *Film and History* 33, no. 1 (2003): 30–40.

Couperie, Pierre. *A History of the Comic Strip*. New York: Crown, 1972.

Coward, John M. *Indians Illustrated: The Image of Native Americans in the Pictorial Press*. Champaign: University of Illinois Press, 2016.

Coward, John M. "Making Sense of Savagery: Native American Cartoons in *The Daily Graphic*." *Visual Communication Quarterly* 19, no. 4 (2012): 200–215.

Coward, John M. *The Newspaper Indian: Native American Identity in the Press, 1820–90*. Urbana: University of Illinois Press, 1999.

Cox, Alex. "A Bullet in the Back." *Guardian*, May 5, 2006.

Coyne, Michael. *The Crowded Prairie: American National Identity in the Hollywood Western*. London: I. B. Tauris, 1998.

Cracroft, Richard. "World Westerns: The European Writer and the American West." In *A Literary History of the American West*, edited by J. Golden Taylor and Thomas J. Lyon, 111–132. Fort Worth: Texas Christian University Press, 1987.

Craig, R. L. "Fact, Public Opinion, and Persuasion: The Rise of the Visual in Journalism and Advertising." In *Picturing the Past: Media, History, and Photography*, edited by B. Brennan and H. Hardt, 36–59. Urbana: University of Illinois Press, 1999.

Creekmur, Corey. "The American Western in Film." In *A Companion to the Literature and Culture of the American West*, edited by Nicolas S. Witschi, 395–408. Chichester, UK: Wiley-Blackwell, 2011.

Dandridge, Eliza Borque. "Cowboys and Indians in Africa: The Far West, French Algeria, and the Comics Western in France." PhD diss., Duke University, Durham, NC, 2017.

Daniels, Les. *Comix: A History of Comic Books in America*. London: Wildwood House, 1973.

Daniels, Les. *Marvel: Five Fabulous Decades of the World's Greatest Comics*. London: Virgin Books, 1991.

Davis, Blair. "*All-Negro Comics* and the Birth of Lion Man, the First African American Superhero." *Inks: The Journal of the Comics Studies Society* 3, no. 3 (2019): 273–297.

Davis, Blair. *Movie Comics: Page to Screen/Screen to Page*. New Brunswick, NJ: Rutgers University Press, 2017.

Davis, Carolyn O'Bagy, and Harvey Leake. *Kayenta and Monument Valley*. Charleston, SC: Arcadia Publishing, 2010.

Deleuze, Gilles. *Cinema II: The Time-Image*. London: Bloomsbury, 2013.

Deloria, Philip J. *Playing Indian*. New Haven, CT: Yale University Press, 1998.

Denning, Michael. *Mechanic Accents: Dime Novels and Working-Class Culture in America*. London: Verso, 1987.

D'haen, Theo. "The Western." In *International Postmodernism: Theory and Literary Practice*, edited by Hans Bertens, 183–194. Amsterdam: John Benjamins, 1997.

Dickstein, Morris. *Leopards in the Temple: The Transformation of American Fiction, 1945–1970*. Cambridge, MA: Harvard University Press, 2002.

Dilworth, Leah. *Imagining Indians in the Southwest: Persistent Visions of a Primitive Past*. Washington, DC: Smithsonian Institution Press, 1996.

Dippie, Brian W. *Custer's Last Stand: The Anatomy of an American Myth*. Lincoln: University of Nebraska Press, [1976] 1994.

Dippie, Brian W. *Remington and Russell: The Sid Richardson Collection*. Austin: University of Texas Press, 1994.

Donovan, Timothy. "Annie Get Your Gun: A Last Celebration of Nationalism." *Journal of Popular Culture* 12, no. 3 (1978): 531–539.

Dony, Christophe. "The Rewriting Ethos of the Vertigo Imprint: Critical Perspectives on Memory-Making and Canon Formation in the American Comics Field." *Comicalités: Études de culture graphique*, 2014. Accessed February 9, 2021. https://doi.org/10.4000/comicalites.1918.

Dorfman, Ariel. *The Empire's Old Clothes: What the Lone Ranger, Babar, and Other Innocent Heroes Do to Our Minds*. Durham, NC: Duke University Press, [1983] 2010.

Early, Gerald, and Alan Lightman. "Race, Art, and Integration: The Image of the African American Soldier in Popular Culture during the Korean War." *Bulletin of the American Academy of Arts and Sciences* 57, no. 1 (2003): 32–38.

Ehrman, John. *The Eighties: America in the Age of Reagan*. New Haven, CT: Yale University Press, 2005.

Engelhardt, Tom. *The End of Victory Culture: Cold War America and the Disillusioning of a Generation*. Amherst: University of Massachusetts Press, 2007.

Fillmore, Gary. *Desert Horizons: Images of James Swinnerton's Southwest*. Cave Creek, AZ: Blue Coyote Gallery, 2009.

Finigan, Theo. "'To the Stables, Robin!': Regenerating the Frontier in Frank Miller's *Batman: The Dark Knight Returns*." *ImageTexT* 5, no. 1 (2010): n.p.

Fischer, Roger A. *Them Damned Pictures: Explorations in American Political Cartoon Art*. North Haven, CT: Archon, 1996.

Fisher, Austin. *Radical Frontiers in the Spaghetti Western: Politics, Violence and Popular Italian Cinema*. London: I. B. Tauris, 2014.

Fojas, Camilla. *Border Bandits: Hollywood on the Southern Frontier*. Austin: University of Texas Press, 2008.

Frayling, Christopher. *Spaghetti Westerns: Cowboys and Europeans from Karl May to Sergio Leone*. London: I. B. Tauris, 1981.

French, Philip. *Westerns*. London: Carcanet, [1973] 2005.

Friedan, Betty. *The Feminine Mystique*. London: Gollancz, 1963.

Fussell, Edwin. *Frontier: American Literature and the American West*. Princeton, NJ: Princeton University Press, 1965.

Gabilliet, Jean-Paul. *Of Comics and Men: A Cultural History of American Comic Books*. Translated Bart Beaty and Nick Nguyen. Jackson: University Press of Mississippi, 2010.

Gaddis, John Lewis. *The Cold War: A New History*. New York: Penguin, 2005.

Gallafent, Edward. "Not with a Bang: The End of the West in *Lonely Are the Brave, The Misfits*, and *Hud*." In *The Movie Book of the Western*, edited by Ian Cameron and Douglas Pye, 241–254. London: Studio Vista, 1996.

Gardner, Jared. *Projections: Comics and the History of Twenty-First-Century Storytelling*. Stanford, CA: Stanford University Press, 2012.

Gardner, Jared. "Storylines." *SubStance* 40, no. 1 (2011): 53–69.

Gardner, Jeanne Emerson. "'Dreams May End, But Love Never Does': Marriage and Materialism in American Romance Comics, 1947–1954." In *Comic Books and American Cultural History*, edited by Matthew Pustz, 94–109. London: Continuum, 2012.

Gilbert, James. *Cycle of Outrage: America's Reaction to the Juvenile Delinquent in the 1950s*. Oxford: Oxford University Press, 1986.

Goetzmann, William H., and William N. Goetzmann. *The West of the Imagination*. 2nd ed. Norman: University of Oklahoma Press, 2009.

Goodman, Paul. *Growing Up Absurd*. New York: Random House, 1960.

Gordon, Ian. *Comic Strips and Consumer Culture, 1890–1945*. Washington, DC: Smithsonian Institution Press, 1998.

Goulart, Ron. *The Adventurous Decade: Comic Strips in the Thirties*. New York: Arlington House, 1975.

Grady, William. "A Baptism of Blood: *Priest* and the Regeneration of Violence on Min-Woo Hyung's Frontier." In *Undead in the West II: They Just Keep Coming*, edited by Cynthia Miller and A. Bowdoin Van Riper, 177–194. Lanham, MD: Scarecrow Press, 2013.

Grady, William. "For a Few Comic Strips More: Reinterpreting the Spaghetti Western through the Comic Book." In *Spaghetti Westerns at the Crossroads: Studies in Relocation, Transition and Appropriation*, edited by Austin Fisher, 213–238. Edinburgh: Edinburgh University Press, 2016.

Grady, William. "Garth Ennis Interview." *Studies in Comics* 3, no. 1 (2012): 17–24.

Grady, William. "Transcending the Frontier Myth: Dime Novel Narration and (Jesse) Custer's Last Stand in *Preacher*." In *Comic Books and American Cultural History*, edited by Matthew J. Pustz, 40–58. London: Continuum, 2012.

Grady, William. "Western Comics." In *The Routledge Companion to Comics*, edited by Frank Bramlett, Roy T. Cook, and Aaron Meskin, 164–173. London: Routledge, 2016.

Grafton, John. *The American West in the Nineteenth Century*. New York: Dover, 1993.

Gravett, Paul. "Hermann: A Man of Characters." *Comic Heroes*, January 2017, 96–101.

Groensteen, Thierry. *The System of Comics*. Jackson: University Press of Mississippi, [1999] 2007.

Grove, Laurence. *Comics in French: The European Bande Dessinée in Context*. New York: Berghahn Books, 2010.

"The Gun Under Fire." *Time*, June 21, 1968.

Hajdu, David. *The Ten-Cent Plague: The Great Comic Book Scare and How It Changed America*. New York: Farrar, Straus and Giroux, 2008.

Hall, Roger A. *Performing the American Frontier, 1870–1906*. Cambridge: Cambridge University Press, 2006.

Halliwell, Martin. *American Culture in the 1950s*. Edinburgh: Edinburgh University Press, 2007.

Hart, Jane Sherron de. "Containment at Home: Gender, Sexuality, and National Identity in Cold War America." In *Rethinking Cold War Culture*, edited by Peter J. Kuznick and James Gilbert, 124–155. Washington, DC: Smithsonian Books, 2001.

Harvey, Robert C. *The Art of the Funnies: An Aesthetic History*. Jackson: University Press of Mississippi, 1994.

Harvey, Robert C. "How Comics Came to Be: Through the Juncture of Word and Image from Magazine Gag Cartoons to Newspaper Strips, Tools for Critical Appreciation plus Rare Seldom Witnessed Historical Facts." In *A Comics Studies Reader*, edited by Jeet Heer and Kent Worcester, 25–45. Jackson: University Press of Mississippi, 2009.

Hassler-Forest, Dan. "Cowboys and Zombies: Destabilizing Patriarchal Discourse in *The Walking Dead*." *Studies in Comics* 2, no. 2 (2012): 339–355.

Hatfield, Charles. *Alternative Comics: An Emerging Literature*. Jackson: University Press of Mississippi, 2005.

Heer, Jeet. Introduction to *Walt & Skeezix: 1923–1924*, by Frank O. King. Montreal: Drawn & Quarterly, 2006.

Heer, Jeet. "Who's [sic] Strip Is This Anyway? The Birth and Rebirth of a Western Comic." In *Ed Leffingwell's Little Joe: The Sunday Comics* by Harold Gray, 5–7. Palo Alto, CA: Sunday Press, 2019.

Hendershot, Cynthia. *Anti-Communism and Popular Culture in Mid-Century America*. Jefferson, NC: McFarland, 2003.

Higgins, MaryEllen, Rita Keresztesi, and Dayna Oscherwitz, eds. *The Western in the Global South*. London: Routledge, 2015.

Higgs, Robert J., and Ralph L. Turner. *The Cowboy Way: The Western Leader in Film, 1945–1995*. Santa Barbara, CA: Praeger, 1999.

Hoberman, J. "How the West Was Lost—Tracking the Decline of an American Genre: From Appomattox to Vietnam to Disney World." *Voice*, August 27, 1991, 49–54.

Hodgson, Godfrey. *America in Our Time: From World War II to Nixon—What Happened and Why*. Princeton, NJ: Princeton University Press, 2005.

Hofstadter, Richard. *Anti-Intellectualism in American Life*. New York: Vintage Books, 1966.

Horn, Maurice. *Comics of the American West*. South Hackensack, NJ: Stoeger Publishing, 1978.

Howe, Irving. "This Age of Conformity." *Partisan Review* 21 (January-February 1954): 7–33.

Howe, Richard J. "Updating Superman: Comic Book Heroes Are Being Modernized." *Wall Street Journal*, April 15, 1970.

"The Hundred Million Dollar Market for Comics." *Publishers Weekly*, May 1, 1954, 1906.

Huxley, David. *Lone Heroes and the Myth of the American West in Comic Books, 1945–1962*. Cham: Palgrave Macmillan, 2018.

Inge, M. Thomas. *Comics as Culture*. Jackson: University Press of Mississippi, 1990.

Ireland, Brian. "Errand into the Wilderness: *The Cursed Earth* as Apocalyptic Road Narrative." *Journal of American Studies* 43, no. 3 (2009): 497–534.

Isabelinho, Domingos. "Sgt. Kirk." In *1001 Comics You Must Read before You Die*, edited by Paul Gravett, 175. London: Cassell Illustrated, 2011.

Jackson, Jack. "The Good, the Bad, the Foreign." *Comics Journal* no. 144 (1991): 50–62.

Jay, Gregory S. "'White Man's Book No Good': D. W. Griffith and the American Indian." *Cinema Journal* 39, no. 4 (2000): 3–26.

Jenkins, Henry. *Convergence Culture: Where Old and New Media Collide*. New York: New York University Press, 2006.

Johnson, Michael K. *Hoo-Doo Cowboys and Bronze Buckaroos: Conceptions of the African American West*. Jackson: University Press of Mississippi, 2014.

Jones, Byron B. "Fred Harman." *Southwest Art* 20 (1990): 134–139.

Jones, Maldwyn A. *The Limits of Liberty: American History 1607–1992*. Oxford: Oxford University Press, 1995.

Juergens, George. *Joseph Pulitzer and the New York World*. Princeton, NJ: Princeton University Press, 1966.

Kael, Pauline. *Reeling*. London: Marion Boyars, 1977.

Kahin, George McTurnan. *Intervention: How America Became Involved in Vietnam*. New York: Anchor Books, 1987.

Kakko, Tommi, and Mervi Miettinen, "'The Image Rules the World': Focalization, Hallucinations and Metalepsis in *The Invisibles*." *ImageTexT* 8, no. 2 (2015): n.p.

Kasson, Joy S. *Buffalo Bill's Wild West: Celebrity, Memory, and Popular History*. New York: Hill and Wang, 2000.

Kennedy, John F. "The New Frontier." Democratic National Convention Nomination Acceptance Address, Los Angeles, July 15, 1960. Shapell Manuscript Collection. Accessed November 21, 2023, https://www.shapell.org/manuscript/jfk-1960-new-frontier-speech/.

Kidman, Shawna. *Comic Books Incorporated: How the Business of Comics Became the Business of Hollywood*. Berkeley: University of California Press, 2019.

Kilpatrick, Jacquelyn. *Celluloid Indians: Native Americans and Film*. Lincoln: University of Nebraska Press, 1999.

King, C. Richard. "Alter/native Heroes: Native Americans, Comic Books, and the Struggle for Self-Definition." *Cultural Studies/Critical Methodologies* 9, no. 2 (2009): 214–223.

King, Geoff. *Spectacular Narratives: Hollywood in the Age of the Blockbuster*. London: I. B. Tauris, 2000.

Kitses, Jim. *Horizons West: Directing the Western from John Ford to Clint Eastwood*. New ed. London: BFI Publishing, 2004.

Kitses, Jim, and Gregg Rickman, eds. *The Western Reader*. New York: Limelight Editions, 1998.

Knobloch, Frieda. *The Culture of Wilderness*. Chapel Hill: University of North Carolina Press, 1996.

Kollin, Susan. "Dead Man, Dead West." *Arizona Quarterly* 56, no. 3 (2000): 125–154.

Kollin, Susan, ed. *A History of Western American Literature.* Cambridge: Cambridge University Press, 2015.

Kopin, Joshua Abraham. "'With Apologies to the Old Masters': Jack Jackson's Citational Practice and the History of Comic Book History." *Inks: The Journal of the Comics Studies Society* 3, no. 1 (2019): 27–47.

Kukkonen, Karin. "Metalepsis in Comics and Graphic Novels." In *Metalepsis in Popular Culture*, edited by Karin Kukkonen and Sonja Klimek, 213–231. Berlin: De Gruyter, 2011.

Kukkonen, Karin. *Studying Comics and Graphic Novels.* Chichester, UK: Wiley-Blackwell, 2013.

Kurtzman, Harvey. *From Aargh! to Zap!* New York: Prentice Hall, 1991.

Kurtzman, Harvey. "War Is Not Glamorous." *The EC Archives: Two-Fisted Tales.* Vol. 1. West Plains, NY: Gemstone, 2005.

Kuznick, Peter J., and James Gilbert, eds. *Rethinking Cold War Culture.* Washington, DC: Smithsonian Books, 2001.

Lamont, Victoria. *Westerns: A Women's History.* Lincoln: University of Nebraska Press, 2016.

Lawrence, John Shelton, and Robert Jewett. *The Myth of the American Superhero.* Grand Rapids, MI: William B. Eerdmans, 2002.

Lee, Peter. "Decrypting Espionage Comic Books in 1950s America." In *Comic Books and the Cold War, 1946–1962: Essays on Graphic Treatment of Communism, the Code and Social Concerns*, edited by Chris York and Rafiel York, 30–44. Jefferson, NC: McFarland, 2012.

Lefèvre, Pascal. "Newspaper Strips." In *The Routledge Companion to Comics*, edited by Frank Bramlett, Roy T. Cook, and Aaron Meskin, 16–24. London: Routledge, 2016.

Lejeune, Anthony. "The Disappearing Cowboy: The Rise and Fall of the Western." *National Review*, December 31, 1989, 23–26.

Lenihan, John H. *Showdown: Confronting Modern America in the Western Film.* Urbana: University of Illinois Press, 1985.

Lenihan, John H. "Westbound: Feature Films and the American West." In *Wanted Dead or Alive: The American West in Popular Culture*, edited by Richard Aquila, 109–134. Urbana: University of Illinois Press, 1996.

Levine, Paul, and Harry Papasotiriou. *America since 1945: The American Moment.* 2nd ed. Basingstoke, UK: Palgrave Macmillan, 2011.

Levy, Beth E. *Frontier Figures: American Music and the Mythology of the American West.* Berkeley: University of California Press, 2012.

Limerick, Patricia Nelson. *The Legacy of Conquest: The Unbroken Past of the American West.* New York: Norton, 1988.

Limerick, Patricia Nelson. "Seeing and Being Seen: Tourism in the American West." In *Over the Edge: Remapping the American West*, edited by Valerie J. Matsumoto and Blake Allmendinger, 15–30. Berkeley: University of California Press, 1999.

Lopes, Paul Douglas. *Demanding Respect: The Evolution of the American Comic Book.* Philadelphia: Temple University Press, 2009.

Luce, Henry. "The American Century," *Life*, February 17, 1941, 61–65.

Lyon, Thomas J., Christine Bold, Gerald Haslam, Glen Love, James H. Maguire, Gregory L. Morris, Tom Pilkington, Diane Dufva Quantic, and Susan J. Rosowski, eds. *Updating the Literary West*. Sponsored by the Western Literature Association. Fort Worth: Texas Christian University Press, 1997.

Lytle, Mark Hamilton. *America's Uncivil Wars: The Sixties Era from Elvis to the Fall of Richard Nixon*. Oxford: Oxford University Press, 2006.

MacDonald, J. Fred. *Who Shot the Sheriff? The Rise and Fall of the Television Western*. New York: Praeger, 1987.

Macy, Christine, and Sarah Bonnemaison. *Architecture and Nature: Creating the American Landscape*. London: Routledge, 2003.

Mainardi, Patricia. *Another World: Nineteenth-Century Illustrated Print Culture*. New Haven, CT: Yale University Press, 2017.

Marwick, Arthur. *The Sixties: Cultural Revolution in Britain, France, Italy, and the United States, c. 1958–c. 1974*. Oxford: Oxford University Press, 1998.

May, Elaine Tyler. "Explosive Issues: Sex, Women, and the Bomb." In *Recasting America: Culture and Politics in the Age of the Cold War*, edited by Lary May, 154–170. Chicago: University of Chicago Press, 1989.

May, Elaine Tyler. *Homeward Bound: American Families in the Cold War Era*. New York: Basic Books, 1988.

May, Lary. *The Big Tomorrow: Hollywood and the Politics of the American Way*. Chicago: University of Chicago Press, 2000.

Maynard, Richard A. *The American Western Film: Myth and Reality*. Rochelle Park, NJ: Hayden Book Co., 1974.

Mazur, Dan, and Alexander Danner. *Comics: A Global History, 1968 to the Present*. London: Thames & Hudson, 2014.

McCloud, Scott. *Understanding Comics: The Invisible Art*. New York: Harper Perennial, 1994.

McDonnell, Patrick, Georgia Riley De Havenon, and Karen O'Connell. *Krazy Kat: The Comic Art of George Herriman*. New York: Abrams, 1986.

McGee, Patrick. *From "Shane" to "Kill Bill": Rethinking the Western*. Oxford: Blackwell Publishing, 2007.

McKinney, Mark. *Redrawing French Empire in Comics*. Columbus: Ohio State University Press, 2013.

McVeigh, Stephen. *The American Western*. Edinburgh: Edinburgh University Press, 2007.

Mihesuah, Devon A. *American Indians: Stereotypes and Realities*. Atlanta: Clarity Press, 1996.

Miller, Cynthia J., and A. Bowdoin Van Riper, eds. *International Westerns: Re-Locating the Frontier*. Lanham, MD: Scarecrow Press, 2013.

Miller, Cynthia J., and A. Bowdoin Van Riper, eds. *Undead in the West II: They Just Keep Coming*. Lanham, MD: Scarecrow Press, 2013.

Moreton-Robinson, Aileen. *Sovereign Subjects: Indigenous Sovereignty Matters*. Crows Nest, NSW: Allen & Unwin, 2007.

Moses, L. G. *Wild West Shows and the Images of American Indians, 1883–1933*. Albuquerque: University of New Mexico Press, 1996.

Murray, Christopher. "British Comics." In *The Routledge Companion to Comics*, edited by Frank Bramlett, Roy T. Cook, and Aaron Meskin, 44–52. London: Routledge, 2016.

Murray, Christopher. *Champions of the Oppressed: Superhero Comics, Propaganda and Popular Culture in America during World War Two*. Cresskill, NJ: Hampton Press, 2010.

Murray, Christopher. "The Pleasures of Persuasion: Comics and Propaganda." In *Critical Approaches to Comics and Graphic Novels*, edited by Matthew Smith and Randy Duncan, 129–141. New York: Routledge, 2011.

Nash, Gerald D. *Creating the West: Historical Interpretation 1890-1990*. Albuquerque: University of New Mexico Press, 1993.

Navasky, Victor S. *Naming Names*. New York: Penguin Books, 1981.

Nelson, Andrew Patrick, ed. *Contemporary Westerns: Film and Television since 1990*. Lanham, MD: Scarecrow Press, 2013.

Nelson, Andrew Patrick, ed. *Still in the Saddle: The Hollywood Western, 1969-1980*. Norman: University of Oklahoma Press, 2015.

Niebuhr, Reinhold. *The Irony of American History*. Chicago: University of Chicago Press, [1952] 2010.

Nolan, Michelle. "Collecting the Western Genre!" *Comic Book Marketplace* 61 (July 1998): 23–26.

North, Sterling. "A National Disgrace and a Challenge to American Parents." *Chicago Daily News*, May 1940. Reprinted in *Childhood Education* 17, no. 2 (1940): 56.

Northern Pacific Railroad. *The Land of Geysers: Yellowstone National Park*. Pamphlet. St. Paul, Minnesota, 1916. Collection of Harold B. Lee Library, Brigham Young University. Accessed November 21, 2023. https://archive.org/details /landofgeyser2691917nort.

Nyberg, Amy Kiste. *Seal of Approval: The History of the Comics Code*. Jackson: University Press of Mississippi, 1998.

O'Sullivan, Judith. *The Great American Comic Strip: One Hundred Years of Cartoon Art*. Boston: Bullfinch, 1990.

Palmer, Lorrie. "'Le Western Noir': *The Punisher* as Revisionist Superhero Western." In *The Amazing Transforming Superhero!*, edited by Terrence R. Wandtke, 192–208. Jefferson, NC: McFarland, 2007.

Patrick, Kevin. "The Contested Frontier: Western Comics and Australian Identity, 1945-1960." *International Journal of Comic Art* 13, no. 2 (2011): 219–243.

Patterson, James T. *Grand Expectations: The United States, 1945-1974*. Oxford: Oxford University Press, 1996.

Polak, Kate. *Ethics in the Gutter: Empathy and Historical Fiction in Comics*. Columbus: Ohio State University Press, 2017.

Polenberg, Richard. *One Nation Divisible: Class, Race, and Ethnicity in the United States since 1938*. New York: Viking, 1980.

Pomeroy, Earl. *In Search of the Golden West: The Tourist in Western America*. Lincoln: University of Nebraska Press, 1990.

Pomeroy, Earl. "Rediscovering the West." *American Quarterly* 12 (1960): 20–30.

Pustz, Matthew J. *Comic Book Culture: Fanboys and True Believers*. Jackson: University Press of Mississippi, 1999.

Pye, Douglas. "Introduction: Criticism and the Western." In *The Movie Book of the Western*, edited by Ian Cameron and Douglas Pye, 9–21. London: Studio Vista, 1996.

Quart, Leonard, and Albert Auster. *American Film and Society since 1945*. 2nd ed. New York: Praeger, 1991.

Rae, John B. *The American Automobile: A Brief History*. Chicago: University of Chicago Press, 1965.

Rakoff, Ian. "Red Ryder." In *1001 Comics You Must Read before You Die*, edited by Paul Gravett, 108. London: Cassell Illustrated, 2011.

Ranelagh, John. *The Agency: The Rise and Decline of the CIA*. London: Weidenfeld and Nicolson, 1986.

Reddin, Paul. *Wild West Shows*. Urbana: University of Illinois Press, 1999.

Refaie, Elisabeth El. "Metaphor in Political Cartoons: Exploring Audience Responses." In *Multimodal Metaphor*, edited by Charles J. Forceville and Eduardo Urios-Aparisi, 173–196. Berlin: De Gruyter, 2009.

Reynolds, David. *America: Empire of Liberty*. London: Penguin Books, 2010.

Rheault, Sylvain. "A Surge of Indigenous Graphic Novels." *Journal of Graphic Novels and Comics* 11, no. 5–6 (2020): 501–521.

Rifas, Leonard. *Korean War Comic Books*. Jefferson, NC: McFarland, 2021.

Roeder, Katherine. *Wide Awake in Slumberland: Fantasy, Mass Culture, and Modernism in the Art of Winsor McCay*. Jackson: University Press of Mississippi, 2014.

Roosevelt, Franklin D. Speech at the Democratic National Convention, Philadel-phia, June 27, 1936. UVA, Miller Center. Accessed November 21, 2023. https://millercenter.org/the-presidency/presidential-speeches/june-27-1936-democratic-national-convention.

Rosaldo, Renato. "Imperialist Nostalgia." *Representations* 26 (Spring 1989): 107–122.

Rosenkranz, Patrick. *Rebel Visions: The Underground Comix Revolution, 1963–1975*. Seattle: Fantagraphics, 2006.

Rothman, Hal K. *Devil's Bargains: Tourism in the Twentieth-Century American West*. Lawrence: University Press of Kansas, 1998.

Russell, Don. *Custer's Last*. Fort Worth, TX: Amon Carter Museum of Western Art, 1968.

Sabin, Roger. *Adult Comics: An Introduction*. London: Routledge, 1993.

Sabin, Roger. *Comics, Comix and Graphic Novels: A History of Comic Art*. London: Phaidon, 1996.

Sandweiss, Martha. "Redrawing the West: Jack Jackson's *Comanche Moon*." In *The Graphic Novel*, edited by Jan Baetens, 115–130. Leuven, Belgium: Leuven University Press, 2001.

Savage, William W. *Comic Books and America 1945–1954*. Norman: University of Oklahoma Press, 1990.

Schatz, Thomas. *Hollywood Genres*. New York: Random House, 1981.

Schickel, Richard. *D. W. Griffith: An American Life*. New York: Simon and Schuster, 1984.

Schlesinger, Arthur M., Jr. *The Vital Center: Our Purposes and Perils on the Tightrope of American Liberalism*. Boston: Houghton Mifflin, 1949.

Scott, Randall W. "European Western Comics: A Kind of Round-Up." *International Journal of Comic Art* 9, no. 2 (2007): 413–424.

Shaffer, Marguerite S. "'The West Plays West': Western Tourism and the Landscape of Leisure." In *A Companion to the American West*, edited by William Deverell, 375–389. Oxford: Blackwell, 2004.

Sheyahshe, Michael A. Introduction to *Moonshot: The Indigenous Comics Collection*, edited by Hope Nicholson, n.p. Toronto: Inhabit Education Books, 2015.

Sheyahshe, Michael A. *Native Americans in Comic Books*. Jefferson, NC: McFarland, 2008.

Shindler, Colin. *Hollywood in Crisis: Cinema and American Society, 1929–1939*. London: Routledge, 1996.

Sides, Hampton. Foreword to *Bury My Heart at Wounded Knee: An Indian History of the American West*, by Dee Brown, i–xvi. 4th ed. New York: Holt, 2007.

Simmon, Scott. *The Invention of the Western Film: A Cultural History of the Genre's First Half-Century*. Cambridge: Cambridge University Press, 2003.

Singer, Marc. *Breaking the Frames: Populism and Prestige in Comics Studies*. Austin: University of Texas Press, 2019.

"Siroc was on the edge of the tall bluff." Illustration. In D. W. Stevens, "The James Boys in Peril." *New York Detective Library* #548. New York: Frank Tousey, 1893.

Sklar, Robert. *Movie-Made America: A Cultural History of American Movies*. New York: Random House, 1994.

Slotkin, Richard. *The Fatal Environment: The Myth of the Frontier in the Age of Industrialization, 1800–1890*. New York: Atheneum, 1985.

Slotkin, Richard. *Gunfighter Nation: The Myth of the Frontier in Twentieth-Century America*. Norman: University of Oklahoma Press, [1992] 1998.

Slotkin, Richard. *Regeneration through Violence: The Mythology of the American Frontier, 1600–1860*. Middletown, CT: Wesleyan University Press, 1973.

Smith, Henry Nash. *Virgin Land: The American West as Symbol and Myth*. Cambridge, MA: Harvard University Press, [1950] 1978.

Spindel, Carol. *Dancing at Halftime: Sports and the Controversy over American Indian Mascots*. New York: NYU Press, 2000.

Stanfield, Peter. "Country Music and the 1939 Western: From Hillbillies to Cowboys." In *The Movie Book of the Western*, edited by Ian Cameron and Douglas Pye, 22–33. London: Studio Vista, 1996.

Stanfield, Peter. *Hollywood, Westerns, and the 1930s: The Lost Trail*. Exeter, UK: University of Exeter Press, 2001.

Stein, Daniel. "The Comic Modernism of George Herriman." In *Crossing Boundaries in Graphic Narrative: Essays on Forms, Series and Genres*, edited by Jake Jakaitis and James F. Wurtz, 40–70. Jefferson, NC: McFarland, 2012.

Stott, Rosemary. *Crossing the Wall: The Western Feature Film Import in East Germany*. Oxford: Peter Lang, 2012.

Stowe, David W. *Swing Changes: Big-Band Jazz in New Deal America*. Cambridge, MA: Harvard University Press, 1994.

Stromberg, Joseph. *Lands of the Lakota: Policy, Culture and Land Use on the Pine Ridge Reservation*. Saarbrucken, Germany: LAP LAMBERT Academic Publishing, 2013.

Susman, Warren I. *Culture as History: The Transformation of American Society in the Twentieth Century*. New York: Pantheon Books, 2003.

Sweeney, Bruce. "Bruce Sweeney Talks with Jaxon." *Cascade Comix Monthly* (May 1980): 3–10.

Swinnerton, James. Interview with Master Sergeant Percy Brown Jr. for Armed Forces Radio, 1963. Accessed November 4, 2012. https://www.youtube.com/watch?v=eeNKnxeR_mM.

Tatum, Stephen. "Postfrontier Horizons." *Modern Fiction Studies* 50 (2004): 460–468.

Taylor, J. Golden, and Thomas J. Lyon, eds., *A Literary History of the American West.* Sponsored by the Western Literature Association. Fort Worth: Texas Christian University Press, 1987.

Teo, Stephen. *Eastern Westerns: Film and Genre Outside and Inside Hollywood.* London: Routledge, 2016.

Tilley, Carol L. "Seducing the Innocent: Fredric Wertham and the Falsifications that Helped Condemn Comics." *Information and Culture: A Journal of History* 47, no. 4 (2012): 383–413.

Tisserand, Michael. *Krazy: George Herriman; A Life in Black and White.* New York: HarperCollins, 2016.

Tompkins, Jane. *West of Everything: The Inner Life of Westerns.* Oxford: Oxford University Press, 1992.

Torgovnick, Marianna. *Gone Primitive: Savage Intellects, Modern Lives.* Chicago: University of Chicago Press, 1990.

Turner, Frederick Jackson. "The Significance of the Frontier in American History." In *The Frontier in American History.* New York: Holt, 1920.

Turner, John W. "*Little Big Man,* the Novel and the Film." *Literature/Film Quarterly* 5 (Spring 1977): 154–163.

Tuska, Jon. *The Filming of the West.* New York: Doubleday, 1976.

US Senate. *Juvenile Delinquency (Comic Books): Hearing before the Subcommittee to Investigate Juvenile Delinquency.* 83rd Cong., 2nd Sess. Washington, DC, 1954. Accessed November 21, 2023. https://archive.org/details/juveniledelinque54unit/page/n5/mode/2up.

US Senate Committee on the Judiciary to Investigation Juvenile Delinquency in the United States. *Comic Books and Juvenile Delinquency—Interim Report.* 84th Cong., 1st Sess. Washington, DC, 1955.

Vizenor, Gerald. *Manifest Manners: Postindian Warriors of Survivance.* Hanover, NH: Wesleyan University Press, 1994.

Walker, Brian. *The Comics before 1945.* New York: Harry N. Abrams, 2004.

Warshow, Robert. "The Westerner." In *The Western Story: Fact, Fiction and Myth,* edited by Philip Durham and Everett L. Jones, 338–351. New York: Harcourt Brace Jovanovich, 1975.

Webb, Walter Prescott. *Divided We Stand: The Crisis of a Frontierless Democracy.* New York: Farrer & Rinehart, 1937.

Wertham, Fredric. *Seduction of the Innocent.* New York: Rinehart & Co., 1954.

Westad, Odd Arne. *The Global Cold War: Third World Interventions and the Making of Our Times.* Cambridge: Cambridge University Press, 2005.

White, John. *Westerns.* London: Routledge, 2011.

Whitfield, Stephen J. *The Culture of the Cold War.* 2nd ed. Baltimore: Johns Hopkins University Press, 1996.

Whitted, Qiana. *EC Comics: Race, Shock, and Social Protest.* New Brunswick, NJ: Rutgers University Press, 2019.

Wildermuth, Mark E. *Feminism and the Western in Film and Television.* London: Palgrave Macmillan, 2018.

Wilson, Edmund. *Europe without Baedeker: Sketches among the Ruins of Italy, Greece, and England.* New York: Doubleday, 1947.

Wister, Owen. *The Virginian*. London: Macmillan, 1902.

Witek, Joseph. *Comic Books as History: The Narrative Art of Jack Jackson, Art Spiegelman, and Harvey Pekar*. Jackson: University Press of Mississippi, 1989.

Witek, Joseph. "Comics Modes: Caricature and Illustration in the Crumb Family's *Dirty Laundry*." In *Critical Approaches to Comics: Theories and Methods*, edited by Matthew J. Smith and Randy Duncan, 27–42. New York: Routledge, 2012.

Witschi, Nicólas S., ed. *A Companion to the Literature and Culture of the American West*. Chichester, UK: Wiley-Blackwell, 2011.

Worden, Daniel. *Masculine Style: The American West and Literary Modernism*. Basingstoke, UK: Palgrave Macmillan, 2011.

Wright, Bradford W. *Comic Book Nation: The Transformation of Youth Culture in America*. Baltimore: Johns Hopkins University Press, 2001.

York, Chris, and Rafiel York, eds. *Comic Books and the Cold War, 1946–1962: Essays on Graphic Treatment of Communism, the Code and Social Concerns*. Jefferson, NC: McFarland, 2012.

Photos and illustrations are indicated by italicized page numbers.